Thought and Character

THE RHETORIC OF DEMOCRATIC EDUCATION

Frederick J. Antczak

THE IOWA STATE UNIVERSITY PRESS / AMES

Every crowd has a silver lining.
—P. T. BARNUM

ACKNOWLEDGMENTS

David Mead, *Yankee Eloquence in the Middle West, 1850–1870,* Michigan State University Press, Lansing, 1951, pp. 40–41. Reprinted by permission of Michigan State University Press.

Selections from "Advice to Youth," "American Vandal," "Sandwich Islands," "The Weather," "Plymouth Rock and the Pilgrims," "Theoretical and Practical Morals," and "Literature" in *Mark Twain's Speeches.* Copyright 1923, 1951 by the Mark Twain Company. Reprinted by permission of Harper and Row, Publishers, Inc.

© 1985 The Iowa State University Press. Composed and printed by The Iowa State University Press, Ames, Iowa 50010

First edition, 1985

Library of Congress Cataloging in Publication Data

Antczak, Frederick J., 1952–
 Thought and character.

Bibliography: p.
 1. Education — United States — History. 2. Democracy. 3. Self-government in education — United States — History. 4. Rhetoric. I. Title.
LA209.A57   1985   370′.973   85–2430
ISBN 0–8138–1781–1

FREDERICK J. ANTCZAK received his B.A. from the University of Notre Dame and his M.A. and Ph.D. from the University of Chicago. He is an assistant professor in Rhetoric and Communication Studies at the University of Virginia.

Thought and Character

THE RHETORIC OF DEMOCRATIC EDUCATION

CONTENTS

ILLUSTRATIONS

PREFACE

A M E R I C A is now engaged in one of its characteristically breath-less rediscoveries of education. Perhaps we need periodically to be reminded of what public education means to democracy. Those reminders need not be confined to endless remastications of commonplaces; we may if we choose push the sloganeering toward serious discussion of the public and personal functions and obligations of which democratic education is to be the basis. This book is, from one angle, an attempt to seize the moment and explore with an interested audience how to think about democratic education.

Democracy itself is a problematic term. It can be used to refer simply to a particular mode of organizing power relationships. But none of the Americans who came to worry about "the problem of democracy" meant merely that; in their attempts at practical solution, it is clear that democracy meant more. To study the rhetorical solutions is to regard democracy as a distinctive culture of thought and character. This book is, from a practical perspective, an examination of the possibilities of that culture and the human identities it nurtures — or, if you will, a meditation on what it is to be American, and what it can be.

My premise is that rhetorical studies can have something valuable to say about such questions. Rhetoric, both as a practice and a field of inquiry, can always use a little popularizing. Our habitual way of thinking about it holds it in some disdain; at best it may seem a necessary evil. But in any democracy civic talk plays a determinative role. This book is, from another view, an investigation into what "success" in playing that role might mean, whether rhetoric might have a distinctive office in democracy, with distinctive functions to perform and obligations to fulfill. More tersely: this book suggests what it would mean for rhetoric to be central in a publicly constitutive, personally liberating democratic education.

I would be remiss to begin a study of education without acknowledging a number of people without whom this project would not have been possible.

This book is dedicated to my parents, whose love, patience, and sense of humor have been abundant and unstinting. My sister and her husband,

Mary Lou and Harold Gray, have always been generous and loving beyond every obligation and expectation. The ethical influence of my grandfather, Joseph Ryszko, is also fundamental in my life, and I cherish it deeply.

I would credit my friends for all their contributions to what I am today in thought and character but, as Twain said, I'm afraid they might sue. Suffice it to say that friends whose support and suggestions have been invaluable include Leonard Hill Lillard, Julie Dean, Doug Stevenson, Michael Subocz, Steven Grohofsky, Thom Miller, Jane Lohrman Taylor, Susan Hendges, John Paul Wenke, Michael Melody, Ann Dunn, Kerry McNamara, Ed Martin, Frederick and Kathy DeVries, Michael DeVries, Chris Stokes, James Grober, S. Steven Block, Stephen Janachowski, Robert Trombley, Elizabeth Morse, Amy Eskin, Monica Johnstone, Richard N. and Sharon Briggs, Rob and Ann Kilkuskie, Scott Kleber, Jim McOmber, and Mary Helen Lewis.

Colleagues have been of enormous help. I wish to thank most warmly William Brandt, Thomas Sloane, and Arthur Quinn for their wise advice and sustaining encouragement. Also due recognition are Herbert Simons, E. P. J. Corbett, and Alan Brinton. James Childress has given deeply valued counsel and friendship. Dante Germino, Erik Midelfort, David Little, Robert Gaines, J. Michael Hogan, and especially James Aune have offered insight and inspiration. William Lee Miller has been a wonderful boss. I particularly want to thank John Sullivan for all his generous and selfless sacrifice.

A word of appreciation goes to the staffs of the Library of Congress, the Alderman Library at the University of Virginia, the Bancroft Library at Berkeley, and the Regenstein Library at the University of Chicago. Some of this work was undertaken with grant support from the National Endowment for the Humanities and the Aspen Institute, and I am grateful to them.

I also wish to thank the many helpful people at the Iowa State University Press, especially Suzanne C. Lowitt for her thoughtful and extremely useful suggestions. Needless to say, I am responsible for whatever error or foolishness may remain.

Finally, my thanks and affection go to my own educators, however undemocratic they had the good sense to be. John Kamyszek, Edward Goerner, Robert Vacca, Joseph Evans, Charles Wegener, Robert Streeter, and Wayne Booth have all been, more than they know, worthy and invigorating influences on my thought and character.

I

The Problem of the Democratic Audience

When a man is holding public office, the greatest thing they can say about him is that he's a man of the people. Then when they find out he is, that's when the trouble starts.

—Representative john young (d-tex.) discussing a former secretary's charge that he paid her a handsome salary in exchange for sexual favors.

The secret of education lies in respecting the pupil.

—Ralph Waldo Emerson

Indulgence, Identification, and Democratic Rhetoric

The worth of a state, in the long run, is the worth of the individuals composing it.

— JOHN STUART MILL

Democracy is based upon the conviction that there are extraordinary possibilities in ordinary people.

— HARRY EMERSON FOSDICK

T H E essential, the identifying characteristic of democracy is that here the people rule. Most obviously this means that the people are empowered to affect, in some sense to control, the future and nature of their community. But more deeply, it means that in democracy the quality of the community and the character of its politics are determined by the quality and character of the people who constitute it. Nowhere, then, is there a more urgent need for the constant instruction and improvement of popular thought and character. Nowhere are the possibilities of education greater—nor, to be fair, are the prospects of its failure anywhere more threatening—than in democracy.

This is a book about the problems and promise of democratic education. It proposes to explore the limits and capacities for intellectual reconstitution inherent in the specifically democratic audience—the distinctive needs it has for such reconstitution and the peculiar problems which, in one of its deeper paradoxes, it stubbornly presents to such reconstitution. The book further proposes to specify instruments of popular education that were somehow successful in addressing such problems, to consider their implications for the theory of democracy. A crucial instrument was rhetoric: we must explore its powers, functions, and obligations and specify its proper role, its distinctive office in democracy. All this pushes toward developing a practical notion of rhetorical success that fits the nature of our politics: rhetoric as central to a publicly constitutive, personally liberating education. This notion is far from original or untested; it nonetheless may shed new light on entrenched notions of the means and ends of rhetoric and education in democracy.[1]

There is perhaps no aspect of public life that takes a worse beating from more sides with greater glee than "rhetoric." We believe, and to a damaging extent attempt to live by, the axiom that talk is cheap. A salesman earnestly promises me to "cut out the rhetoric and get down to business." A senator compliments a presidential address by saying, "I liked particularly the tone of the speech, especially the lack of rhetoric."[2] The suffragettes' old slogan makes sense to us still: "deeds, not words," they insisted, implying a distinction that their audience was to find clear, immediate, and in no way problematic. Clearly we are part of that audience; we can without hesitation conflate the art of rhetoric to the knacks of "trickoric." Think of how we talk about those knacks: covering up and jazzing up; waffling, sugar coating and fudging, stonewalling and smokescreening; what we call "hype," what P. T. Barnum called "humbug." Rhetoric in this view only indulges audiences with what they want to hear in order to manipulate them, rather than submitting them to what they ought to hear, in order ultimately to liberate them. What could be farther from the ideal of democratic education, of disciplining those capable if not always cooperative minds into needed new capabilities?

Rhetoric's disrepute likely arises in considerable part from the seamy purposes it has so often been made to serve, especially recently. To be florid about it — which in such serious matters may not always be be a bad thing — slick public deceptions have been uncovered from Boys' Town to the Oval Office.[3]

It is beyond doubt that bad rhetoric does degrade our shared life; insofar as it misrepresents the bases of decision, limits the alternatives, or distorts the process, bad rhetoric diminishes the extent to which we make our own decisions in self-government. But while bad rhetoric deserves condemnation, perhaps good rhetoric deserves some popularization. The capacity for offenses against the democratic character of our community cannot be denied, and the severity of its most egregious offenses ought not be downplayed. But these events also demonstrate, if only by lurid contrast, the practical value of its better uses and the public importance of being able to distinguish good from bad. One positive contribution rhetoric can make is to teach us how better to recognize and ferret out deceit. The first presidential resignation in our history was earned by rhetoric: it was not so much the illegal break-ins into the Watergate, but the subsequent obstructions of justice that constituted the legal and political grounds for President Nixon's removal. But it was also rhetoric that revealed the offenses and that made the charges stick, deploying the complex proofs intelligibly and, as the lawyers said, "actionably." Act we did, firmly if reluctantly, not immobilized by the gravity and the sadness of the situation. Barbara Jordan's eloquent invocation of the Constitution to open the hearings of the House committee, Howard Baker's persistent refocusing of the question, Gerald Ford's unassuming words of healing and national reunification all helped to give us the necessary heart as a people to press the matter to a worthy, determinate, and sharable conclusion. In short, rhetoric has sometimes been an ailment to the body politic; but it has also actively participated in some purgations and cures.

On another level, rhetoric's current disrepute may also stem from a distinction imported from modern philosophy. In our unexamined attitude of "deeds, not words," we assume a distinction between the supposedly hard stuff of reality and the fundamentally immaterial embellishments of language. The philosophical merits of the distinction have been for some time a matter of contention.[4] Yet in many intellectual specialties—indeed, in the specialized discourse of field after field—the distinction seems to be dissolving.[5] For the purposes that intellectual specialties might serve in the context of the way we live now, the distinction between reality and rhetoric seems less meaningful, relevant, useful, true.

Thus the occasion presents itself for renewed inquiry into the rhetoric of democratic education. This inquiry begins by pursuing in the American experience Tocqueville's first and most pressing observation about democracy in America: "the first duty imposed on those who now direct society is to educate democracy."[6] Many of those who "directed" American society came to the same conclusion; a variety of educational enterprises had been undertaken even in the Republic's infancy. But the need for democratic education was felt with even greater urgency after the turn of the century.

What sort of audience for democratic discourse did Americans constitute? One of their favorite orators and most persistent advocates, the reserved and gentle Ralph Waldo Emerson, described his audiences this way:

> Masses are rude, lame, unmade, pernicious in their demands, and need not be flattered, but schooled. I wish not to concede anything to them, but to tame, drill, divide, and break them up, and draw individuals out of them![7]

The hope of democracy, the keystone of democratic faith is the individual, drawn out from the mass to achieve all of his or her uncommon potential.[8] This process of intellectual reconstitution is never an easy task. But members of the democratic audience presented special problems to the enterprise of education. To those who would individuate them, they presented a distinctive resistance to claims of special authority and a peculiar appreciation of being like everyone else, a "regular guy." To those who would reconstitute them intellectually, these auditors afforded a restlessly shifting attention—and both the most urgent needs and the greatest opportunities for democratic education.

The problem of the democratic audience emerged concussively in the election of 1840. The presidential canvass had become the focal point of American politics expressing the public character of the whole people; and the newly democratized American audience elected, against all their supposed political principles, a president who literally didn't know enough to come in out of the rain. The ancient William Henry Harrison saw fit to deliver, on a blustery March day, the longest inaugural address ever. He had worn only the lightest topcoat so as to prove his own vigor and symbolically the health of the Republic. Thus when Harrison immediately fell ill and died barely a month into his term, it could not help but seem a little portentious. But even more portentious was the nature of the public persuasion that effected this outcome—persuasion that, from the perspective of even those most sympathetic toward democracy, demonstrated more clearly than any results ever could the character of the democratic audience and the problems they presented to intellectual reconstitution.

Americans turned out to be shifty and shallow auditors, but they were also particularly receptive to new ideas. By nature they were an ambitious lot, confident of their abilities if they could only find their main chance. As a result, the typical American would try his hand at many endeavors and was perfectly willing to flit from one enterprise to another. This shifting generated a kind of momentum of its own. Even successful ventures were regularly and quite cheerfully abandoned when new opportunities beckoned; and these tempting new opportunities were so frequently so implausible that there arose a real question as to the democratic audience's abilities to discriminate among alternatives.

This versatile if shallow ingenuity in the Americans also had an immediate educational benefit: The democratic audience was unusually receptive to new ideas. Yet a subject's superior intellectual merit was no guarantee that it would have proportionate persuasiveness; there was a characteristic need to present a message's attractiveness in an especially immediate and tangible way. Otherwise, left to themselves, Americans would merely dabble.[9] Thus, exasperatingly, the same characteristics—confidence and ambition—that made Americans a broadly receptive audience also made them shifty and shallow in their intellectual commitments.

The democratic audience also had an unstinting faith in equality. Political equality was translated to presumed equality of every sort, even intellectual equality. This presumption of equality made Americans, once they were actually engaged in a discipline, willing to exercise their own judgment. But it also made them peculiarly resistant to one of an educator's most valuable tools—his personal authority.

> When it comes to the influence of one man's mind over another's, that is necessarily very restricted in a country where the citizens have all become more or less similar, see each other at very close quarters, and, since they do not recognize any signs of incontestable greatness or

superiority in any of their fellows, are continually brought back to their
own judgment as the most apparent and accessible test of truth.[10]

"There is a general distaste," Tocqueville concluded, "for accepting any
man's word as proof of anything." But since "somewhere and somehow
authority is always bound to play a part in intellectual and moral life,"
Americans came to respond to different kinds of personal authority. "Generally speaking, they look into themselves or into their fellows for the
sources of truth." When they didn't have an opinion of their own, they
responded not to superiors but to "representative" figures, characters they
identified with as being like them. In the not very long run, the emphasis or
equality generated a pressure downward on individual intellectual excel-
lence toward this sort of least common denominator with which all good
democrats identified. There is a real tension between egalitarian notions of
authority and those employed in an intellectual discipline. A discipline implies hierarchy, ranking: all ideas are not equally good or profitable, and no
assertion of an individual will can make them so. Thus any discipline implies a critique that was unlikely to sit well with an audience of equalitar-
ians who stood "ready to deny anything which they cannot understand."[11]

Here again, the same principle that made Americans an audience peculiarly worth talking to in their characteristic questioning attitudes and
acuteness of mind also made them a more difficult audience. In all these
respects, painfully enough, the same societal condition that made Americans an audience interesting and vital to address—democracy itself—made
them difficult to address successfully. The problem for the intellectual reconstitution of the democratic audience was not to eradicate their vices,
even if that were possible, lest the audience's virtues be eradicated as well.
The problem was rather to find a way to convey the message of intellectual
discipline that could animate the virtues and enervate the vices—or, ideally,
to reconstitute those vices into virtues too.

As the democratic audience emerged, institutions of popular education
were developed, the most successful of which was the circuit of public
speech. The circuit provided a forum for, among others, prospective educators of the democratic audience. Some failed to establish sufficient authority to make their case, but others had some success at reconstituting their
audiences intellectually. We shall examine three of the most distinguished
educators, Ralph Waldo Emerson, Mark Twain, and William James.

If this inquiry is to get very far in understanding these intellectual
reconstitutions of the American audience and their implications for rhetoric and democracy, it must respect the diversity among these speakers and
messages and the ways they connected in different rhetorics of democratic
education. Still, two critical concepts undergird the whole study: the classical idea of indulgence will help evaluate and hierarchize levels of rhetorical

approach; the modern notion of the identification of self in a field of selves will help explicate the rhetorical successes achieved.

Plato and the Levels of Approach

Plato envisioned two sorts of rhetoric: one which is a rhetoric of indulging the audience rather than in any way reconstituting it, "mere flattery and disgraceful declamation; the other which is noble and aims at the training and improvement of the souls of the citizens, and strives to say what is best, whether welcome or unwelcome to the audience." But if such a rhetoric was to be preferred, Plato nonetheless warned of a considerable problem in addressing it to democratic audiences. The good orator bringing his not-always-palatable message into competition with indulgers was like a doctor with his castor oil competing against a pastry chef arraying his sweets before a jury of children "or of men who have no more sense than children." Of course intellectual and moral discipline was good for democratic audiences; the rhetorical problem was how to get them to swallow it — especially, to extend the metaphor, since too much sugar coating can alter the chemistry of the exchange, reducing its potence and value.[12]

No one states the difficulties of addressing democratic audiences more harshly than Plato. Perhaps even too harshly: what is interesting about the American audiences, as is revealed in the rhetoric, is the peculiar set of characteristic virtues that, for whatever they may prove to be worth, Plato did not anticipate. But even Plato admitted possibilities for a rhetoric than could be more interestingly "successful," a rhetoric that would improve the audience's thought had to involve their character — and in some sense the character of the speaker himself.

In his dialogues explicitly concerning rhetoric, the *Gorgias* and the *Phaedrus,* Plato has Socrates achieve some undeniable rhetorical success. In the *Gorgias,* Socrates tames a character named Polus, the "wild colt" of the dialogue, and even silences Callicles, a grown-up and more powerful version of the *Republic's* Thrasymachus. The rhetoric by which Socrates accomplishes all this resolutely avoids invoking the opinion of the masses, "what others may say." Instead Socrates persistently returns to a personal engagement with the audience he addresses: "I shall produce one witness only of the truth of my words, and he is the person with whom I am arguing . . . with the many I have nothing to do, and do not even address myself to them."[13]

Successful rhetoric personally engages both speaker and audience in the search for intellectual and moral reconstitution. In the *Phaedrus,* Plato has Socrates go outside the gates of the city, for the only time in all the dialogues outside the reach of the public. Face to face with a beloved friend, Socrates can productively explore the nature of rhetoric, of love, and of the soul itself. Individuals had to be engaged and drawn out of the mass: while indulgence might generate mass appeal for purposes of manipulation, the unconceding mutual discipline of thought and character could serve the higher purpose of releasing individuals "from the yoke of custom and convention" and could open intellectual and moral possibilities that constitute a truer freedom.[14] But while this sort of reconstitutive mutual engagement of the identities of speaker and audience was far better rhetoric than indulgence could be, Plato warned that it would never be easy and perhaps sometimes impossible to invent successful rhetoric for a democratic audience.

This study speaks in terms—indulgence, vulgarization, popularization—of largely the same range of rhetoric that Plato delineated. The *indulgence* of the democratic audience played shamelessly to the audience's commonplaces for purposes of the speaker's gain. Rhetorical indulgence meant no significant intellectual reconstitution of its audience—but also meant considerable and corrosive appeal.

Then there was a sort of middle range of rhetorical ambition: *vulgarization* of ideas at least tried to change the audience's mind about some thing, but only about a particular conclusion. It still based its arguments on the mass habits of thought; it did not attempt to reconstitute listeners into a new way of thinking that might allow them to think for themselves, or rather *as* themselves.

Finally, some few lecturers—Emerson, Twain, and James among them—genuinely tried to reconstitute their audiences intellectually. They aimed at the training and improvement of their listeners' thought and character, and they were not deflected by the possibility that such reconstitution might be unwelcome. Their rhetorical success consisted precisely in making it welcome, making it—in all its rigor and discipline—popular. I choose the word *popularization* for this level of rhetorical approach cognizant of its supposedly pejorative connotations; indeed in a way I am invoking them. For what distinguished this rhetoric was its popular success: it *worked* for the democratic audience, worked in two senses. It managed to respect the integrity of the intellectual discipline, but it also found rhetorical resources for presenting the discipline in a way that engaged the thought and character of the democratic audience.

For all the diversity among lecturers and messages, there was one constant among them; on the circuit of public speech the rhetoric of democratic education was a rhetoric of identification. The speaker had to be a sort of representative figure—representative in the sense of being one with, one *of* the democratic audience, of course; but representative too of the discipline he wanted to popularize. He was like them, only more so by virtue of his way of thinking. The promise, the draw, the *lift* of this democratic rhetoric was that in identifying with the speaker's character and thought, the listeners could become more themselves.

To offer such promise plausibly was a difficult task. To appreciate such rhetoric adequately, we must examine our very notion of rhetorical success.

Burke and Booth: Identification and "Success" in Rhetoric

Are the prospects for success in rhetoric any different in the American democracy from what they were in Plato's Athens? Its possibilities for achieving power seem in no important way diminished, at least if the avidness with which power is pursued is any index. Indeed, they are amplified with the development of new media of communication. More discouragingly, there are new causes for an American audience to submit to indulgence more eagerly and suffer manipulation more readily.

The audience of public discourse that Plato had in mind consisted of the "citizens," a small percentage of the whole population including only those sufficiently wellborn to have a material stake in the city they inherited. These citizens enjoyed the full benefit of education into the Athenian way of life: not only exposure to those few readily identifiable subjects that in the simpler life of Athenians a man could and should know; but education in the public values of the community, the constitutive values that gave Athens its distinctive character as a community and defined the range of meaningful identity within which Athenians might find themselves.

Few of these conditions have obtained in our democracy. "Citizens" has never included everyone, of course; but over time the category proved flexible, including first the landed gentry but eventually more and more of "the common people." Many of these new American citizens did not have a huge material stake in the community; indeed, their driving motivation was often precisely an improvement of their material lot. Most of them had little or no formal education, at a time when there was a wild multiplication of intellectual specialties and a corresponding increase broadly perceived in the needs to know. Moreover, in the United States what was trumpeted as most distinctive about the community's character was that it might change, that the range of identity was not and could not be decisively defined. Jefferson had anticipated revolution at regular intervals; Paine had suggested that what Americans were about was beginning history over again. Nothing seemed to constrain who they might become as a community or as individuals. While Americans were engaged in the constant process of inventing and constituting America, they were also engaged in the exhilarating and bewildering adventure of inventing and identifying themselves.

Two contemporary thinkers, Kenneth Burke and Wayne Booth, suggest that the study of rhetoric can illuminate such processes of constitution and identification. They claim that identification—not persuasion, as traditional theory had always contended—is at the heart of the rhetorical enterprise.

"A doctrine of *consubstantiality,* either explicit or implicit, may be necessary to any way of life," writes Burke. "For substance, in the old philosophies was an *act;* and a way of life is an "acting-together"; and in acting together, men have common sensations, concepts, images, ideas, attitudes that make them *consubstantial.*"[15] In any interaction, including the rhetorical interactions between speakers and democratic audiences, human substance may be shared. The physical and symbolic differences that are the occasions of communication must be located and bridged if speaker and audience are to become "consubstantial," to share such substance. But when they do, insofar as they do, they are identical, identified. For Burke, what rhetoric fundamentally does and what rhetorical studies fundamentally explore is identification.

Wayne Booth incorporates identification in his notion of the human self as a field of selves. For Booth, "the primary mental act of man is to assent . . . 'to take in' and even 'to be taken in' " by others in rhetorical exchange.[16] By understanding and being understood, by taking in other selves, we expand our moral and intellectual capacities, we extend our identities ourselves. We human beings are not only made of bones and muscle, or even muscle memory and nerve synapses. *As human,* we are made of the reasons and people whom we engage rhetorically—those who persuade us and those whom we work to persuade. We have literally a personal stake in our rhetoric, in the people we are moved to stand with and the ideas we are moved to understand.

Burke and Booth will be useful in developing a notion of rhetorical success to apply to enterprises of democratic education. As Booth says, "the reality that is most decisively made in every kind of rhetoric is people."[17] This is the real dynamic in the rhetoric of democratic education; for Burke and Booth, as for democratic audiences, intellectual reconstitution inextricably involves human character. A rhetoric's success in democratic education will involve adjustments of ideas to people and people to ideas— a mutual reconstitution of thought and character.

None of these matters are self-evident or even simple enough to be taken in at a glance. Perhaps the most intelligible and persuasive way into all this is to begin at the historical beginning—the beginning of a broad public awareness that public education was fundamental if democracy was not to destroy itself. The single event in which the need and character of the democratic audience emerged most provocatively was the election of 1840.

Emergence of the Democratic Audience: Election of 1840

Mentioning this 1840, we must say that it marks an epoch in *our* political and social doctrines. The famous election of that year wrought a much greater revolution in us than in the government. . . . We for our part frankly confess — and we care not who knows it — that what we saw during the presidential election of 1840 shook, nay, gave to the winds, all our remaining confidence in the popular democratic doctrines.

—ORESTES BROWNSON

S E L D O M do the results of an election induce serious reflection on first principles. Professional politicians are prepared by experience in their trade to endure setbacks, convinced that anything they can lose in an election can be regained, that no defeats are fundamental, that no reversals are so profound they cannot and will not be reversed, and reversed again. The Democrats lost the White House in 1840. In the off-year elections, however, they would bounce back resiliently, scoring important gains in Congress; in 1844 they would turn out Whig incumbent John Tyler and turn back that most persistent of Whig presidential aspirants, Henry Clay. In that election, their successful banner carrier would be James Knox Polk — a dark horse who only months before had been so obscure that he could win his party's nomination only after the convention suffered a long and harrowing deadlock between two other candidates.

Such are the vagaries of electoral politics. Defeat augurs nothing worse than the beginning of another campaign, this time with better gimmicks to snare attention, catchier slogans, and, perhaps, a new, more marketable candidate. Life goes on.

But to a few other Americans, "Democracy" was less a partisan affiliation than a personal creed — so much so that historian Arthur Schlesinger, Jr. has dubbed them the "doctrinaire democrats."[1] They included practical men like William Leggett, Theodore Sedgwick, and many of the other so-called "locofoco" politicians; intellectuals like Robert Dale Owen, George H. Evans, Frances Wright, and Orestes Brownson; and literary figures like Ralph Waldo Emerson and the great poet of democracy Walt Whitman. For these ardent believers in democracy, the early nineteenth century had been an exhilarating time, a time that was now beginning to bear its fruits. The nation had been undergoing a political reconstitution that went to the very roots of politics, the results of which would now begin to emerge.

The reforms of the day amounted to a practical working out of a classic theoretical clash in American thought, a clash so essential that it had received its first articulation from the founding fathers themselves. The more traditional idea of America as a democratic republic had been challenged by the newer—and from the perspective of these observers, decidedly better—conception of America as a direct democracy. These were not mutually exclusive notions; in practice, they had admitted of a certain amount of compromise and interanimation. But by the turn of the century this accommodation seemed to have reached its practical limit: the basic question of American politics had become a choice between the differing notions of what America was to be in its thought and character, of how informed and active an audience of public discourse it was to become. At issue was the degree to which the common people would be trusted with self-government, and conversely, the degree to which government would instead be delegated to the so-called "best men." At stake was the fundamental character of American democracy.

By 1840 the question had been decided tolerably clearly in favor of broad democratization; but the role that the people would adopt in democratized America was still being formulated.[2] Because the masses had only recently been enfranchised with significant political influence, the election of 1840 had been expected to demonstrate revealingly how they would tend to use it and how the very potentials of that use would reconstitute public discourse and politics. Though some awaited the results with foreboding, the doctrinaire democrats were supremely confident of the outcome, convinced that the people would prove their intellectual and moral abilities to fulfill their duties, and to do so in such a way as to constitute a society intellectually and morally worth living in.

For the doctrinaire democrats, 1840 was not just another presidential election, nor did its adverse results present merely technical questions about how one campaign malfunctioned and how the next one should be tinkered together. Those results could not even be adequately interpreted from a narrowly partisan, won-lost standpoint, for in the eyes of the doctrinaire democrats it was not simply an electoral phenomenon. It held for these observers broad implications both about their young nation and about the ultimate limitations and possibilities of democratic societies as political audiences—audiences for the public discourse necessary to the nation's and democracy's survival and prosperity. And those implications, they felt, struck at the very root of their democratic faith. In the words of Orestes Brownson,

> Mentioning this 1840, we must say that it marks an epoch in *our* political and social doctrines. The famous election of that year wrought a much greater revolution in us than in the government; and, we confess, here on the threshold, that since then we have pretty much ceased to speak of, or to confide in the "intelligence of the people."[3]

Why did the so-called doctrinaire democrats feel the essential principles of their democratic faith threatened by the election of 1840? In narrow partisan terms, the outcome could only be seen as the defeat, however embarrassing, of their candidate; but in a larger view, it was the sudden, shocking revelation of the fundamental vulnerability characterizing the democratic audience which had emerged.

Martin Van Buren had been elected president decisively in 1836, despite some grumbling in his own party. The doctrinaire democrats viewed his performance with approval and identified with him strongly as their candidate in 1840. In standing for reelection, Van Buren held not only the electoral advantages of incumbency, but the greater popular advantage of having been designated the "crown prince" by "King" Andrew—Andrew Jackson, Van Buren's revered predecessor, whom he had served both as secretary of state between 1828 and 1830 and as vice president for Old Hickory's second term, 1832 to 1836. No endorsement could have struck the common people—the traditional constituency of the party ever since Jefferson four decades before—more favorably, for Jackson was the unquestioned favorite of the masses.[4]

By 1836 Van Buren's slickness and subtlety as a political operator had earned him the popular monickers "The Red Fox" and "The Little Magician." In his early days in New York State politics he had decisively outfoxed the established DeWitt Clinton machine, replacing it with his own socalled Albany Regency; and upon entering the national scene, he had outmaneuvered the brilliant and powerful John C. Calhoun, Jackson's first vice president, for the role of anointed successor. Such aptitude seemed to his contemporaries like a sort of political magic; but no sooner had Van Buren cast his ultimate political spell and won the White House for himself than he encountered a problem that even a political wizard of his powers could not transmogrify: the Panic of 1837.

Perhaps the best way to understand the Panic, a terrible depression whose economic effects were still being felt six years later, is as America's first mass loss of nerve. In the growth years since the recession of 1819, runaway expansion—"overbanking and overtrading," as the incumbent Democrats tersely diagnosed it—had created an unnerving amount of debt

MARTIN VAN BUREN. *Library of Congress.*

and questionable currency. These sorts of monetary entities depend for their value largely on the amount of credence that people give them, and in the boom times of the late twenties and early thirties such credence was easy—because profitable—to give. But certain economic events had changed the situation by 1837. Painfully for Van Buren and devastatingly for the common people who were hit hardest by the Panic, most of those events had resulted from the monetary policy of Andrew Jackson, Van Buren's political patron and the common people's champion.

The most prominent element in Jackson's monetary policy had been the destruction of the Second Bank of the United States. By a strictly political calculation, Jackson's resolute campaign against the bank indisputably was a brilliant and profitable move: by his championing of what he portrayed as the common people's cause against "that Monster" and against the privileged classes which he claimed it represented, Jackson cemented a long-standing personal relationship with that constituency.[5] But these common people were the first to suffer the economically disruptive effects of the bank's destruction: its demise removed the only influential check on the emission of paper by state banks, thus in effect fostering questionable banking practices. When the economic climate began to change, these practices literally were called to account.

There was also another sense in which Jackson's economic policies had contributed significantly to the conditions of the 1837 depression; but this time the sin was not of commission, but of omission. The economic trends that were allowed to arise under Jackson's laissez-faire, a central tenet of the democratic faith as Old Hickory practiced it, transformed the vital economic relationships in a subtle way. This change eventually exposed the vulnerability of the American economy.

The uncontrolled expansion of investment naturally had brought on more absentee ownership, divorcing ownership from management. This combined with the rise of cities to enfeeble the neighborly, or at least paternalistic, sentiments with which many of the first American capitalists had regarded their workers in towns and villages. "Slowly, private morality and business morality grew apart. Slowly, the commercial community developed a collection of devices and ceremonials which enabled businessmen to set aside [for purposes of their business] the ethic which ruled their private life and personal relations."[6] Slowly, in short, the vital economic relationships were becoming impersonal.

> There was a price—a high price—Americans paid for "go ahead." They no longer had the security of a tightly integrated society in which all persons had a place and knew their responsibilities and what was expected of them. In the past everybody had belonged; all were important to each other and to society as a whole. Individuals, no matter what they did for a living or what their social position, had the comforting

knowledge that they were needed and wanted. And this strong sense of belonging and participation were buttressed by the powerful links of family, community responsibility and church membership. But "go ahead" changed all that. With men and women on the move, scrambling to achieve material success, they had no time for the needs of others. Their responsibility was to themselves and their own goods. . . . They needs of the community in maintaining a stable society were problems for "others" to bother about.[7]

As a result of this change in the fundamental economic relationships, it was "every man for himself" in a way unprecedented in American history when the reversal in the general financial conditions came.

The beginning of this reversal occurred outside of the American sphere of influence entirely: a depression struck England. This quickly sent the price of cotton skidding downward. The suddenly squeezed investors of the Old World did not hesitate to liquidate their New World holdings and did so on a large enough scale to make money tight here. Then, in his last year in office, Jackson signed the Specie Circular. This law effectively drained gold and silver from the monetary centers, both on the seaboard and in the West, undercutting the relative credibility and value of paper. Land prices promptly plummeted. As the monetary situation continued to decay, there spread "a sudden wave of doubt . . . now the mood of America began to change dramatically. From being a nation of people who would boast, with Phillip Hone, that they could 'run faster, sail smarter, dive deeper, and fly further than any other people on the face of the earth,' Americans rushed to foreclose; planters and farmers were in despair as they looked for additional sources of credit; businessmen and laborers became alike distrustful and uneasy."[8]

What could Van Buren have done to stem the mounting tide of events? Economic historians disagree about so complex a question. Possibly some kind of central monitoring of credit, had it been exercised early enough and energetically enough, could have helped control one of the Panic's major causes; more probably, it was too late by the time Van Buren took office to do much of anything except to try to cushion the depression's effects. But both these sorts of measures would have run contrary to the laissez-faire theory of economics to which the Democratic party in general and Jackson and Van Buren in particular subscribed. In the hindsight of subsequent historical events, many ways have been found to criticize this belief that pure laissez-faire economics served the interests of common people. Our perspectives enjoy the advantage of history: the subsequent rise of monopolies and trusts in the absence of federal intervention and the success of "safety net" programs may qualify some of our ideas on the matter. But through all the controversy, no scholar of the period has suggested that Van Buren ever broke faith with the economic policy or ideology of his mentor;

nor has it ever been alleged that the besieged new president failed to do everything he could have done—within, that is, the limits of those ideas. If part of the responsibility rested with Van Buren, surely the people could be expected to see that a considerable part had also been earned by their unimpeachable favorite, Old Hickory himself. Yet, come election time, the people did not for a moment indict the Great Man. Instead, they erroneously—hypocritically—invoked him in laying the blame for the materially shakier state of the nation on his faithful political heir.

Despite their large-scale affiliation with the Democratic party, most doctrinaire democrats probably could have accepted the Whig victory in 1840 with the detached tolerance characteristic of idealists had the campaign been an intelligent disputation of the issues—had the people been offered the opportunity to learn about these complicated and difficult matters, to identify their interests for themselves, and to decide the question in something like the corporate process of reasoned deliberation that is the keystone of democratic faith. And in point of fact, there actually were attempts at rational discussion in the campaign. In *The Log Cabin,* for example, Horace Greeley patiently explained the case "for protection, a sound and uniform currency, distribution, and a restriction of executive privilege."[9] But the election—popularly called "the great commotion"—of 1840 was characterized by profoundly different techniques of campaigning, whose efficacy in swaying the democratic audience replaced the familiar, Jackson-ordained Van Buren with little-known William Henry Harrison— and whose nature caused distress and not a little despair on the part of believers. As a Whig banner of 1840 very accurately proclaimed, "We stoop to conquer!"[10]

A crucial factor in the Whig strategy was the somewhat unusual character of their candidate. It was at least vaguely possible to perceive him as presidential timber: he *had* caused a minor electoral ripple in the presidential canvass of 1836 on the strength of a modest military reputation resuscitated from the War of 1812. But to the Whig kingmakers, Harrison offered a singular virtue as a candidate, or at least a singular utility. He was, bluntly, "a man of no known views." During the campaign his critics came to call him "General Mum."[11] Indeed, his proponents plotted to present him this way:

> If Gen Harrison is taken up as a candidate . . . let him say not one single word about his principles, or his creed—let him say nothing— promise nothing. Let no Committee, no Convention—no town meeting ever extract from him a single word, about what he thinks now, or what he will do hereafter. Let the use of pen and ink be wholly forbidden as if he were a mad poet in Bedlam.[12]

This stance made sense for a party that claimed to be based on "not men, but principles" yet somehow never managed to issue a platform. As one strategist had advised, "in politics, as in Philosophy—it is unwise to give more reasons than are necessary." Thus it was with some truth that Harrison's critics observed that "on most major issues, Harrison's views were carefully concealed, doubtless even from himself." But the way these critics, including the doctrinaire democrats, viewed Harrison was one thing; the way the common people were brought to see him was quite another. The popular point of view was carefully shaped by the Whig strategists, and objective onlookers recognized this shaping as a classic exercise in the misuse of rhetoric—in the perversion of the arts of persuasion to defraud the gullible electorate and in the misuse of those skills to lessen the status and reformulate the role of persuasion itself in the democratic process of decision making.[13]

In the personal mythification of the candidate, predictably much was made of (and manufactured from) Old Tip's war record; but even more interesting was what happened to simple biographical facts. Harrison was a prosperous landowner with a comfortable farmhouse overlooking the well-settled Ohio River; but, for the purposes of the campaign, he was transformed into "the Cincinnatus of the West": a common farmer once more called to service by his grateful, again-needful nation from his plow and his beloved, if humble, log cabin on the edge of the wilderness, whose "latch-string . . . was always out for the ever-welcome visitor." Poverty and common breeding had suddenly become the chic political fashion: "Wealthy Whigs put on 'cowhide boots, felt hats and homespun coats' in order to register their humble circumstances and thus woo the voters more successfully." More prominent ones (including even Daniel Webster), knowing that they could not credibly sell themselves as log cabin born, did the next best thing: publicly regretting the conditions of their upbringing, they explained that close relatives or at least intimate associates had been frontier bred. "Shrewd men in politics . . . paid lip service to the common man, managing to explain their own origins, their careers, and their political beliefs in terms that were highly flattering to Tom, Dick, and Harry. . . . Common men there were in abundance." Public discourse was filled with such personal details, some apochryphal, an occasional few otherwise—but details which, even if true, seemed to the critics of democracy politically trivial.[14]

Meanwhile, encouraged by each success, the Whigs launched a full-scale campaign of totally contrived personal slander against the Democrats in general and Van Buren in particular:

> Whig editors sneered at their General's critics as "Eastern office-holder pimps." Nor did the new masters of demagogy neglect their opponent, the portly and decorous little Van. If Harrison was the "Cincinnatus of the West," Van Buren was "a man who wore corsets, put cologne on his

Harrison Campaign Poster. *Library of Congress.*

whiskers, slept on French beds, rode in a British coach and ate with golden spoon from silver plates when he sat down to dine in the White House." In Thurlow Weed's thoughtful language, Van was a "grovelling demagogue" who had "slimed himself into the Presidency." In a startling reversal of party name-calling, the Democratic candidate was called the symbol of a "bloated aristocracy."[15]

As personalities came to the fore of the campaign, the discussion of issues receded. Of course issues can be used for political hucksterism too. What may be less recognizable is that a rhetoric of personal identification — a rhetoric appealing to the speaker's character — can at its best bring to the public mind and conversation matters of intellectual, moral, and political substance. Since issues may pass and new ones arise, the particular stands a candidate takes are sometimes less revealing than the characteristic ways he recognizes, formulates, and thinks through political problems. For example, arguably the character of the candidate was the best single indicator of what to expect from the administrations of a Theodore Roosevelt, a Calvin Coolidge, a Harry Truman, a Richard Nixon. Clearly, however, the rhetoric of 1840 was not crafted to communicate the substance of the candidate's thought and character; it was not an "ethos-based" rhetoric at its best, but rather at its most indulgent. In this it seemed, disturbingly, only to be giving the audience what it wanted, indulging what it craved; attempts to introduce substance into the nation's political discussion gave the voting public more than it wanted to think about. The consistent behavior of that democratic audience was to ignore issues and to accept the images uncritically, as if they comprised the kind of language in which Americans now preferred to carry on their political discussion. The public was assured that Old Tip had magnificent principles and was not to be bothered with any nitpicking discussion about what those principles were. When such a discussion somehow did arise, the people's handlers dealt with it in two ways: they rendered it less possible in itself by changing or obscuring the usual relationship between words and meanings; and they rendered it irrelevant to the larger process, by reconstituting that process into another kind of politics.

Obfuscation of the issues and misrepresentation of opposing candidates' stands were hardly novel in electoral politics. Genuinely new in 1840 was the concerted and successful attempt to reduce the ability of political language to communicate — by means of awkward, unusual phrasing, by rhythmic but not necessarily meaningful slogans, and by a whole raft of neologisms that acquired what meanings they had only through usage during the course of the campaign.[16] James Fenimore Cooper observed, "the confusion over terminology sometimes amounts to a kind of political lunacy"; "lunacy" was the only alternative when political sense could no longer be made.[17]

Three of the new words introduced to describe kinds of 1840 politicking still are in use today: "ballyhoo," "hoopla," and "buncombe" ("bunk"). They refer to the barnstorming techniques that the Whigs used in place of substantive discussion—used not only to obscure substantive embarrassments linguistically, but to render them irrelevant to the process of democratic decision making as they hoped to reconstitute it. Torchlight parades were held, complete with bands, flags, and—thoughtfully—fake Indians to recall Old Tip's military victories. The common folk were invited to free barbeques. Model log cabins were dragged and huge "victory balls" were rolled enormous distances by puffing faithful, one all the way to Baltimore from Allegany County, Maryland. And of course all these rollicking mass activities were amply fueled with hard cider, dispensed in smaller versions of Old Tip's inescapable log cabin. "Free cider and torchlight parades," Cooper concluded, "had much to do with the confused vision of American voters during the giddy campaign of 1840."[18] Campaigning to the new, democratic audience was no longer intended to clear the vision of the deliberating electors so their choices could be rationally—that is, freely and independently—made; it was aimed instead at confusing that vision sufficiently to make any rational choice impossible and to reduce the grounds for individual political decision to gut feelings of emotional or even physical sorts.

That this was a reconstitution of the democratic process, of the way politics is conducted in a democratic society, is perhaps most apparent in the humiliating diminution of the role played by the individual voter. Once he had been treated as the sovereign citizen whom the campaign was in some measure to inform and to educate, so that he might make a rational, free decision. But that had been a different rhetorical situation, with a more select, better-educated electorate for an audience. Now the electorate had been expanded to include a new kind of voter who had by 1840 obviously come to dominate it; the commensurate new kind of politics treated him as a boozy reveler who was to fall obediently into the now-staggering step of the political parade, over whose direction he exercised no influence. Those giant victory balls, for all their silliness, might have provided the campaign's most insidious image. Elections had been thought of as the function in which the American was simultaneously most fully a citizen and most fully free, in making as he judged fit his country's decisions. But now elections were not to be construed by the voter as his individual decision, with individual responsibility, about what should be done; instead, they were to be seen as mass registers of political momentum—and heaven help anyone who didn't "keep the ball rolling!" and jump on the bandwagon in time; as the president of the Whig convention announced, "the Avalanche of the people is here!"[19] In rhetorical terms, the issue was whether the democratic audience was to be addressed and moved in its identity as a mass, in which case persuasion would be a simple matter of impersonal, *de*personalizing momenta; or if democratic rhetoric was to address its audience as individual, morally independent human beings, as free citizens, in which case persuasion would actually involve ways of thinking.

The politics of 1840 diminished the role of the citizen individually and the status of politics as a communal function. What the doctrinaire democrats found so disheartening in the politics of 1840 was that the emergent democratic audience had bought it all enthusiastically: Harrison 234, Van Buren 60 was the final tally of the electoral college. In defeat, astonishingly, Van Buren had received nearly 400,000 *more* votes than he had obtained in his victorious 1836 campaign: the popular vote had increased by a startling 54 percent over that of 1836.[20] Clearly Harrison's victory resulted not so much in restructuring the traditional political alignments, but in rousting out and capturing the great numbers of the new voters.

It was Orestes Brownson who, echoing Alcuin, had once passionately declared his allegiance to the "vox populi"; "the voice of the people is the voice of God; and when God speaks, who dare deny that he will be heard and obeyed?" But now Brownson, perhaps the "most implacably logical" and surely one of the most devoted of all those who believed in democracy felt himself nonetheless inexorably led by the results of the election to conclusions once unthinkable, but now inescapable:

> Truth had no beauty, sound argument no weight, patriotism no influence. They who had devoted their lives to the cause of their country, of truth, justice, liberty, humanity, were looked upon as enemies of the people, and were unable to make themselves heard amid the maddened and maddening hurrahs of the drunken mob that went for "Tippecanoe and Tyler too." It was a sorry sight, to see the poor fellows rolling huge balls and dragging log cabins at the bidding of the demagogues, who were surprised to find how easily the enthusiasm of the people could be excited by hard cider and doggerel rhymes. . . . An instructive year, that 1840, to all who have sense enough to read it aright. What happened then may happen again, if not in the same form, in some other form equally foolish, and equally pernicious; and, therefore, if we wish to secure to ourselves and our posterity the blessings of freedom and good government, we must secure stronger guaranties than popular suffrage and popular virtue and intelligence.[21]

To Brownson and a great number of his colleagues, the election of Harrison augured something deeper and far worse than a political defeat. The people had frivolously deserted their true interests and faithful leaders, "all for a song, hard cider, and a shabby little military hero." Not only had the people been deceived; the startling fact was that the people could be hoodwinked so badly but feel so exultantly good about it. The democratic character which Brownson saw emerging in 1840 brought him to doubt the most fundamental abilities of the people to fulfill the public duties with which they would be entrusted in any democratically organized society: "Suffrage rests for its basis, as a guaranty of freedom and good government, in the assumed intelligence and virtue of the people," he wrote. "Its grand maxim is 'The People can do no wrong.' Now this may be very beautiful in theory, but when we come to practice, this virtue and intelligence of the people is all a humbug." By 1840, even for doctrinaire democrats, the powers of rhetoric had demonstrated that the theory of democracy could no longer be an unquestioned invocation of the people's voice.[22]

For so radical a doubt, there is no consolation in the perspective that Arthur Schlesinger, Jr., offers: "Though a long view is perhaps inadequately comforting in the short run, the election of 1840, if a setback for the Democrats, was not necessarily a setback for democracy. In a sense, it was the most conclusive evidence of the triumph of Jackson. Conservatism had carried the election, but it had to assume the manner of the popular party in order to do it." Unfortunately, the problem of the democratic audience did not occur to concerned observers as merely one of style or manner; even as articulated by the most sympathetic and optimistic of them, the problem was one of substance, or, to be more precise, one of lack of substance. When Walt Whitman had looked closely at the democratic audience, he had seen in them nothing less than the stuff of poetry; yet he could not help but also notice "the shallowness and miserable selfism of these crowds of men, with all their minds so blank of high humanity and aspiration—then comes the terrible query, and will not be denied: 'is not Democracy of human rights humbug after all?' "[23] Even the faith of Ralph Waldo Emerson had been shaken: "Will it not be dreadful to discover," he worried, "that this experiment made by America, to ascertain if men can govern themselves, does not succeed?"[24]

The year 1840 was a watershed for the democratic faith in America. It was in the results of this election that the character of Americans as constituting a democratic audience emerged clearly enough for all to see. It emerged as an issue itself, for it would help determine the nature of American democracy and the role of the common people in it. The qualities that characterized this democratic audience seemed even to its most sympathetic observer to constitute a fundamental problem for its intellectual and moral abilities to take up a significant role in a society worth living in.

Characterizing the Democratic Audience: Age of Egalitarianism and Andrew Jackson

What we lovingly admire, that, in some degree, we are.
—*Historian* JAMES PARTON,
on Andrew Jackson

BY the election of 1840, when the democratic character of the American audience of public discourse had emerged for even its most doctrinaire supporters to see, many of its distinguishing traits seemed to present serious public problems. The nature of those problems and the character of the democratic audience may be most intelligible in terms of the process in which they developed. Years before their dismaying emergence in 1840, that process had begun in the peculiar physical and moral conditions from which America distinctively grew. It intensified in political changes that made the presidential election the focal point of politics, the most forceful expression of the political character of the whole people. It culminated in the emergence of Andrew Jackson, a leader "created by his contemporaries to embody the characteristic virtues they ascribed to themselves as a people," a hero who "was the nation's image of itself."[1]

To understand the nature and causes of what happened in 1840, we must turn back the pages of history to the Age of Jackson. This chapter will sketch the process of democratization as it reconstituted American rhetoric and politics in such a way that a Jackson could emerge as a representative figure; examine the characterisitics of Jackson that made him appealingly, identifyingly representative and the characteristics of his audience that made so many identify with his representation; discuss the historical dubiousness of these apparent characteristics and the implications for rhetoric of this sort of representation and identification; and show how the short-

comings, virtues, and needs of the emerging democratic character are accessible to study as rhetorical phenomena, as they were accessible to practical
recharacterizing and reconstitution in the rhetorical process.

America was not the only legatee of the Western cultural heritage; if in
some sense it "produced" us, it also produced nations of different characters. We can take a cue from Alexis de Tocqueville, who began his classic
account of *Democracy in America* by sorting out the conditions that gave
our inheritance its peculiarly American twist.[2] The awesome physical facts
of separating ocean and threatening wilderness made life in the newly discovered continent quite different from that in settled Europe; this was literally a "New World" in which different demands were placed on society and
different social organization came to be required, as John Smith's famous
"no work, no eat" order manifested. In settling a harsh new environment,
the privileges of the gentry were not always welcome or even supportable;
in the common susceptibility of men to factors like hunger and fear, a
certain kind of equality was imposed. The fullest and most forceful argument for "The Significance of the Frontier in American History" was presented by Frederick Jackson Turner: "the true point of view in the history
of this nation is not the Atlantic coast," he contended, but the frontier at
each stage of its advance; and "to study this advance, the men who grew up
under these conditions and the political, economic, and social results of it,
is to study the really American part of our history."[3]
    Turner's theory of the frontier as safety valve attempts to explain how
the frontier broke down the established class structures and offered opportunities for advancement to men of industry and talent. The theory has
been subject to considerable criticism and qualification: one may suspect,
for example, that the class breakdown may not have been as prompt and
complete as Turner portrays it; that advancement more than occasionally
was affected by established, "unearned" factors like family prestige and
fortune; or that the opportunities were not equally available – not as available, for example, to the new urban poor as the entrepreneurs of the West.[4]
Yet one may still concur in the general notion that the frontier broke down
some established class structures and offered *some* new opportunities for
advancement to men of industry and merit. Perhaps more importantly, it
offered the sense of opportunities; people of the time found the notion of
the possibility for advancement increasingly credible, so much so that their
belief eventually generalized to the characteristically American "myth of
the self-made man" and "the doctrine of self-improvement." In fact, among
the social forces promoting democratization in the eighteenth and nineteenth centuries, "the most powerful force of all was, no doubt, the general
quest for knowledge and self-improvement." In this quest, Americans be-

came "a people in motion"; "a breathless cupidity perpetually distracts the mind from the pleasures of the imagination and the labors of the intellect and urges it on to nothing but the pursuit of wealth." This common characteristic, in short, amounted practically to a materialism so pure as to be a kind of idealism.[5]

The idea that merit, taking its main chance, led directly to advancement was to find more and more support in observable fact. Consequently it grew in popular credence to the extent that it began to reorder the very assumptions Americans made about their situation and possibilities:

> "If he had not talents and virtues, would he not have remained in obscurity?" Behind that "if" lies the assumption that the world is a world of justice, an ordered world in which God permits "effects to follow their appropriate causes." Because they did not doubt that virtue does not receive its own reward, believers in the myth of the self-made man were not arguing from cause to effect; they were arguing from effect back to cause.[6]

If the period was not quite Turner's age of frontier egalitarianism it was at the time broadly and confidently thought to be and treated as if it were so. This confidence and the wide-ranging ambition it engendered characterized the age so well as to become a permanent part of the national identity.

During this period democratization was also progressing on the specifically political front. The deliberations of governmental units like the town meeting—which for simple reason of geography operated with an important degree of independence—were fostering the skills, and perhaps more tellingly, the moral habits of self-determination. "Americans by the hundreds," as Charles and Mary Beard put it, "learned to practice and think about the arts of government." Tocqueville observed that even in normal circumstances, "men generally stick more tenaciously to their habits than to their lives." In extraordinary circumstances this became all the more applicable, for these habits and the basic rights to exercise them were sanctified by the sacrifices of the Revolution and its subsequent mythology.[7]

In this period not only the habits but the issues of self-government became a familiar part of the popular consciousness. The public debate in America was an active and broadly attended one from the early 1760s through the Constitutional Convention, including works of such enduring quality as Edmund Burke's speeches "On Moving Resolutions for Conciliation with the Colonies" and "On American Taxation"; Tom Paine's *Common Sense; The Federalist Papers* of Hamilton, Madison, and Jay; and Benjamin Franklin's great use of autobiography as political and cultural argument, *The Autobiography.*

But it should also be noted that significant events of political democratization continued to occur even after the adoption of the Constitution. In the early nineteenth century extremely influential political democratizations were enacted in three different areas: in voting qualification requirements, in the procedure of determining members of the electoral college, and in the nomination of presidential candidates.

Between 1812 and 1821 six new Western states entered the Union with constitutions providing for "universal" — that is, white manhood — suffrage, or something functionally like it. Meanwhile, four of the older states lowered property qualifications substantially or dropped them entirely, allowing the vote to the growing classes of small farmers and poor laborers. These laws effectively broadened the base of political power, as election figures of the time vividly demonstrate. The year 1824 is the first election from which we have relatively complete statistics, and even these statistics were probably unrepresentative as a result of that year's peculiar electoral situation: the triumphs of particular candidates in certain states — William Crawford in Virginia, Jackson in Pennsylvania and in his home state of Tennessee — were widely taken for granted, and undoubtedly a significant number of voters in these states lost interest. In any event, the total vote in the 1824 election was in the neighborhood of 355,000. While general interest was unquestionably heightened in the campaign and election of 1828, the rise to approximately 1,155,000 votes cast nevertheless is sizeable. In the ensuing years, while the population did not quite double, the total vote tripled, culminating in that 54 percent increase of the popular vote in 1840.[8] But not only were more people voting; because of democratizing reforms on two other levels, votes were counting for more.

At the turn of the century only two states determined their delegates to the electoral college by popular vote. By 1824, however, all but six states had changed their method of selection to allow voters to elect the delegates directly; eight years later, only South Carolina was still employing its old indirect procedure.[9] At the same time the procedure for nominating candidates for the presidency changed. The old system of congressional caucus was replaced by that distinctively American innovation, the national party convention. Delegates to such conventions were elected by various methods, involving varying degrees of democratization; but all of the methods were adopted to facilitate an increased degree of popular representation, if not popular control.

The net effects of these changes were that they "gave a popular dimension to the presidential contest, created or enhanced the need for state party machinery . . . and made the presidential election the dramatic focal point of American politics."[10] The doctrinaire democrats could find the presidential election of 1840 more portentous than any other because the presidential election now expressed more forcefully than any other canvass the political character of the whole people. All these changes — in voter qualification, in the selection of presidential electors, and in the nomination of presidential candidates — included dramatically more Americans in their country's public life and by 1840 had distributed significantly more political power among them.

Thus the special significance of the election of 1840 was that through it, the character of the democratic audience emerged in identifiable fashion. Even ardent believers in democracy recognized that character and its peculiar vulnerabilities and were forced to qualify their belief. The year 1840 was an unmistakable sign — or symptom, as some insisted — of not only the broadening but the reshaping of the American public sphere. It also signaled the full development of the peculiar needs that this reconstitution created, needs so serious that the emergence of the democratic audience could no longer be overlooked or denied. But it had not, of a sudden, emerged fully grown, the wide-eyed surprise of some observers notwithstanding. The democratic audience had developed and exhibited its identifying characteristics years earlier, although most observers were slow to grasp its implications. In distinctively democratic manner, the democratically characterized American public had raised to be its leader a representative figure who embodied qualities by which it identified itself. Andrew Jackson seemed to be a hero against the odds in the scramble of life, an outsider who, in championing equality of opportunity, became the direct representative of the people.

> The rise of Andrew Jackson and the other "new men" who came to the fore after the end of the Virginia Dynasty was widely regarded as the ascension of self-made common men — albeit men of unusual ability and determination — to the highest levels of government. That humble origins — actual or alleged — were all the rage in the era of "Tippecanoe and Tyler too!" was a sign that the people would no longer settle for leadership by an elite. Tom, Dick and Harry insisted on leaders in their own image.[11]

> In rising from log cabin to White House, he had repeatedly displayed those qualities of industry and initiative that everyone agreed were essential to individual success. In his relentless search for the main chance, he had been merchant, lawyer, planter, speculator, and officeholder. He could, and did, drive a hard bargain, and he believed in the Calvinistic doctrine of the efficacy of hard work. In every respect he was a representative figure of the acquisitive age in which he lived.[12]

> The spirit of an age sometimes descends to future generations in the form of a man...his countryman saw their image and spirit in Andrew Jackson.[13]

In Robert Remini's words, "the Revolutionary Age of Andrew Jackson changed much of America's way of life." It was during this period when Jackson captured and dominated the imagination of the common people that the role those masses would play in American life was first being formulated. The age "established the nation's basic political practices and patterns"; it was during Jackson's public life that many aspects of the character of American democracy, which long before had been theoretically described and given legal definition by the founding fathers, were being worked out practically. Thus the presidency of Andrew Jackson "stands at the beginning of the modern America we have inherited."[14] Jackson was, in a peculiar but rhetorically relevant sense, the most "representative" figure of American culture in the early nineteenth century: the events of his career and the qualities of his character (or at least, the qualities of what Americans took to be his character) corresponded with the identifying and enduring characteristics of the democratic audience that was then still emerging.

Jackson as the Hero against the Odds

From start to finish, the War of 1812 was full of bizarre anomalies. For example, one of the prime reasons why the United States went to war had been the set of British orders-in-council—orders that Britain repealed two days before hostilities were declared. The treaty that finally ended the war did not settle, nor even bother to address, a single one of the remaining points of contention. In so strange a conflict, Andrew Jackson's celebrated victory at New Orleans fit right in; for this battle, the most famous of the war, took place after the treaty ending the war had been signed and the war was officially over.

Over the course of the conflict, the Americans had been suffering more than their share of serious military reverses; but perhaps the more serious blows were being dealt to the young nation's self-image. "The buoyant optimism which had marked the opening of the war," as Remini puts it, "had given way by the end to gloom and despair."[15] This change of heart must have seemed at least somewhat warranted to the average American: by the beginning of 1815, Washington—the capital of the young nation itself—lay in ashes, the Hartford Convention was in session, and cities up and down the East Coast were in a positive uproar over rumors of an approaching British armada. The *Salem Gazette* was even considering whether the union was not already "virtually dissolved"; the *Boston Daily Advertiser* published the view that a British victory at New Orleans would actually be good for the country, in that it would expose the weakness of the administration and rid the union of Louisiana, "a curse to the nation," to boot. Meanwhile, money lenders in New Orleans refused to loan money or advance funds, even for so short a period as sixty days, in confident anticipation of a change of government in the interim. When word spread that the British were approaching New Orleans, the most positive position that the proadministration press would venture was that "if the British succeeded, they will know they have been in a fight." Far more representative of American sentiment was the *New-York Evening Post's* straight-forward assumption that the enemy had celebrated Christmas in New Orleans, and it was even alleged that the administration already had in hand an official account of the city's fall, but feared to release the news. In sum, the mood of the country was one of pervasive despair. Then burst the news of the crushing triumph of Andrew Jackson.[16]

GLORIOUS!!!
Unparalleled Victory!

ALMOST INCREDIBLE VICTORY!!
Glorious News.

RISING GLORY OF THE AMERICAN REPUBLIC![17]

The papers blared the joyous tidings to an astonished nation, and soon thereafter they were printing news of the peace. Modern treatments of the War of 1812 deplore as a matter of course "that the Atlantic Cable had not yet been laid in 1815 so that the needless carnage of the Battle of New Orleans could have been averted"; but it is one register of what Jackson's victory meant to his young nation that contemporary appraisals of the battle, its losses notwithstanding, unabashedly maintained the contrary view. "How fortunate it is for the U.S. that the peace did not arrive *before* the attack was made," one editor gushed; "the brilliant and unparalleled victory at *New-Orleans* has closed the war in a blaze of glory," rhapsodized another, who concluded that the victory of Andrew Jackson had "placed America on the very pinnacle of fame."[18] It is clear that the country was particularly inclined to believe that Jackson had outwitted the British, and with his legendary Tennessee frontier marksmen had outfought them; to believe, that is, that Jackson in particular and Americans in general had successfully defied the odds. What is striking about the persuasiveness of this belief for Americans is how very much its subscribers cheerfully overlooked in order to maintain it. The mythification of Andrew Jackson, like that of Washington before him, had become a persuasive political factor — even though that myth flatly contradicted publicly known facts.

Jackson's conduct of the battle, while undeniably creative and audacious, was known to have been something short of uniformly brilliant. Before the fighting even started, Jackson almost squandered the invaluable aid of Jean Lafitte's Baratarian pirates. The grounds on which Jackson first publicly scorned their help were curious ones for either the military mastermind or a democratic hero: though he conceded that as fighters the Baratarians were courageous, capable, and experienced, Jackson for a time held himself above consorting with the "hellish banditti." He relented at the insistence of a specially formed committee of New Orleans's leading citizens — its "first men," from whom the general at last found it appropriate to accept this kind of advice. Then, in his preparations for the battle, Jackson committed a careless and potentially devastating error. To close the many waterways that led to the city, Jackson had commanded that large trees be felled across them. An effective tactic — had he closed all of the bayous in a systematic way. The British advance force, 1,600 men, simply searched the water passages until they found an unclogged one — the waterway, appropriately enough, that the locals called Bayou Bienvenue. Jackson had carelessly left open a vital artery; and as even the most sympathetic of observers admitted, had the British marched directly on the city, the defenses as Jackson had deployed them could not have withstood such a sizeable onslaught at that point of attack.[19]

Moreover, luck in the form of British stupidity and of favorable weather conditions were factors as influential in the American victory as Jackson's tactics had been. The redcoated invaders made gross logistical errors like using hogsheads of sugar to fortify gunnery emplacements — which would have been rather a better tactic if hogsheads of sugar had sufficient density to stop bullets. As it was, the Americans simply had to shoot into the British artillery emplacements to inflict a disheartening number of casualties before any direct battle had yet been joined. When the British finally did decide to attack, they sent their main strike force directly across the cypress swamps where they promptly bogged down, losing invaluable time and equipment. Perhaps more astonishing was the British decision to attack on a day so foggy that their attacking troops could not even see where the American positions were, so they could not determine in just which direction they had to proceed. After wandering about and incurring heavy casualties for more than an hour, the confused and desperate British decided to dig in and make the best of their situation, wherever they happened to be. For three hours a ferocious battle was pitched — with the redcoats below the guns of the Americans, who were nearly invisible in the remaining fog and rising battle smoke. The casualty count can be (and of course was) interpreted as an evidence of Jackson's military genius; or it can be seen as an index of the inferiority of the British position and how astonishingly long it took the hapless British command to make the simple realization that their troops were sitting ducks: while 2,057 British were killed, only 11 Americans died.[20]

But the many auxiliary causes involved in the British defeat are, of course, not quite the right stuff from which personal myths are made. The understanding of the Battle of New Orleans that satisfied the American public was partial and selective; Americans evidently suffered as an audience the common tendency to simplify situations. But there was one curious peculiarity: the kind of essentials to which this particular audience strongly tended to reduce matters were qualities of personal character. What had to be taken into account about the battle did not include tactical blunders of the enemy or accidents of condition, however influential they might have been. What was worth remembering about New Orleans was Jackson's undeniable courage, *his* cleverness, the heroism of *his* success.

Apparently the reason only these particular qualities were remembered about Jackson's victory was that they corresponded resonantly with characteristics inherent in the democratic audience. "In the original American populistic dream, the omnipotence of the common man was fundamental"; the common man's ability to triumph over even the most difficult situation was crucial to the way the average American understood himself in the early nineteenth century. Indeed, this "can-do" confidence had been becoming an identifying national characteristic. And it was a characteristic with practical consequences: Americans had become "an optimistic people, and, being optimistic, they were profit-minded and risk-minded. . . . They admired boldness and respected material success." It is likely that the war had temporarily shaken this confidence. But now, after a period of national malaise and self-doubt, Americans had been given reason to believe again in this element of the American myth, reason in a sense to believe again in themselves: Jackson's bold and very material success in the battle of New Orleans — the triumph of the American hero against the odds.[21]

Jackson Entering the Scramble

Jackson's subsequent rough-and-ready governorship of Florida and his growing reputation as an Indian fighter were other prominent components of his personal mythification. They conformed to, perhaps even flattered, the American's vision of himself as the industrious and insuperable white man, courageously wresting the virgin wilderness from a variety of savage heathen who didn't exploit it very profitably anyway.

But Jackson's business provided a more important point of contact; that he had tried his hand at many enterprises with mixed results only endeared him the more to the restless age, famed for its wandering imagination and its short attention span for ideas and projects that didn't deliver immediate profit:

> Jackson himself was by no means unfamiliar with the entrepreneurial impulse that gave Jacksonian democracy so much of its freshness and vitality. An enterpriser of middling success, he could spontaneously see things from the standpoint of the typical American who was eager for advancement in the democratic game of competition — the master mechanic who aspired to open his own shop, the planter who hoped to be a judge, the local politician who wanted to go to Congress, the grocer who would be a merchant. He had entered the scramble himself in a variety of lines, as a professional man, a merchant, land speculator, a

planter, an office-holder, and a military chieftain. He understood the old Jeffersonian bias against the overgrown government machinery, the Westerner's resentment of the entrenched East, the new politician's dislike of the old bureaucracy, and the aspiring citizen's hatred of privilege.[22]

Jackson as the Political Outsider

When Jackson threw his hat into the political ring, his image as the man of the people continued to grow — and sometimes by providence as much as by design. In 1824, for example, the candidate whose stands were the most populist in the political terms and directions of the day was not Jackson, but Jefferson's lumpily uncharismatic protégé Senator William Crawford. But it happened that Crawford and the two other major candidates, Henry Clay and John Quincy Adams, held prominent positions, and it was common knowledge that each of them was backed by powerful political machines; as such, they came to be seen as representatives of entrenched special interests and minority factions, their avowed democratic convictions notwithstanding. And in an egalitarian age, nothing was more difficult for the mass of Americans to relate to, to be led by, or to identify with politically than entrenched power. Since Jackson as a relative newcomer was not seen as entrenched, by the weird luck of this process of elimination he became the candidate to whom the masses turned for political identity: "Few politicians have profited more from defeat than did Jackson in 1824. Entering the campaign as a military hero, he had emerged from the struggle as a symbol of democracy."[23] And what more fortunate time to become recognized as the candidate of the masses than precisely that period in which they emerge as a distinct and increasingly self-conscious electoral force?

If the election of 1824 led the specifically democratic audience to distinguish Jackson as their candidate, however, it was a distinction that could only have been sustained on the basis of personal style. Far from taking a definably different stand on the issues, Jackson kept trying to shift the rhetorical focus from consistent stands and reasoned evaluation to matters of personality; here, the campaign of Harrision — "General Mum," "Old Tip" — found a comprehensive model. Perhaps sneaking a quick glance at the electorate themselves, Adams's handlers took up precisely the same strategy. As the startled Fenimore Cooper saw it, "the question is entirely of men, there being scarcely a measure of policy that is likely to be affected by the result."[24]

Of the two candidates, however, Jackson's campaigns seemed generally freer from the clutter of substantive discussion: "In New York it was said no one in the Democratic caucus that nominated Jackson knew precisely what his principles were. One Pennsylvanian wrote to another, 'the great mystery of the case to me is that the South should support General Jackson avowedly for the purpose of preventing tariffs and internal improvements, and that we should support him for a directly opposite purpose!' " Old Hickory was attracting votes not by taking any persuasively distinct positions, but simply for being Old Hickory. Jackson's support, in Schlesinger's words, sprang from nothing more intellectually sophisticated than "the glowing enthusiasm for the Hero of New Orleans, and was largely uninformed by ideas, beyond a vague impression." But what other kind of impression could he have given the democratic audience? "Up to the time of his inauguration, Jackson had contributed neither a thought nor a deed to the democratic movement." In this respect Jackson benefitted enormously from the democratic audience's tendency to translate, and often to reduce, issues into terms of personalities, thought into terms of character.[25]

Nonetheless the outcome of the election of 1824 was closely contested among the four candidates, and its ultimate disposition stirred one of the greatest electoral controversies in American history. Jackson had won a small plurality of the electoral college ballots, but John Quincy Adams and Senators Henry Clay and William Crawford also had received considerable support—curiously, all as "Democratic Republican" candidates—so that no one managed a majority in the electoral college. The Constitution provided that "if no person have such majority, then from the persons having the highest numbers not exceeding three on the list of those voted for as President, the House of Representatives shall choose immediately, by ballot, the President."[26] Thus Crawford was eliminated from consideration, and Henry Clay, whose voted total was the least of the remaining three, was placed—or rather, visibly placed himself in the position of power broker, able to throw the election either to Adams or to Jackson as he chose.

Clay could have found some factors in Jackson's favor: since Old Hickory was from a western state, there was probably a greater confluence of sectional interests between him and Clay of Kentucky than between Clay and Adams of New England. Moreover, Jackson *had,* after all, been the choice, from a crowded field of candidates, of a plurality of the people. But after a period of fretful fence-sitting, Clay toppled over to Adams—and Jackson's supporters, along with a great many of the more disinterested observers, thought they knew why. Clay was not the least ambitious of American politicians: he would remain an active presidential candidate for another quarter century. Jackson clearly presented a more permanent obstacle to these presidential ambitions. John Quincy Adams was far from a savvy machine politician and seemed far less likely than Old Hickory to put together anything like the "Virginia Dynasty," which had given the country four of its first five chief executives (that Jackson successfully engineered the nomination of Van Buren in the teeth of initial resistance seems to bear out this appraisal). When the newly elected President Adams promptly appointed Clay secretary of state, Jacksonians howled, bitterly decrying the "unholy deal"; Jackson gained the image of the outsider, unjustly denied the presidency by entrenched powers; and the campaign of 1828 was on.

As publicly eye-opening a lesson as the campaign of 1840 would be, it was the presidential campaign of 1828 that taught insiders about the changed nature of democratic politics: "it was the campaign of 1828 that taught politicians the unforgettable lesson that an attractive candidate is likely to do very well if his friends and supporters spend money lavishly, have dozens of partisan newspapers scattered all over the union, concert their actions in Congress with the end in view always of promoting his chances in the next election, and span the country with a fine network of committees that are capable of organizing the campaign, disseminating propaganda and dispensing the vital ingredients in liquid or solid form that were assured to be the way to the voter's heart." The mythifications and misrepresentations that elected "Old Tip" Harrison merely amplified antecedents in the election of Old Hickory; as the *Democratic Review* of June 1840 moaned, "We have taught them to conquer us!"[27]

The popular conception that the ragged Jacksonians berated Adams in every possible way—as an overeducated, effete aristo, a former pimp for the czar of Russia, and, most slanderously of all, "a Federalist in sheep's clothing"—is quite true; but it should be noted that stalwarts of the austere Adams also "contributed their share of bitterness. They denounced Andrew Jackson as ignorant and hot-tempered, an irresponsible butcher of men, a liar and a blasphemer, a co-conspirator with Aaron Burr. They asserted with smirks and sneers that he had lived in sin with his Rachel before they had been legally married. They cited Jefferson as declaring that this wild Tennessean was unfit for the presidency and that his election would be dangerous to the public safety." Name-calling and deliberate misrepresentation—appropriately fueled and lubricated at the well-stocked political rallies—took on a role more prominent and more influential in the rhetoric of both sides than it had played in any election before:[28]

> The election of 1828 was not fought over great issues. . . . Questions important to the nation, it is true, were before the public eye—the tariff, land policy, internal improvements—but on these questions there were no clear-cut party stands. It was, rather, chicanery, slippery tactics, and downright falsehoods upon which the politicians relied to win the contest.[29]

In the clash of personalities, Jackson soon came to have all the better of it, and Adams's virtures were perverted into disadvantages distancing him from the common man. Richard Hofstadter claims that the single most powerful and important reaction was a new American anti-intellectualism.

> He [Adams] had studied in Paris, Amsterdam, and the Hague, as well as at Harvard; he had occupied Harvard's chair of rhetoric and ora-

tory; he had aspired to write epic poetry; like Jefferson, he was known for his scientific interests; he had been head for many years of the American Academy of Arts and Sciences; and as Monroe's Secretary of State, he had prepared a learned scientific report on systems of weights and measures which is still a classic.

Adams's administration, nonetheless, seemed to prove "the unsuitability of the intellectual temperament for political leadership in early eighteenth-century America." Anti-intellectual sentiment had really "made its way into our politics" as an influential factor in 1828, and it helped to turn the incumbent Adams into "the chief victim of the reaction against the learned": when the votes were tallied, the representative of the common man had been elected president.[30]

Jackson as "The Direct Representative of the People"

Probably the most persuasive democratic symbol of Jackson's political career was the famous inauguration party of 4 March 1829. The old man, garbed with conspicuous modesty in his plain black suit, delivered his inauguration speech to an excited and unexpectedly large crowd. Most were too far from the rostrum to hear much of what he said, but they cheered delightedly anyway and followed him in what seems to have been a spirit of almost carnival festivity down Pennsylvania Avenue to the White House. Jackson had his reception thrown open to all, "from the highest and most polished down to the most vulgar and gross in the nation." The symbolic value of this gesture was not lost on ardently democratic observers; for "the great number of new voters who exercised their franchise during the Jacksonian era and who flocked to Washington to cheer their approval of Old Hickory upon his inauguration, justified all the efforts of professional politicians and did, in fact, link them [the new voters] closer to the operation of government. Seeing these masses, reading the constant rise of the number of voters exercising the ballot, and looking at the candidates elected to office—every one of them, not simply Jackson alone—provided all they needed to argue that popular government had indeed arrived in the United States."[31]

For months afterward, pro-Jackson publishers did their best to make sure the legend was spread: "it was a proud day for the people," Amos Kendall exulted; by welcoming all comers, Jackson had proven that he was *"their own president."* Adherents of this way of looking at the inauguration party had a benign tendency to gainsay what happened next.

There was a mad rush to congratulate the Hero, and to get a share of the punch, ice cream, cake, and lemonade. But glass and china were smashed in the ensuing melee, ladies fainted, men's noses were bloodied. The President, saved by a cordon of his friends from being pressed against the wall, or even trampled, had to make his escape by a back door to his rooms at Gadsby's Tavern. The mansion was only saved from futher damage by taking the bowls of punch out on the lawn, the crowd following the refreshment.

"To the fastidious Justice Story, 'the reign of King Mob' seemed triumphant." It seemed that the great democratic gesture admitted of another interpretation; Story was a Justice of the Supreme Court, protégé of the great John Marshall and heir to another, older American tradition. The educated and wellborn for whom Justice Story spoke understood the inauguration party as a symbol of *dis*enfranchisement — the ill-advised and rather ungrateful disenfranchisement of the very kind of people who had made the country what it was, in favor of a class of citizens whose qualifications were, to put it politely, suspect, and whose behavior was literally enough to make the White House count the silverware at their departure. This suspicion was shared by several presciently sceptical observers of the American scene, even by Tocqueville, the great prophet of democracy: he energetically derides the "vulgar" and "obscure" little members of the House of Representatives, contrasting them to the greatly more distinguished, if more entrenched, members of the Senate:

> There is scarcely a man to be seen there whose name does not recall some recent claim to fame. They are eloquent advocates, distinguished generals, wise magistrates and noted statesmen. . . . Whence, then, comes this vast difference? I can see only one fact to explain it: the election which produces the House of Representatives is direct, whereas the Senate is subject to election in two stages.

Tocqueville generalized that democratic republics should make "more frequent use of election in two stages, unless they are to be miserably lost among the shoals of democracy."[32]

From a self-proclaimed "friend of democracy" this is a startlingly harsh indictment; but the direct enfranchisement of the common people was a prospect about which at least a few acute critics were growing uneasy long before "the election of General Harrison . . . seemed to demonstrate the vulnerability of the electorate."[33] It was the direct enfranchisement of this electorate that all of America saw symbolized in Jackson's inauguration party: some, in the open door of the White House; others, in the shards of glass and china, the muddied carpets, the broken furniture. In either case, "It was the People's Day, the People's President, and the People shall rule!"

> That was the sum and substance of it, according to most contemporaries. It was the end of limited republicanism, established under the Constitution, restricting government to the few — the educated, the well born, the property owners. Here was the beginning of truly popular

government in America — at least in spirit. And for the next eight years, under the administration of President Andrew Jackson, that spirit, in several particulars, was translated into political reality.[34]

Two of these particulars are also useful in revealing democratic characteristics developing in the American audience: the desires for equality in political and economic affairs.

Jackson and Equality of Opportunity

If the common man was now man enough, citizen enough to visit the president, it was natural for him to feel himself good enough to *become* the president, or any other officeholder in government. This feeling was strong enough that Jackson could justify even his most controversial policies by appeal to it, to the feeling of equality of qualification. It was in his annual message that Jackson articulated a policy by which his administration would be identified thereafter:

> Office is considered as a species of property; and Government rather as a means of promoting individual interests than as an instrument created solely for the service of the People. Corruption in some and in others a perversion of correct feelings and principles divert Government from its legitimate ends, and make it an engine for the support of the few at the expense of the many.
>
> The duties of all public offices are, or at least admit of being made, so plain and simple that men of intelligence may readily qualify themselves for their performance. . . . In a country where offices are created solely for the benefit of the people, no one man has any more intrinsic right to official station than another.[35]

A policy of rotation in office implied interchangeability of officeholders, and what could be more equalitarian than that? Jackon's policy thus was recognized and vindicated as a broad-based equalitarian measure. But like the heroism of New Orleans, what may be most interesting about the appeal involved here is how it retained its persuasiveness even when it showed itself not to conform very scrupulously to reality. The policy as Jackson *practiced* it — the "spoils system" with which he is so closely indentified — was neither broad-based nor equalitarian.

Only 919 of 10,093 federal officeholders were replaced in Jackson's first two years; for his whole two-term tenure, the figure barely edged over 10 percent. Granted, this turnover rate significantly exceeded that of the Adams administration: Adams had dismissed fewer than 10 officeholders. But in no way was it the wholesale housecleaning that Jackson seemed to have promised, or that his opponents had anticipated and feared. Worse, the policy readily adapted itself to a genuine spoils system in which public office became "a species of property" again — *partisan* property. The practical effect of the policy of rotation in office on democratic politics was to make appointment a kind of prize for support — or, seen from a more operational angle, an instrument of party discipline. The letters of Samuel Swartwout, one of Jackson's stalwarts who did gain appointment, describe clearly and rather pungently how the principle of rotation of office could be understood. "I hold to your doctrine fully," Swartwout wrote, "that no d — d rascal who made use of his office or its profits for the purpose of keeping Mr. Adams in, and General Jackson out of power, is entitled to the least lenity or mercy, save that of hanging"; to a friend, he confided, "whether or not I shall get any thing in the general scramble for plunder, remains to be proven; but I guess I shall." To say that he happened to guess correctly here is something of an understatement: Swartwout was appointed — over Van Buren's objection, no less — to the cushy position of collector of the port of New York.[36] Swartwout was so to distinguish himself in his conduct of this trust that when he ran off to Europe in 1839, he became the first American to steal a million dollars.[37]

But should the father be held responsible for the sins of the sons? If the policy of rotation was perverted by his underlings and especially by his successors, ought Jackson be blamed for the perversions? Arguably not. But a characteristic of what happened in Jackson's wake is how comfortably it all fits with Jackson's own execution of the policy.

It is difficult to break down Jackson's appointments meaningfully along partisan lines, because at the time there simply did not exist two distinct parties. The Federalist party of Washington and Hamilton had fallen into such wide popular disrepute that in 1824 and again in 1828, every candidate prominent enough to draw a single electoral vote identified himself as a "Democratic-Republican" — even John Quincy Adams. The Whig party, on the other hand, would not be recognized as a real alternative until 1836. But if there weren't distinct parties as such, there were clearly demarcated classes, divided along monetary, social, and educational lines. In this respect, appointment under Jackson was unmistakably business-as-usual, and Jackson, the "first man of the people," was unmistakably another president of the entrenched classes: "Old Hickory's choices were about as atypically rich, educated, and of the most prestigious ethnic and social elites as those of the Adams and Jefferson Administrations."[38] Yet these facts notwithstanding, Jackson's mere articulation of the notion of democratizing political opportunity struck something in the American consciousness so powerfully and so close to home that common people felt themselves to share in Jackson's presidency — even though they really did not share much more of the political spoils.

But politics was not the only or even the most popular realm in which

Americans — now, to an increasing extent, a self-consciously ambitious, hustling people — sought equality of opportunity. Jackson represented *economic* precepts to which the democratic audience subscribed. Specifically, as president, he now embodied characteristics they admired when he waged his self-admittedly epic battle against the Bank of the United States. His obsessive pressing of the "Bank War" became popularly understandable (and laudable) in fighting the good fight against privilege of the economic kind, against the monstrous perversion of the ends of government to the advantage of the rich and powerful. In this, Jackson personally represented the virtues of merit and industry in even the humblest members of society against the undemocratic perquisites of birth and position — undemocratic not because they would end in unequal results, but because, it was alleged, they were usurping special competitive advantages.

> When Jacksonians talked about equality, they were not thinking in literal terms of everyone being equal. They realized that everyone was not equal — and maybe there was some advantage to that. Talent varied, abilities differed. What they did believe and were committed to was the notion of equality of opportunity. Everyone should have the opportunity to make it, to get ahead to achieve financial success. No one should have special privileges that work to the disadvantage of others.[39]

Jackson's classic characterization of his personal struggle against the bank, "that monster," is found in his veto of the bill to recharter:

> It is to be regretted that the rich and powerful too often bend the acts of government to their selfish purposes. Distinctions in society will always exist under every just government. Equality of talents, of education, or of wealth cannot be produced by human institutions. In the full enjoyment of the gifts of Heaven and the fruits of superior industry, economy, and virtue, every man is equally entitled to protection by law; but when the laws undertake to add to these natural and just advantages artificial distinctions, to grant titles, gratuities, and exclusive privileges, to make the rich richer and the potent more powerful, the humble members of society — the farmers, mechanics and laborers — who have neither the time nor the means of securing like favors to themselves, have a right to complain of the injustice of their Government. There are no necessary evils in government. Its evils exist only in its abuses. If it would confine itself to equal protection, and, as Heaven does its rains, shower its favors alike on the high and the low, the rich and the poor, it would be an unqualified blessing. In the act before me there seems to be a wide departure from these just principles. . . . Many of our rich men have not been content with equal protection and equal benefits, but have besought us to make them richer by act of Congress. By attempting to gratify their desires we have in the results of our legislation arrayed section against section, interest against interest, and man against man in a fearful commotion which threatens to shake the foundations of our Union.[40]

ANDREW JACKSON. *Library of Congress.*

Jackson reduced the complexities of the bank issues to a simple matter of personal confrontation: the bank represented economic privilege, Jackson represented the cause of equal opportunity for even the mass of common people, and this led inevitably to a face-to-face showdown. "The Bank is trying to kill me," Old Hickory told Van Buren, "but *I* will kill *it!*"[41]

This way of understanding issues by identifying with aspects of the "representative" personality became so deeply characteristic of the democratic audience that it began to reconstitute the way American politics was conducted. Jackson could now describe the proper role of the president as "the direct representative of the American people."[42] Thus the presidential election came to be viewed as essentially a choice between personalities, between prospective personal representatives.

It must be repeated that this can be an altogether legitimate way of doing politics: that a "rhetoric of issues" may admit of as much cant as a "rhetoric of personal identification." But in the practice of Jacksonian politics, a rhetoric of personality led to reshaping the substance of politics — led, indeed, to distortions that were inflicted by both followers and leaders.

An issue-based politics at its best formulates and accounts for itself in terms of public knowledge — the recognized realities held in common, at least commonly enough to reconstitute a publicly intelligible vocabulary and the set of topics commonly seen as relevant to the community's way of life. That these realities are held in common provides the opportunites for checks on assertions, replies, counterassertions, in short, a real and politically influential res publica. But a politics of personality admits of decision making (and even *issue* making) on strictly personal considerations. Along this line, Nathaniel Niles, a New England Democrat and diplomat who was close to the leading members of his party in Washington, remarked that those who had a real hold on Jackson held their status "not because they like what the General liked, but because they hated what the General hated."[43]

One of the most famous and influential abuses of this kind occurred during Jackson's first term: the Peggy Eaton incident. The new wife of Jackson's Secretary of War John Eaton was a woman of highly questionable reputation. The wives of cabinet members from the genteel South predictably conspired to snub her and did so in the most pointed and obvious way possible. For purely personal reasons, President Jackson particularly resented this criticism and harassment. He and his own beloved Rachel — who died, to Jackson's profound shock, shortly after the 1828 election — had suffered the same sort of social ostracism when they were first married, Rachel's divorce from her first husband having been of questionable legality. Thus Jackson, a man with a long memory for insults, reacted bitterly against those who blackballed Peggy Eaton and most bitterly against those he considered responsible for the trend. Since it was essentially a southern movement, and since the wife of the southern vice-president led cabinet wives in their campaigns against Peggy, Jackson's wrath was settled on John Calhoun, the undisputed leader of the Old South and vice-president of the United States.

Calhoun had been made vice-president partly because it forged a useful political coalition and partly because Jackson saw him as his logical successor. But when Calhoun and his cohorts snubbed Peggy Eaton, and sly Secretary of State Martin Van Buren, a widower, made an obvious point of squiring her about, Jackson dumped Calhoun in as unceremonious a manner as he could manage. New York's Van Buren was elevated quickly to a place of unique trust, to the vice-presidency in the second term, and onto Jackson's coattails for the 1836 presidential election. Both the issues of future succession and of contemporary political coalition were of manifest public significance; Jackson was willing to make his dispositions of them both on principles of an essentially private nature. "Throughout the controversy, some of his more courageous advisers dared to tell him that Peggy's reputation was not altogether undeserved and warned him that the 'Eaton trouble' was so ludicrous and degrading that it was beneath the notice of the President of the United States. They were right, of course, but of far greater historical significance is the fashion in which Jackson demonstrated that he was willing to destroy a coalition — no matter how essential it seemed to his political career — whose members did not reflect his wishes," his essentially personal wishes.[44] When presidential politics could become personal politics, the most far-reaching sorts of policy decisions — inherently public decision — could be formulated and decided on inappropriately personal bases.

This change in the way presidential politics were understood and conducted represented a profound change in American political theory and practice. The theorists of *The Federalist* had conceded "it was desirable that the sense of the people should operate in the choice" of the president. But they also asserted that "it is equally desirable that the immediate election should be made by men most capable of analyzing the qualities adapted to the station, and acting under circumstances favorable to deliberation and to a judicious combination of all the reasons and inducements which were proper to govern their choice. A small number of persons selected by their fellow citizens from the general mass will be most likely to possess the information and discernment requisite to such complicated investigations." Madison's statement of the fundamental point is characteristically pithy: "the executive power will be derived from a very compound source. The immediate election of the President is made by the states in their political character."[45] But in practice, presidential elections soon began to operate differently. Electors were chosen less and less to exercise their own informed and discerning judgment and more and more merely to reflect the judgment of the people. The issue amounts to a fundamental clash in democratic thought—a clash over the nature and meaning of the concept of "representation."

Two notions of representation competed in the consciousness of the young nation. Representation had first been understood as properly an elitist, active function—a kind of trusteeship or stewardship. The good representative, in this view, was an exceptional man, a man who towered over his day much in the manner of George Washington. As Edmund Burke said, "Representatives should be superior men of wisdom and ability, not average or typical or even popular men." And they were to be regarded as especially fit for the responsibilities of their position in consequence of their special personal qualities. This superiority was of different natures for different thinkers—for Burke, it lay "in judgment, virtue, and wisdom derived from experience."[46]

Whether it was moral or intellectual in nature, the representative's superiority authorized him some special degree of independence from the instruction of his constituency. Thomas Hobbes even contended that for government to fulfill its function effectively, the independence authorized to the "sovereign representatives" had to be absolute; virtually nothing he could do, then, could be misrepresentative of his constituency, because they had entrusted him with authority before the fact. But whatever the extent of independence granted to the representative, and whatever the kind of accountability to which he might subsequently have to submit, the function of representation was seen in this formulation as a fundamentally independent one. In this understanding, the representative deserves his position because of special personal qualities, his special qualifications. If he was "typical" in any sense, he was typical of the best in his constituency, his audience for the purposes of public discourse. And his position is characterized as one of special personal authority: "To say that we send our representatives to Congress is not to say that we have sent our servants to the market. We have simply designated the person or persons to whose judgment or will we have subordinated ourselves."[47] The "trustee" concept was essentially elitist and active: the leader is somehow a special man, and he may exercise authority with consequently special freedom.

In the alternative understanding of representation that evolved, to be in any way special is to be *mis*representative. In the era when common people were emerging as a political force, representation came to be understood as a descriptive or mirroring function: the representative was supposed to be typical of his constituency, to reflect it passively, without personal originality or independence. Even crusty John Adams had remarked that "a representative legislature . . . should be an exact portrait, in miniature, of the people at large, as it should think, feel, reason, and act like them"; and "the perfection of the portrait consists in its likeness."[48] That is, this view meant a change in what a representative was expected — and allowed — to do and to be.

> Representing is not acting with authority or acting before being held to account, or *any kind of acting at all.* Rather, it depends on the representative's characteristics, on what he *is* or is *like,* on *being* something rather than *doing* something. The representative does not "act for" others; he "stands for" them, by virtue of a correspondence or connection between them, a resemblance or reflection.[49]

The belief in the fundamental equality of men subverted the notion of being led by superiors; democratic man came to pay attention to more typical figures, personae with whom he could identify. And this was a tendency that became so basic and enduring a trait of the American character that it has flourished even up to our own day: it underlies, for example, the development of the epithet "a regular guy" as a compliment; and it surely helps to account for the interest of man-in-the-street interviews. In a more aristocratic time, to be "regular" would mean to be merely ordinary, which would hardly seem much of an accomplishment; and the reactions of the average man-in-the-street would carry no particular interest and certainly no special importance or authority at all.[50]

This shift in democratic meaning affected government at all elected levels, from state houses through Congress to the presidency itself. Because the presidential canvass had become the focus of electoral politics, a profound change occurred in the character of the presidency: "The notion that the President is in charge of the government became a fact accepted by the American people." The people blamed Van Buren for presiding over the Panic of 1837 and brusquely turned him out of office at the next election. "Yet the previous depression, in 1819, had no such effect on the President. James Monroe was not blamed for the catastrophe"; the Era of Good Feeling continued, the feeling largely unruffled, and Monroe was reelected overwhelmingly in 1820, receiving all the electoral votes but one. "Obviously," concludes Robert Remini, "something had happened between the presidencies of James Monroe and Martin Van Buren."[51]

What had happened was the recircuiting of the patterns of political power — and the way political power was understood — to center on the president, and Jackson was largely responsible. His bank veto set a crucial precedent: the nine previous presidential vetoes had been justified on constitutional grounds. Jackson's argument against the recharter of the bank, however, was not that recharter would be somehow unconstitutional, but quite simply that it would be a bad law. It was now the province of the president to make such judgments, judgments that previously had been considered legislative in nature, and within his powers to use the veto on such grounds. Later, leaving no room for doubt, Jackson responded to a Senate censure with an official *Protest* that stands as "the most sweeping and straightforward defense of the presidential powers ever made by a chief executive of the United States." Tocqueville was wrong for once in his prediction that Jackson's tenure would enfeeble the office of the presidency. In practical effect, perhaps Jackson's "most permanent influence was this conception of the President's office and his enlargement of executive authority. Jackson, rather than having weakened the powers of the presidency, had changed them in focus and in nature. The president was now to be held personally responsible by the people, the direct source of his power, for the events of his administration. [52]

The kind of appeal that a presidential candidate had to project changed commensurately:

> It says something about the new style of politics during this Jacksonian age that all the Presidents of both parties, beginning with the Hero in 1828, had nicknames: Jackson was "the Hero" or "Old Hickory"; Van Buren, elected in 1836, was "the Little Magician"; then came "Tippecanoe and Tyler too," otherwise known as William Henry Harrison and John Tyler; James Knox Polk was "Young Hickory," elected in 1844; and finally, in 1848, Zachary Taylor was called "Old Rough-and-Ready." The six Presidents who preceded Jackson never had such nicknames. The democratization of the presidency obviously included some inelegant side effects. [53]

The trend to personalization through nicknames, as John William Ward explains, was specially in response to the new situation in American politics. "The democratic leader faces a delicate task. He must lead men and still be one of them. According to a naive democratic philosophy of equality, the vertical distance that separates the leader from the led must be denied. One of the easiest ways to lessen that distance is through the nickname, which lessens the august character of the leader while at the same time it increases the emotional allegiance given him." [54] If the focus of American politics had become presidential politics, the focus of presidential politics had become the personal relationship between the fully enfranchised, sovereign common people and their direct representative, the president.

It is possible, of course, to argue that democratization was more apparent than real; and in fact, ever since the publication of Arthur Schlesinger, Jr.'s great argument for the economic and political reality of the democratization. *The Age of Jackson,* the most significant Jackson scholarship has been dedicated to debating this proposition in particular spheres of influence. Richard Hofstadter, for example, attacks the image of the young Jackson as the quintessential democrat.

> Because Andrew Jackson came into prominence on the Tennessee frontier, he has often been set down as typical frontiersman; but many patent facts about his life fit poorly with the stereotype. From the beginning of his career in Tennessee, he considered himself to be, and was accepted as an aristocrat, and his tastes, manners, and style of life were shaped accordingly.[55]

Harold Syrett presses the attack even more vigorously:

> While serving as a delegate to Tennessee's constitutional convention, a Representative in Congress, a Senator, a member of his state's highest court, and the first American governor of the Florida territory, Jackson did not once espouse a policy that was designed to aid the majority or to weaken the control of the minority over the government. If as Frederick Jackson Turner has asserted, democracy was a product of the frontier, it flourished in that region in spite of the efforts of the nation's most famous Westerner and the era's most renowned democrat.[56]

Another way democratization may have been more apparent than real is expressed in Edward Pessen's attack on the notion, common from Tocqueville's time to our own, of the entrepreneur as a representative American figure: "These restless men on the make should not be confused with the bulk of the nation's workingmen or small farmers." Jackson was, in Pessen's view, of no meaningful help to the aspirations of the larger classes of common people. "There is no evidence," he concludes, "that during the Jacksonian era the poor made dramatic movement up the social ladder."[57]

Nor did Jackson's bank policy escape criticism in its effects on common people. "It might have been possible—and it would have been far wiser—for him to have made a deal with Biddle, trading recharter of the bank for more adequate government control of the Bank's affairs," criticizes Hofstadter; "it would have been possible to safeguard democratic institutions without such financial havoc." Glyndon Van Deusen defends the bank, pointing out that "it made only 20 per cent of the country's bank loans, the note circulation was only about one-fifth of the nation's total, and it had only one-third of the total bank deposits and of the specie held by American banks. It was, moreover, subject to charter revision"; Van Deusen condemns the bank war as a mere personal vendetta, since "these are not the aspects of monopoly banking."[58]

These critics make their case cogently; they seem to demonstrate at least the lively possibility that democratization during the period was more apparent than material. But this criticism may be off the mark. Even if democratization was quite as illusory as these critics claim, it still did not prevent Jackson from being perceived as the representative democratic figure; nor did it prevent Americans from identifying with this image. The characteristics of Jackson that we have examined corresponded so persuasively with what the emerging democratic audience was and wanted to be that everything else took on a practical irrelevance. "Whether democracy had *really* come to America can be debated," Remini concedes. "In fact, many present-day historians have gone to great pains to prove the phrase 'Jacksonian Democracy' a contradiction in terms. But they miss the important point. The people at the time believed democracy had come to America." And – as Pessen himself admits – "in history oftentimes what people think is true is more important than what in fact was . . . the era's consciousness was itself a vital element in the life of the time. Part of the reality of the era was a belief – distorted though it might be – in the central importance of Andrew Jackson, and of the campaigns he and his party waged in behalf of the common man." The result of that belief was the very real reconstitution of the American audience into one with certain specifically democratic characteristics. "Mere rhetoric" – in some cases, the "merest" of rhetoric with the most casual connection to the historical facts – had become a powerful public reality. Andrew Jackson was the key representative figure of American politics in the nineteenth century because with him, identification with a democratic character became the most effective mode of persuasion of the popular audience – the most effective way to reconstitute that audience's character.[59]

That character had distinct and powerful virtues to which rhetoric could appeal. Americans saw themselves as potential "heroes against the odds"; increasingly confident in their can-do attitudes, they were willing and even eager to "enter the scramble" and get ahead. But while their character fostered these admirable ambitions, it also led them to distinctive and very serious problems and vulnerabilities.

In their far-flung search for the lucky strike, Americans developed a Jacksonian propensity to flit from one occupation to another. The typical American of the early nineteenth century would try his hand at many endeavors, just as Jackson had shifted back and forth from law to soldiering to farming to politicking. This far-reaching if sometimes superficial ingenuity, Tocqueville remarked, constantly "turns each man's attention to new thoughts"; as an audience, Americans were receptive to all sorts of new ideas.[60] On the other hand, this same active character prevented much commitment to any one project, unless of course that project promised an immediate material profit, a "cash-value." Sometimes not even that was enough; many a fortune won in one endeavor was quickly gambled away in another, suggesting a certain inability to discriminate qualitatively among alternatives. The can-do assertion of the individual will seem to make every option, even the most outlandish, equally promising, equally exploitable. It is no coincidence that it was in this period of their history that Americans discovered "you can't make a silk purse out of sow's ear" – to their surprise, and unconcealed disappointment.

But even when Americans had settled on a project, they were not likely to submit to its discipline very patiently. More probably, they would look for short-cuts, "angles," and this too had a problematic consequence. When Tocqueville examined the effects of democracy on the intellectual dimensions of life in America, it was his unequivocal — rather uneasy — assessment that it led to a shallowness of approach, which in the long run struck Tocqueville as radically impoverishing. "Democratic man likes generalizations," he wrote. "Most men who live in times of equality are full of lively yet indolent ambition. They want great success at once, but they want to do so without great efforts. These contrary instincts lead them straight to generalizations . . . to make bad use of that type of conception and espouse them with injudicious warmth." This character of democratic life militates against proper habits of thought; reflection on principles gives way all too easily to thinking exclusively about easy generalizations and rough applications.

"Democratic social conditions and institutions involve most people in continual activity, but habits of thought useful in action are not always helpful to thought. The man of action has often to make do with approximations . . . the seasonableness of an idea is much more often useful to him than its strict accuracy."[61]

How serious a problem do these democratic characteristics of intellectual shiftiness and shallowness present? Tocqueville took them seriously enough to offer what he expected to be a troublingly suggestive analogy with China:

> Three hundred years ago, when the first Europeans came to China, they found that almost all the arts had reached a certain degree of improvement, and they were surprised that, having come so far, they had not gone further. Later on, they found traces of profound knowledge that had been forgotten. The nation was a hive of industry; the greater part of its scientific methods were still in use, but science itself was dead. That made them understand the strange immobility of mind found among this people. The Chinese, following, in their fathers' steps, had forgotten the reasons which guided them. They still used the formula without asking why. They kept the tool but had no skill to adapt or replace it. So the Chinese were unable to change anything. They had to drop the ideas of improvements. They had to copy their ancestors the whole time in everything for fear of straying into impenetrable darkness if they deviated for a moment from their tracks. Human knowledge had almost dried up at the fount, and though the stream still flowed, it could neither increase nor change its course.

On this ground, the intensity of the doctrinaire democrats' concern in 1840 seems genuinely justified. Inherent in the democratic audience was a characteristic that was entailed in some of their important virtues — but, if left unaddressed, also threatened to hurt or even to destroy democracy. "If the lights that guide us ever go out, they will fade little by little, as if of their own accord. Confirming ourselves to practice, we may lose sight of basic principles, and when these have been entirely forgotten, we may apply the methods derived from them badly, we might be left without the capacity to invent new methods and only be able to make a clumsy and an unintelligent use of wise procedures no longer understood. . . . We therefore should not console ourselves by thinking that the barbarians are still a long way off. Some peoples may let the torch be snatched from their hands, but others stamp it out themselves."[62]

Another democratic characteristic of the American audience grew out of the sense of being the outsider — albeit always in the process of irresistibly insinuating himself in. The newly enfranchised American had a natural aversion to entrenched authority; his equalitarian impulses readily generalized this aversion to any authority whatever, in the belief in his own competence that many Americans were achieving. "Seeing that they are successful in resolving unaided all the little difficulties they encounter in practical affairs, they are easily led to the conclusion that . . . nothing passes beyond the limits of [their] intelligence." Not only was this tendency involved in the rush of anti-intellectualism that marked the early nineteenth century, as Hofstadter observed, it may also help account for the unusually high turnover rate for incumbents during the period. In the four decades between the publication of the Monroe Doctrine and the outbreak of the Civil War, Americans had only one two-term president — Andrew Jackson.[63]

But some "authority is always bound to play a part in intellectual and moral life. The part may vary, but some part there must be." To meet this requirement, Americans developed a tendency "to seek by themselves and in themselves for the only reason for things." Given their equalitarian premises, they felt they could equally well "look into themselves and their fellows for the sources of truth." That is, while they had grown far less willing to "believe blindly in any man or any class . . . they are readier to trust the mass, and public opinion becomes more and more mistress of the world. . . . For they think it not unreasonable that, all having the same means of knowledge, truth will be found on the side of the majority."[64]

It was this tendency of democratic men to identify one with another that received poetic expression for the century at the pen of Walt Whitman.

> One's self I sing, a simple, separate person,
> Yet utter the word Democratic, the word En Masse
>
> . . . .
> The modern Man I sing.[65]
>
> I was looking a long while for Intentions,
> For a clew to the history of the past for myself
>   and for these chants — And now I have found it —
> It is in Democracy (the purport and aim of
>   all the past)
> It is the life of one man or one woman to-day —
>   the average man of to-day.[66]

The most celebrated, significant, and stirring embodiment of this characteristic of democratic man to identify with his fellows is the comprehensive, representative ego of Whitman's "Song of Myself."

> I celebrate myself, and sing myself,
> And what I assume you shall assume,
> For every atom belonging to me as good belongs to you
> . . . .
> I acknowlege the duplicates of myself, the
>   weakest and shallowest is deathless with me.
> . . . .
> I am possess'd
> Embodying all presences outlaw'd or suffering
> . . . .
> Magnifying and applying came I,
> Outbidding . . . Lithographing . . . Buying
> . . . .
> All this I swallow, it tastes good, I like it well,
>   it becomes mine, I am the man, I suffer'd,
>   I was there.
> . . . .
> Of these one and all I weave the song of myself.[67]

Whitman showed most winningly that this equalitarian tendency had positive as well as negative dimensions. But even James Fenimore Cooper, who on the whole was not a softheaded observer of democratic behavior, had to concede that "a general elevation in the character of the people" was "the principal advantage of democracy." Not only were more new thoughts being entertained; there were more people entertaining the ideas, and this had an edifying mass effect. Tocqueville was astonished at the extent "that good qualities were common among the governed." Yet these good qualities were "rare among the rulers . . . and it must be recognized that this tendency has increased as democracy has gone beyond its previous limits. It is clear that during the last fifty years the race of American statesmen has strangely shrunk."[68]

Cooper has an explanation ready:

> The tendency of democracies is, in all things, to mediocrity, since the tastes, knowledge, and principles of the majority form the tribunal of appeal. This circumstance, while it certainly serves to elevate the average qualities of a nation, renders the introduction of a high standard difficult. Thus do we find in literature, in the arts, architecture, and in all acquired knowlege a tendency in America to gravitate towards the common center in this, as in other things; lending a value and estimation to mediocrity that are not elsewhere given.[69]

It is Cooper's assertion that, given free rein, this tendency readily leads to abuses like "a disposition in the majority to carry out the opinions of the system to extremes, and a disposition in the minority to abandon all to the

current of the day"; for in any society organized in the democratic manner
in which America had been reconstituted, "there is a besetting disposition
to make public opinion stronger than the law. This is the particular form in
which tyranny exhibits itself in a popular government," and "the most
insinuating and dangerous form in which oppression can overshadow a
community is that of popular sway." Ultimately, this "disposition to defer
to the public" chronically comes "in opposition to truth and justice."
Tocqueville called this opposition nothing less than "the *tyranny* of the
majority," and judges it "the Greatest Danger to the American Republic."[70]

Here we find another democratic characteristic which, it left unaddressed, can bring the end of democracy, or at least of a democracy worth
living in. But here too, the role of the true friend of democracy gains
definition. This dangerous democratic characteristic, this "penalty that is
paid for liberty . . . depends on the very natural principle of flattering
power. In a monarchy, adulation is paid to the prince; in a democracy, to
the people, or the public. Neither hears the truth as often as is wholesome,
and both suffer for the want of the corrective." If a lover of democracy is
disturbed by its inherent shortcomings, then it is up to him precisely as a
function of that love not to indulge the shortcomings but to administer
their corrective and notwithstanding the differing opinion of the common
man, tell the truth as he sees it. Otherwise, this equalitarian impulse would
limit what was thinkable for the common man, and thus, in Tocqueville's
view, the same cause that "turns each man's attention to new thoughts" also
"would induce him freely to give up thinking at all."[71] The paradox of
American rhetoric was that entailed in some of the greatest of democracy's
virtues were some of its most threatening vices.

Cooper noted in summary that "while we see in our democracy this
manifest disposition to defer to the wrong in matters that are not properly
subject to the common sentiment, in deference to the popular will of the
hour, there is a simple boldness in the use of personalities." The personalities who represented — and, on the strength of their personal appeal, sold —
ideas and issues were no longer the almost mythologically "better man," of
whom the almost worshipped George Washington had been the archetype.
It appeared that America was no longer inclined to follow its extraordinary
and excellent men: Tocqueville calls it "a constant fact that the most outstanding Americans are seldom summoned to public office." Instead, reconstituted democratically, it espoused a still personal but more direct notion of representation: Americans as a democratic audience were drawn to
and literally identified with men who seemed like them — of whom the archetype was Andrew Jackson.[72]

The democratic audience that emerged and demanded response in 1840 had developed its peculiar virtues and vices, had literally been character-ized, in the intellectual, social, political, and cultural process that climaxed in the Age of Jackson. Those who felt bound to make a response to the problem of the democratic audience were bound precisely by their loyalty to the democratic way of life, which that problem threatened. They would find Americans characteristically a receptive, educable, and altogether worthy audience — *if* ways could be invented to deal effectively with its other democratic characteristics, or, better yet, to incorporate them all into a new discipline.

To understand the nature and causes of what happened in the wa-tershed year of 1840, we had to turn back to the Age of Jackson. To understand the implications of 1840, we must turn to the most important and intriguing scene of democratic education, the circuit of public speech.

Education of the Democratic Audience: The Circuit of Public Speech

Nobody ever went broke underestimating the intelligence of the American people.

— H. L. MENCKEN

Society not only continues to exist *by* transmission, *by* communication, but it may fairly be said to exist *in* transmission, *in* communication.

— JOHN DEWEY

T
HERE had never been an educational movement like it. Never had a nation undertaken to prepare so many of its people for so full a role of citizenship. The problem of the democratic audience — its urgent need for education and the peculiar educational possibilities and difficulties inherent in its democratic character — had emerged in America during the first few decades of the nineteenth century. Before that century ended, a crusty British peer named James Bryce arrived in this country to study the *American Commonwealth* in all its important political and social dimensions. Assaying the state of popular education, Lord Bryce — far from a softheaded observer and never much disposed to spare criticism he deemed merited — could only marvel: "The average of knowledge is higher, the habit of reading and thinking more generally diffused than in any other country."[1] The problem of the democratic audience had been addressed, Bryce concluded, with a great measure of success. Popular education, to some extent at least, was working — working in at least two ways, because two distinct kinds of challenges had confronted popular education. It had been called to respond of course to educational needs, interests, and goals of an individualistic nature; it had been required moreover to fulfill a larger, a public, a constitutive kind of function.

It would be difficult to find any climate that would have been more congenial to individualistic, private motives than the United States in the flush, burgeoning 1800s. The representative American, "living in the midst of an expanding economy, saw opportunities for money-making on every hand. Untrammeled by any feudal heritage, stimulated by the conditions of his environment, blessed by social philosophers, he was in a singularly fortunate position to lay the foundations for economic developments that were to make the American economy one of the wonders of the modern world."[2]

But individual ambitions arising from these conditions grew so rabid so rapidly that as early as the 1830s, when Tocqueville was first examining the character of democracy in America, he found it had developed a peculiar and very serious need for some restraint on aspirations—a restraint merely in order to keep civil society social and civilized.[3] Private motives had become an identifying trait of the American character, to which American education had to be addressed. Thus popular education also confronted another kind of problem, ultimately one of even larger proportions and greater priority.

> The first educational task of the new nation was to transform an entire people from subjects to citizens—from a people used to being governed by an aristocracy to a people able to govern themselves in a democracy.[4]

The aggregation of newly enfranchised Americans had to be taught how to constitute a functionally unified nation. Put another way, the young democracy needed to reconstitute itself into a new and better kind of audience for public discourse. The masses of common people could no longer be merely passive eavesdroppers on the conduct of community business; they had been entrusted with a more active role. Nor, entrusted with civic responsibility, could they be allowed to lapse into myopic selfishness. The mission of popular education in the United States was to teach the ever more sovereign people how to be discerning listeners and, ultimately, society's responsible agents. And it was an especially urgent mission, even as such missions go, for there was a constant stream of critical new public issues for which the democratic audience would immediately be held responsible. The women's rights movement was beginning. Various attempts to popularize valuable new scientific knowledge and technical procedures were being undertaken. Powerful moral campaigns were being waged for temperance in the use of alcohol and for the abolition of slavery in the United States.

The diversity of these sorts of issues imposed a commensurate diversity of demands on public instruction. The touchstone, perhaps, of the success that American education achieved was its own pluralistic nature—its capacity to respond with equal diversity, for "Americans of the midnineteenth century were untiring inventors of cultural and educational institutions."[5]

The public school movement was initiated by Horace Mann to improve, expand, and standardize the tutelage of children in the basic, "grammatical" skills, while the issue of compulsory, publicly funded basic education was forced into the public consciousness and onto the political agenda. The Sunday school movement used the focal status that churches enjoyed in most communities to extend such education further—and not only, as commonly imagined, in evangelizing directions. The national library movement, perhaps most underestimated in its practical influence, made more and better books far more generally available; the resulting expansion of the American reading public was nothing short of explosive.[6] "Circuit-riding" lawyers brought instruction and entertainment, as did extensive stump speaking by public figures. In an explicit egalitarian spirit, the Morrill Act of 1862 created land-grant colleges to instruct farmers' children in both modern agricultural techniques and the enduring subjects of a liberal education. State-funded universities were founded to make higher education more possible for the common citizen. Black colleges emerged in a courageous and at least partly successful attempt to fulfill the same purpose. And although this list provides some representative examples, it falls far short of exhausting the innovations of democratic education in nineteenth-century America. Popular education was nothing if not pluralistic, both in its means and in its ends.

Historians of education like Malcolm Knowles and Lyman Bryson contend that this pluralism was as distinctive a characteristic of public education in American as it was of the American character; in fact, the success of public education seems to them to have sprung from its compatibility with the American character. In most countries, Knowles observes, the aims and the institutional forms of public education tended (as they still tend) to be rather strictly unified. In England and Sweden adult education focused specifically on the training of workers for present competence and was dedicated to continuously refashioning the national culture—the assumption being that the national culture could be defined in a way which everyone would recognize and to which everyone would assent.[7] Knowles adds the useful modern example of Russian education, whose character and purposes are controlled to a significant extent by whatever overall economic and social strategy the government is currently pursuing.

"In the United States, on the other hand, the national adult educational movement has proliferated . . . in response to myriad individual needs and interests, institutional goals, and social pressures." Public instruction, in being free to diversify, was consequently free to enter all the different dimensions of American life as they developed. The result was that popular education had "penetrated to more phases of life in America than in any other country," and had, in effect, "expressed the complexity and vitality of American life."[8]

Moreover, the particular shape of American public education's success paralleled the leveled equalitarian lines of American life. Few new intellectual peaks were immediately scaled, and the plane of culture was not suddenly elevated. But that cultural plane was sufficiently *broadened* to attract and involve far more of the emerging democratic audience into disciplines that were thought to be as valuable politically as they were valid intellectually. Of all the branches of public instruction, one was regarded as "the most significant venture in popular education in the United States"; from the Age of Jackson to the Age of Radio, the nation's dominant institutional form of adult instruction was the circuit of public speech, carried on first under the auspices of the lyceum, then in the tents of the chautauqua.[9] Beyond this dominance, what is worth our attention about the circuit is that is was widely deemed, among all the venues of popular education, as the most representatively, identifiably American. From its first appearance, the circuit won this reputation: while helping to found Boston's first lyceum society, the Reverend Asa Rand opined, "I like the lyceum because it is *adapted* to the genius of our population through its *social* and *republican* character." The circuit maintained its eminence throughout the century, and when President Theodore Roosevelt returned to Lake Chautauqua in 1905, he declared with characteristic restraint that it was still "the most American thing in America," and "typically American, in that it was typical of America at its best." The circuit's distinctive repute even spread beyond the shores of America: when Count Ilya Tolstoy was asked his reasons for coming on the circuit to speak, "he replied gravely, 'there is only one real reason for living, and that is to acquire knowledge, experience. I have been told that this — this Chautauqua — is distinctively American. I am furthering my understanding of the American people.' "[10]

This chapter proceeds on Count Tolstoy's premise: that the characteristics of the American audience were somehow accessible in the rhetorical process of the lecture circuit. If so, rhetorical studies may be able to discover and articulate something original about them. So this chapter examines the rhetorical success of the circuit as a branch of democratic education — what it accomplished, given what it had to work with in American life. In that process, it addresses and attempts to qualify some misconceptions of the limits of American life. Given the hard-driving, hungry, ambitious American of the democratic audience, there have appeared among some historians of the period (most notably Schlesinger, Pessen, Van Deusen, and Syrett) and especially of the lyceum and chautauqua circuit (most egregiously, Hurlbut and Horner) a tendency to reduce the possible range of American motives to too narrow a notion of self-interest. Democratic life in general is consequently portrayed as essentially and incorrigibly private, thereby overlooking the ways by which community life in a democracy became and remained peculiarly, characteristically vital. In such a context, the rhetoric of democratic education is conceived only as a mode of private address—a rhetoric that serves the interests of private individuals, but can never fundamentally reconstitute those interests into a common interest, nor reconstitute the private individuals into a public individual. Such individuals do not have, cannot have, any of the significant suasive connection to each other or community with each other that Americans, as the rhetoric of democratic education shows, did enjoy in their circuit experience.

Such a picture of democratic life in general and of democratic education in particular is apparently quite tempting; it is disturbingly common among the circuit's chroniclers. But it is an inadequate description on three counts. First, in its reduction of American motives and democratic life, it is an inaccurate and partial account of America as community. Next, simply as a historical conception of the nature and function of the circuit of public speech in America, it overlooks the possibilities for identification of the community in speech. And finally, as a notion of what rhetoric can be and can do, especially in democratic society, it misunderstands and seriously underestimates the intellectual and moral resources of democratic education.

America as Community

Tocqueville, who explicitly worried about the effect of private ambition and aspiration, also detected a very different kind of tendency in the way democratic life was constituted in America. All their private motives notwithstanding, Americans would "pitch in" and help in public concerns.

> Private people do not think that their duties have ceased because the representative of the public has come to take action. On the contrary, everyone guides, supports, and sustains him.

Tocqueville suggests his explanation for this peculiar characteristic by contrasting it with European behavior: "often to an European, a public official stands for force; to an American, he stands for rights"; furthermore " in Europe, the criminal is a luckless man fighting to save his head from the authorities . . . in America he is an enemy of the human race, and every human being is against him." American public life was constituted differently, and apparently in a more productive way for public purposes. Of legal forms, this is obviously true: here, the people were empowered to rule, and they honestly felt that they themselves determined the law of the land, or at least significantly influenced it by their electoral decisions—whence came, very probably, that unusual respect for "their" law and those especially helpful attitudes and habits toward "their" government that Tocqueville reported.[11]

But "in the long run, the sum of private undertakings far surpasses anything the government might have done."[12] If America really was a community, it would show not only in the formal ways it was put together, but also (and perhaps more significantly) in the normal ways it would work together. And it did: a different and richer sense of the public — of the value and possibilities of a genuine community life — was in evidence, shaping the basic relations of the American way of life.

The inclination to form diverse kinds of vigorous new relations ran deep in the American character — and it was something that Americans learned how to do particularly well. "Better use has been made of association and this powerful instrument of action has been applied to more varied aims in America than anywhere else in the world." The sheer proportions of this tendency to associate is revealed in how it reached into every corner of American life: "public security, trade and industry, and morals and religion all provide the aims for association in the United States." And the tendency of association was so qualitatively important to American life that the use of its essential instrument, the press, became "the principal, and, so to say, the constitutive element in freedom."[13]

This communal tendency became so prominent a part of American life and character that its existence could not be ignored; against the individualistic background of the Age of Jackson, it seemed such an obtrusive anomaly that it almost demanded explanation. Americans themselves developed a unique interpretation, genially brushing off this public phenomenon as an enlightened, long-range extension of their private, selfish motives. The concept of "self-interest, properly understood" achieved the status of popular dogma and was regularly invoked to account for any behavior between the most transparent avarice and the most open-hearted philanthropy. Americans seemed to take a special, almost perverse pleasure in elucidating this theory; they seemed to Tocqueville to "enjoy explaining almost every act of their lives on the principle of self-interest properly understood. It gives them pleasure to point out how an enlightened self-love continually leads them to help one another and disposes them freely to give part of their time and wealth for the good of the state." It was Tocqueville's suspicion that this account could hardly tell the whole story. "One sees people carried away by the disinterested spontaneous impulses natural to man. But the Americans are hardly prepared to admit that they do give away to emotions of this sort," he observed. "I think that in this they often do themselves less than justice."[14]

What are we to make of Americans' surprising traits of unselfishness, generosity, and public spirit? How can we most credibly account for Americans' inclination — and perhaps more tellingly, their ability — to identify with each other, from which they gained motivation and guidance for subsequent attitudes and behavior? Tocqueville's suspicion is difficult to dismiss.

It seems a little inadequate to explain all this as merely the precipitate of self-regard. What we think of today as selfishness often tends to quash concerns with the world outside of the individual ego and can enervate the impulse to enter that world and confront its richness frankly; but what was billed as selfishness in America propelled attention outward, activated the impulse to engage the world, and provided consistent motivation to succeed more broadly. Ordinary selfishness again is often useless for determining specifically what to do next; the selfishness of these Americans constantly helped them locate practical direction that was "clear and definite." Selfishness as we know it tends to affect people adversely in their personal morality and in their citizenship; this queer "selfishness" of the Americans was consistently a positive factor in their behavior, a factor whose "discipline shapes . . . orderly, temperate, moderate, careful and self-controlled citizens." It is possible Tocqueville's suspicion was incorrect and that our definitions are anachronistic; but if this was selfishness, then "self" in the American democratic context must have had a richly expandable meaning. When the circuit addressed and helped expand that meaning, it became an instrument for American life constantly to restore and reshape and replenish and reconstitute itself.[15]

The Community in Speech

Josiah Holbrook was born in 1788, the son of a prosperous Connecticut farmer. He went to Yale in 1806 and gradually earned a reputation for diligence if not quite brilliance. Working with one of the college's finest educators, a chemist and mineralogist named Benjamin Silliman, young Josiah developed a passion for science. After a time, however, doing science was not enough for him; he began looking for a way to popularize scientific knowledge and technical procedures among his fellow citizens. He attempted to organize a manual labor school, with little success. Then, in 1825 he heard about what was happening in Europe.

In England a certain Henry Lord Brougham - a flamboyant attorney and colorful M.P., ultimately to become lord chancellor—was founding something called mechanics institutes. Workingmen were taught mechanics, geometry, astronomy, and hydrostatics, along with chemistry and its application to the industrial arts. The characteristic pedagogical methods were "the use of lecture-demonstration courses organized by public-spirited citizens and the assembling of local libraries of technical books." A similar movement sprang up in France under the guidance of a Baron Dupin, a conscious imitator of Brougham. Upon hearing of all this, Holbrook promptly set to establishing something like this institution in the United States.[16]

He called his institution "the lyceum," borrowing the name from Aris-

totle's renowned school in Athens. Later, the claim that the American lyceum had inherited a "democratic spirit" from its Athenian model was put
forward by its boosters, who in the flush of their enthusiasm were little
daunted by the fact that Aristotle's Athens was no longer a democracy. The
lyceum's original style of education was mutual instruction among its members, most of it done by lecture and demonstration as in its European
forebears, although as A. A. Wright insisted, another model might have
been Benjamin Franklin's Junto.[17]

In 1826 — scarcely thirty months after the first mechanics institution
had opened in London and about a month before the first local lyceum
officially started its operation in America — Holbrook published "The Constitution for the American Lyceum for Science and the Arts." This constitution provided the terms in which lyceum participants spoke about — the
terms in which they came to their shared understandings of — what they
were doing.

The lyceum as Holbrook envisioned it had six "purposes" or "advantages":

1. lyceums would diffuse knowledge more generally;
2. the nature of the information communicated would in the long run
   be "useful" and "practical";
3. lyceums would exert a good moral influence;
4. lyceums would exert a good political influence;
5. lyceums would be a thrifty form of public education;
6. lyceums would have a beneficial effect on the other forms of education in a community, particularly on its common schools.[18]

Holbrook went on to make some useful organizational suggestions that
most local lyceums adopted: it would be delegated to "curators," for example, to take care of the society's educational property and also to choose the
lecturers (a function of increasing controversy and importance as the lyceums varied their fare); and the money to run the program would come
from the yearly subscriptions of its members and from admission fees
charged to nonmembers at the door.

Holbrook did not explicit limit what might be taught in the lyceum
programs — in another publication, he mentions "mutual instruction in the
sciences . . . or any other branch of useful knowledge" — but he did make it
abundantly clear that scientific and technical instruction was to come first.
To assist in this instruction, Holbrook — a resourceful Yankee — organized
what amounted to an independent business to equip lyceums and other
community institutions of education in the rather extensive manner that
Holbrook thought proper. What was a lyceum anyhow, he contended, de-

fiant of contradiction, without a good eolopile, a conductometer, an arithmometer, or that faithful old standby, a pneumatic cistern?[19]

Ten dollars would buy the basic equipment for a grammar school: a globe, a set of geometrical apparatus ("solids, transposing figures, diagrams"), an arithmometer (a numeral frame with 144 balls), and an instrument called an orrery. Holbrook sold what he deemed "the essential lyceum apparatus" — specimens in natural history, illustrations, and books — for $75.00. The set of "mechanical powers," costing $15.00, illustrated the principles of the lever, pulley, screw, inclined plane, screw-and-axle, and wedge; and with this set, Holbrook threw in the seductive bonus of a hydrostatic bellows. Chemistry equipment, available for $25.00, would include a pneumatic cistern with a compound blowpipe and two glass holders, retorts, flasks, flexible and glass tubes, a pyrometer, a conductometer, two concave reflectors, a lampstand, and an eolopile (a reaction engine powered by steam). Geology was Holbrook's favorite science and geological cabinets were made popular in early lyceums. The basic labeled set of twenty common rocks sold for a thrifty $3.00, and $5.00 purchased the complete set of fifty specimens, including the "elements of rocks." Ever the entrepreneur, Holbrook also published a great deal of supplementary material to explain the uses of the equipment and sometimes for more general topics. These included *Scientific Tracts,* intended as substitutes for lyceum lectures, twenty-four numbers per year at $1.50 per set; *Family Lyceum,* a four-page weekly paper; a series of "Penny Tracts," self-educational essays, works in the fine arts, drawing, and geology.[20]

The equipment employed in the early lyceum might give the impression that it conducted merely technical instruction. But, argues lyceum historian Carl Bode, even these instruments were facilitating a broader sort of education: they were

> the keys to a new world. The vistas they opened up were limitless.
> Much of the scientific instruction in the early lyceum was practical — a
> knowledge of "mechanical powers," for instance, would make a better
> machinist. Some instruction, however, was more than merely imme-
> diately practical; it was in a real sense liberal and humane. Of this kind,
> the orrery, a small clockwork model of the solar system, was the best
> example. Its lessons included little that the mechanic could use at his
> bench but much that would allow him to understand the heavens he
> saw above him and the universe he inhabited.[21]

The lyceum movement spread quickly throughout New England and the East; in 1831 there were 800 to 1,000 town lyceums and perhaps 60 county lyceums.[22] By the early 1830s it had established outposts in the wilds of the opening West — in Ohio, Michigan, Indiana, as far northwest as Wisconsin and as far southwest as Missouri (curiously, the lyceum never achieved much institutional success in the South; possibly this was because, as Bode suggests, the old plantation aristocracy was more interested in physical activities and was anyhow more engaged in the matters leading up to the Civil War, already looming on the horizon. In any case, the South responded to the lyceum with "an indifference amounting to contempt"[23]). By the early 1840s there were between 3,500 and 4,000 communities that sponsored lyceum lectures, and by the mid-1840s hardly any northern towns of 1,000 or more people lacked one.[24] But in an equalitarian age, some localities were manifestly more equal than others in intellectual resources, particularly in good lecturers. What town in the West would not exhaust its cultural possibilities more quickly than, say, Concord, Massachusetts? From its own membership, the Concord lyceum could draw an Emerson, a Thoreau, an Edward Everett Hale; and from the immediate neighborhood, it could and did attract Oliver Wendell Holmes, David Starr King, Henry Ward Beecher, Louis Agassiz, Charles Dana, James Russell Lowell, Theodore Parker, Horace Greeley, and Wendell Phillips. Naturally, towns less richly blessed began to import speakers, and very quickly the fundamental purpose of the local lyceum changed: "the lyceum in the sense of a local, public, adult education movement was finished by about 1840"; demand for "better talent" — the locution was revealing — transformed local lyceums from institutions of mutual instruction to sponsors for lecture series.[25]

At first each speaker was hired to deliver a series of connected lectures — sometimes as many as five or six, usually at least three — on consecutive nights, allowing for a broader development of a topic. The precedent for this procedure had been set by Ralph Waldo Emerson. In fact, Emerson's example shaped many of the lecture circuit's fundamental practices. "Emerson was the first professional lecturer, and it has been said of him not only that he created the profession, but that he gave the lyceum of this country its form and character."[26] The success Emerson enjoyed with series like *Representative Men, English Traits,* and *The Conduct of Life* created a market for similar series across the country. Emerson also set an example of publishing his lectures as essays, which very significantly extended the reach of the lyceum's influence. Later, the local lyceum sponsored a "course" of lectures, each by different individuals on different topics. We shall examine the consequences; but first, let's have a taste of the savory diversity that the new practice made possible: a tolerably representative program is that of the Salem lyceum in the winter of 1838–1839.

SALEM LYCEUM LECTURES, 1838–1839[27]

Series: *The Character, Customs, Costumes, etc., of the North American Indian*	—GEORGE CATLIN
"Causes of the American Revolution"	—JARED SPARKS
"The Sun"	—HUBBARD WINSLOW
"The Sources of National Wealth"	—C. H. BREWSTER
"Common School Education"	—C. T. TORREY
"The Capacity of the Human Mind for Culture and Improvement"	—EPHRAIM PEABODY
"The Honey Bee"	—H. K. OLIVER
"Popular Education"	—R. C. WINTHROP
"Geology"	—PROF. C. B. ADAMS
"The Legal Rights of Women"	—SIMON GREENLEAF
"Instinct"	—HENRY WARE, JR.
"Life of Mohammed"	—H. J. WARD
"Life and Times of Oliver Cromwell"	—H. W. KINSMAN
"Memoirs of Count Rumford"	—A. C. PEIRSON
"The Practical Man"	—CONVERS FRANCIS
"The Poet of Natural History"	—J. L. RUSSELL
"The Progress of Democracy"	JOHN WAYLAND
"The Discovery of America by the Norsemen"	—A. H. EVERETT
"The Satanic School of Literature and Its Reform"	—SAMUEL OSGOOD
"The Education of Children"	—HORACE MANN

The lecture circuit flourished throughout the late 1830s and early 1840s; even so, at this stage of development it was hardly much of a business proposition. No fees were paid any lecturer in the first few years, and even after payment became the accepted practice, it was widely reported that for poorer lyceums in his vicinity Emerson "would make an address for as little as five dollars and three quarts of oats for his horse." It never became altogether uncommon for speakers who had a message that they particularly wished to present to appear for free. Wendell Phillips drew top dollar for his noncontroversial material (notably his celebrated and extremely popular lecture on "The Lost Arts"), but never charged to speak on abolition.[28]

In 1840 the average fee paid by the prosperous Concord lyceum was only $10.00 plus expenses. Over the next fifteen years, larger amounts were occasionally paid. In 1849, Daniel Webster demanded—and was frequently offered—an astonishing $100.00 for his lecture on the history of the Constitution, part of the drawing power of which, it was said, was its price. But even as late as the season of 1855–1856, Concord's average fee was still only $20.00. When the lyceum showed a year's profit of only $4.69, fees promptly returned to $15.00.[29]

The price of admission was similarly modest. For the first twenty years of the lyceum, a ticket — one seat at one lecture — cost only $0.25. A pass for a whole season's "course" of lectures usually cost between $1.00 and $2.50. The lyceum audience's expectations about prices were deeply ingrained, as was vividly illustrated in the case of Henry Ward Beecher. A preacher who grew famous for his wit and flamboyance, Beecher commanded top dollar almost from his first appearance on the circuit in 1840. But after more than a decade in lyceums across the country, Beecher hired a "literary agent." Beecher's already high asking price inflated dramatically, and the inflation was visible in ticket prices. In 1855, for example, Beecher returned to the Ohio circuit for the first time after engaging his agent. Admission there still averaged only $0.25, but to pay the "forty parson-power preacher," prices had to be increased, even doubled. People still attended in reasonable numbers, but they brought fundamentally changed attitudes to their listening. They were no longer coming to be edified by a wise and articulate man of God; they attended to be entertained by a celebrity, toward whom different personal attitudes were appropriate. "Mr. Wells, the Chicago showman, will let his fifty-cent lion roar at Concert Hall tonight," one paper announced; "Grand Literary Circus!" headlined another. Beecher's popularity endured into the 1870s — and actually increased after the handsome parson was hauled into court in a paternity suit that eventually ended with a hung jury.[30]

For the most part, however, costs stayed low; they were *kept* low intentionally, because most lecturers who toured the circuit in its early years and most of the audiences whom they addressed didn't conceive of the enterprise in which they were involved as simply, or even essentially, a business venture. Rather, they considered it an educational vehicle, and as such a community asset, performing an important public function. The advantages of the lyceum, as Holbrook had originally promised, were public ones: positive effects on other vehicles of public education, wholesome moral influence on the community and especially on its young people, and above all certain specifically political benefits. Many Americans had only recently been accorded the privileges of citizenship, few of whom had previously enjoyed the advantages of education. It therefore became an explicit public priority to equip the new rulers for their new responsibilities, to make them less vulnerable to demagogues, in short "to transform an entire people from subjects to citizens."[31] But the lyceum also addressed another function in democratic community life, one even more crucial — and, so to speak, "constitutive."

Communication and the Constitution
of Democratic Community

"Democracy is more than a form of government," John Dewey observed. "It is primarily a mode of associated living, of conjoint communicated experience." Thus democratic society "not only continues to exist *by* transmission, *by* communication, but it may fairly be said to exist *in* transmission, *in* communication."[32] This way of thinking perhaps requires explication, because it challenges some popular modern commonplaces about the nature of man, the nature of democracy, and the possibilities for their relationship. It begins with the notion that a democratic community can be—and perhaps always must be—more than a collection or an aggregation, more than a mere *heap* of individuals who are no more than accidentally, incidentally connected, and who remain essentially separate and private; that constituting a community is more than a simple process of addition; and that living in that community is more than a matter of sustained juxtaposition.

Rather, it seems that one of the things that a community does, simply in virtue of being a community, is to provide and to explicate a common, unifying set of meanings. It is, after all, from our communities that we receive the fundamental beliefs, ideals, hopes, practices, customs, commonplaces, concepts of success and failure, concepts of happiness and misery by reference to all of which we begin to make sense of the world we live in, the things that happened to us, and even, in a certain sense, ourselves. A radical claim, that. It asserts not only that one's community of discourse provides him at least some of the tools necessary to disinter and interpret his past and to discern and understand his present. It asserts, moreover, that through ongoing "conjoint community experience," one's community helps envision and shape one's future. The community not only informs one's *understanding* of the future, but plays a continuing role in its actual *formulation,* its *constitution*—in the evaluations and aspirations out of which we make the decisions that help make our futures. The ancient claim that the community is prior to the individual is in this sense reinvigorated: past, present, and future, the community provides the unique context in which each individual can fully become who he or she is.

Education is the sharing, the communication of what is held in common, the "renewal of the meanings of experience through a process of transmission." It is in virtue of a certain res publica—the set of public things, things held in common—that an aggregation becomes a community. Education is the way the community insures that these public things, these shared meanings, are *kept* in common; this continuously reconstitutes the community *as* a community. It is perhaps clearer in this light how education—without in any direct sense being partisan—serves not only individual interests, but also a crucial public, community function, a function that is "political" in the highest sense: "men live in a community in virtue of the things which they have in common; and communication is the way in which they come to possess things in common."[33] The lyceum was the form of democratic education that was structured most effectively to enable its audiences "to fashion what one commentator called 'common ground.' The rules of the lecture system enforced discourse directed toward the political, moral and spiritual precepts that transcended sectarian, partisan and social division. . . . In addition, the popular lecture was a ceremony, which in form and content brought the public into self-conscious existence. It was a collective ritual that invoked the values thought to define and sustain the community as a whole." Thus the lyceum "not only expressed a national culture; it was one of the central institutions within and by which the public had its existence."[34]

The lyceum was an instrument of democratic education, an instrument for the communication of, the communing in, the meanings of life in the democratic community. In this communication (communion/community), the lyceum provided means for "the widening of the area of shared concerns, and the liberation of a greater diversity of personal capacities" that, says Dewey, "characterize a democracy." Here Dewey is expanding the term "democracy" to apply both to explicit political organization and to the character of the community's whole way of life. This notion of "democracy" is less tidy and fashionable than simply to regard it as referring only to a certain organization of government, a particular mode of arranging power relationships. This latter understanding is tidier, in that it need never even raise questions about the distinctive character, excellences or ends of the community, and it is more fashionable in that it formalizes a popular view of the individual as constitutively prior to and independent of the community. These advantages notwithstanding, what it does not do very well is to illumine this part of our history; even to address, let alone to explain, the publicly constitutive functions clearly served by the circuit of public speech. Dewey, on the other hand, focuses on such processes: "democracy" as it becomes charged with human identity becomes a distinctive culture of thought and character—a culture very literally, in the sense of a place where thought and character are rooted and nourished and nurtured, and grow into their identifyingly human possibilities.[35]

Democratic citizens participate in the common interests in such a way that "each has to refer his own action to that of others, and to consider the action of others to give point and direction to his own." This relationship helps break down what Dewey called "those barriers of class, race, and national territory which kept men from perceiving the full import of their activity." A democratic community presents its citizens with "more numer-

ous and more varied points of contact," but it also presents "a greater
diversity of stimuli to which an individual has to respond; they consequently put a premium on variation in his action. They secure a liberation
of powers which remain suppressed as long as the incitations to action are
partial, as they must be in a group which in its exclusiveness shuts out many
interests." Democratic education must make available a variety of personal
possibilities to respond to the peculiar variety of demands that life in this
community presents.[36]

This said, Bode's claim for lyceum education—that it was, even at its
most technical, a liberalizing education—takes on its full import. The democratic audience had a special need for just that sort of education, because
of that characteristic liability to intellectual narrowness discussed in Chapter 3. And that need was especially urgent, since unaddressed narrowness in
the people would have particularly severe political consequences in a democracy. This was still another characteristic of the democratic audience
that, left to itself, would eventually come back to damage or even destroy
its democratic constitution and character.

Tocqueville observes that Americans spend most of their time thinking
about their own private affairs and enterprises, tending to overlook issues
that didn't strike them as immediately relevant to their individual concerns.
But issues would arise publicly that citizens were forced to have opinions
about—those "public things" that were the foci of community life and
discourse. Americans employed their egalitarian principles to approach this
problem. If all men were politically equal, then it was no huge jump to the
conviction that all minds were equal too. Americans would identify with
the opinion of the majority, figuring "that, all having the same means of
knowledge, truth will be found on the side of the majority." And to the
majority's dicta, Americans clung with irrational tenacity. "What struck me
most in the United States was the difficulty experienced in getting an idea,
once conceived, out of the head of the majority," Tocqueville reflected.
"Once an idea has taken root there, it would seem that no power on earth
can eradicate it."[37]

Unfortunately, the opinion of the majority was not always enlightened.
Tocqueville devoted two full chapters of his study of democracy in America
to the tyranny of which the majority was capable. But it was capable of its
tyranny specifically when the audience could be reduced from the active
agents of democracy to passive members of the mass, when citizens accepted opinions uncritically rather than thinking for themselves. This was,
surprisingly, a state into which Americans found it easy to lapse: "I know
no country in which, speaking generally, there is less independence of mind
and true freedom of discussion than in America."[38]

The problem was exacerbated by the growing influence of intellectual
specialties on American life. The alternative to understanding such special-

ties is to be ruled by an aristocracy of experts, the specialists; and "to be a citizen under the rule of experts is to be restricted to giving a mild 'yes' or an emphatic 'no' to someone else's decisions." But "this reduces citizenship to a false logical base. Questions which can be answered yes or no are seldom worth asking. When the function of citizenship loses its creativeness, it also loses its meaning."[39] What was needed was the kind of broadening that would enable listeners to think creatively for themselves about new endeavors and new issues, even new *ways* of thinking, of judging what a good idea or a good reason for action might be. In this way, the "citizens/auditors" could deliberate more comprehensively about their world and act more independently on their future.

This is not merely an evaluative point in the theory of democracy, but it is also descriptive of the circuit's distinctive educational appeal: the connection of thought to character.

> Facts, it was constantly pointed out, were more readily available elsewhere. Judging from what was most popular—i.e., those lectures people were most willing to pay to hear—audiences expected lecturers to place their particular topic or kind of knowledge in a broad, interpretive context . . . it was the connection of the specific topic or theme with some more comprehensive view that rendered thought and knowledge ultimately useful, at once "practical" and "ennobling," to use terms frequently employed in praise of lectures. Thus, the good lecture was at once instructive and inspiring; it "elevated and enlarged the understanding and gave broader and more comprehensive views" of the self, the nation, the world, mankind, or nature.[40]

Ultimately, of course, this sort of broadening was not only a political, but also an intellectual duty. Without it "the only meanings possible would be those purchaseable from experts," and this is "precisely what any person with a grain of intellectual self-respect will refuse to do—to take meanings second-hand." But in any case, the community value of the lyceum lay in its intellectually broadening function, since "democratic society is peculiarly dependent for its maintenance upon the use . . . of criteria which are broadly human." As Eduard Lindemann put it, "We cannot have broad and generous societies composed of narrow and limited citizens."[41]

In sum, public speech (or communication, or rhetoric) on the lyceum circuit performed functions that were, in the fullest sense, politically significant, because they were constitutive of the democratic audience, the American community. In fact it "came to be looked upon as a panacea for all the dissolute tendencies of the young, and as a pleasurable means of engendering literary taste and culture."[42] In all those unique ways in which there was a specifically American community, it had become and it grew as a community in speech.

This was the function that the lyceum proudly served — sometimes. But sometimes the democratic community-in-speech became something of a Babel. Contemporary enthusiasm to the contrary, the lyceum was not an unqualified success, and considering the nature of its audience and the rapidly changing world that was its scene, perhaps the success it did achieve *could* not be permanent. Those achievements required a constant maintenance to prevent informed opinions from degenerating into commonplaces that were no longer really understood, only mechanically invoked; and they required constant renewal, to keep up with this world's peculiarly rapid changes and to replace those opinions when something more accurate or incisive or useful or fitting came along. The lyceum could be employed as an instrument to reconstitute its audience intellectually and, in the largest senses, politically. Sometimes it was used this way very skillfully, and that skill will be the object of our attention in later chapters. But even in the form of a speech, communication is a two-way street. If the lyceum reconstituted its audience, its audience also reconstituted the lyceum. It did so gradually, but in the long view very drastically. Although the results occasionally provided some of the unique flavor and charm of the circuit, they ultimately produced an unmistakable pattern of intellectual degeneration and degradation.

> "The lyceum is my pulpit," Emerson once said. . . . When Starr King was asked what he lectured for, he answered "F.A.M.E. — Fifty And My Expenses." . . . Oliver Wendell Holmes remarked to Herman Melville and some others that "a lecturer was a literary strumpet, subject for greater than a whore's fee to prostitute himself."[43]

Herman Melville appeared on the circuit while he was thinking about and writing *Moby-Dick, Pierre,* and *The Confidence Man;* but instead of discussing them, he found himself compelled — because it was far more lucrative, and because it was far less frustrating — to deliver hack lectures on pseudocultural topics like "Lives of the South-Sea Savages" and "Statuary in Rome." Oliver Wendell Holmes felt forced to pitch the intellectual level of his lectures lower and lower. The lectures that he delivered in the 1840s were informative and occasionally tackled very demanding topics like "The Natural Diet of Man" and "The History of Medicine." In the 1850s, however, he largely "abandoned science and history in favor of literature, rather trivially treated." In 1851–1852, a representative season, Holmes offered three lectures of varying intellectual depth: he was contracted to deliver "The History of Medicine" eight times, the much lighter "Lectures and Lecturing" twenty-two times, and the positively frothy "Love of Nature" all of forty-one times. Even Emerson, hardly a crowd pleaser by nature, felt tempted to adjust to this audience and had to enjoin himself firmly not to say "what his audience expected to hear, but what was fit for him to say."[44]

The nature of the circuit's rhetorical situation was being transformed. "Lyceum programs began to change into those heterogeneous courses of lectures on travel, history, biography, foreign affairs and the art of living"; the new, lighter topics came directly as "a result of audience demand. A housewife would never throw on her cloak and leave a warm house to hear about the chemistry of paint, but she would step through snow drifts to hear about 'The Romance of the Sea' or 'The Life and Death of Napoleon Bonaparte.' " Further, as early as 1840 in some veteran lyceum towns in New England, "the public had seen and heard a celebrity on the platform, their curiosity was satisfied, and they rarely . . . sustained interest in a series of appearances by a single lecturer. The people thus unwittingly encouraged the advent of the travelling lecturer who carried one manuscript across the land, reading it night after night in different communities." Developed arguments that shed their light broadly gave way to mere flashes of brilliance, popular not for what they illumined, but for how colorful they were.[45]

As a result of such audience demands, "everyone from respectable Harvard professors to phrenologists or outright quacks" hit the lecture circuit; and more and more frequently they were coming to entertain rather than to instruct. Ultimately, we might pan some of these speakers as considerably less worthwhile than others. But to understand what a lyceum meant in the life of a local community in the mid-1800s, what it meant to an attraction-starved audience whose doughty members—many of them "leather-aproned artisans" and "farmers with dirt on their shoes" who "did not feel the social necessity of wearing suspenders inside their coats on lecture nights"—we must appreciate and perhaps even enjoy, the dazzling variety of speakers, purposes, and relations with the audience that began to appear in the 1850s.[46]

> A substratum of itinerant charlatans squeezed an income from popular interest in current fads and superstitions. The spirit-rappers found a ready audience for their ghostly exhibitions, and in their wake came a horde of debunking lecturers who looked under the spirit-rapper's table and exposed the contrivances of his art, and finally there were the mesmerists, and phrenologists, the astrologists, the mathematical wizards, the female "physicians" and the fakirs who, for a dime or a quarter, were eager to prove the truth of their testimonials by edifying and amusing the people. There was ample justification for Thomas Brown's succinct statement: "all creation is scrambling up to the platform."[47]

Examples of rhetorical indulgence on the circuit might include the "table-thumping" spiritualists, some of the hack politicans bidding for quick popularity, and the more sycophantic of the "common sense philosophers." But phrenology was probably the most popular of these rhetorical quackeries on the circuit and perhaps most representative of the open appeal to audiences' baser susceptibilities. It asserted that the brain was divided into some thirty "organs," each with its particular function, and that the contours of the skull "paralleled" the brain in a way that could be read by physical inspection. Although it appeared in more responsible forms elsewhere, as it was popularized on the circuit phrenology "offered a quick, easy way to the understanding of human nature—with the promise that if it could be understood, it might then be manipulated or at least taken into account." Thus it was promised that "the respectable merchant . . . could tell which clerk to trust and which to discharge out of hand. If the bumps of conscientiousness on the upper rear side of the head were missing—or worse, still, replaced by hollows—then the wretched clerk could expect short shrift. And the merchant might even tell by the bumps and hollows who would quickly buy from him and who would not . . . the rake, by a brief examination of the back of a young lady's neck could tell whether her 'amativeness' was full-bodied or not—and proceed accordingly." When expounded by convincing spokesmen like George Combe, "the uses of phrenology appeared infinite."[48]

As increasing amounts of this grade of material clogged the lecture courses, even speakers who had proven their talent and worth felt forced to water down their speeches or change their topics altogether. Holmes is probably the most representative figure, in that "he recapitulated the shift in lecture topics which characterized the lyceum as a whole. Not that his change was entirely undeviating; he had one or two early lectures which were not on science and an outstanding later one was. Overall, however, he fitted the trend. Moreover, he did so consciously. He once explained, rather contritely it seems, to Emerson, 'I am forced to study effects. You and others may be able to combine popular effect with the exhibition of truths. I cannot.' Increasingly Holmes tailored his lectures for the public. As it became lighter-minded, so did he."[49]

And it was in no uncertain terms that Holmes described how light-minded that public ultimately became:

> A thoroughly popular lecture ought to have nothing in it which five hundred people cannot all take in a flash. I tell you, the *average* intellect of five hundred persons, taken as they come, is not very high.[50]

In the years after the Civil War, the lyceum became more and more a vehicle for popular entertainment, at the expense of popular instruction. One indication was that, for the first time, buffoon-style comedians like Josh Billings, Artemus Ward, and "the Reverend Petroleum Vesuvius Nasby" were being featured and becoming popular. Another was that hack politicians like Davy Crockett discovered how to use the lyceum platform to make their reputations out of exotic and often apocryphal frontier stories. Still another was that the lyceum, where once a Wendell Phillips, a William Lloyd Garrison, a Fanny Wright came to deliver their messages of fierce integrity, was looked upon as *properly* a vehicle for tamer and more diaphanous material. "The Philadelphia Press of 28 January 1861 — to take a late example — found a good deal to praise in the clever Park Benjamin, who was to speak on 'Fact or Fiction.' It sent him its good wishes: 'As he never makes offensive political observations wholly alien to his subject.' " What the audiences came for — the purpose of public speech — was no longer to be instructed and to better themselves, but merely to see popular personalities *perform:* "it was mankind's fondness for menageries that brought many people to see the 'lions' of the lecturing profession." Simultaneously, another sort of degeneration was occurring: "as the decades of the lyceum went on, the lectures on education as related to democracy almost entirely disappeared — in fact, it is a reasonable deduction that the total number of lectures on general education (once the staple of lyceum courses) from any point of view went down." No longer were audience members regularly receiving the general, liberating kind of education that would help them put their peculiarly diverse and pluralistic world together. It's true that right up to the very end of the lyceum's popularity in the 1800s, there were intrepid lecturers who bucked the trend and struggled against audience expectations to engage in serious speech; their skill — and perhaps their courage — deserves our attention and recognition.[51] Still, the *average* quality of the lyceum lecture is more accurately described in an editorial that J. B. Holland wrote for *Scribner's Monthly* in 1872.

> There was a time when a lecture was a lecture. The men who appeared before the lyceums were men who had something to say. . . . Now a lecture may be any string of nonsense that any literary mountebank can find an opportunity to utter.[52]

But as the lyceum declined, another forum for public speech was on the rise: the chautauqua circuit. "The lyceums made up a winter system of lectures and entertainment; the chautauquas were a summer extension of the system. Lyceums were respected fare in towns and cities; chautauquas flourished largely in smaller centers and rural areas."[53] Chautauqua was founded in 1873 by the Reverend John Heyl Vincent and businessman Lewis Miller as a permanent settlement on the shores of Lake Chautauqua in New York State. Each summer, thousands populated this unusual summer resort to be part of an educational program on nondenominationally religious and broadly political topics, aimed at first particularly at teachers. After a summer or two at Chautauqua, many visitors founded some similar kind of "chautauqua" in their own communities. But like the lyceum, chautauqua eventually changed form in a fundamental way; and in fact it is probably better remembered for the gaudy era of the traveling chautauqua.

It was always a big day when the chautauqua caravan came to town. A large part of the company usually arrived in a noisy parade. The locals would string welcoming banners across the streets from second-floor windows or lampposts, or cluster flags at the lampposts' tops. When its presence had been sufficiently trumpeted, the company proceeded to the chautauqua ground itself. A team of muscular young workers had been dispatched there in advance to transform some ordinary empty and fairly flat field into a site fit for a chautauqua. A bandstand had been nailed together, bunting hung from the limbs of trees, and signs posted to advertise this year's attractions in full — some might even say hyperbolic — detail.

Dominating the scene was the chautauqua tent: huge, faded brown, torches posted to illuminate the platform, its flaps adjusted for the weather — tied back to admit whatever breeze a sweltery August night might manage, or closed to the sudden downpours of the Great Plains. Hundreds would pack the tent that night and all the succeeding week to hear some of the greatest orators and most profound thinkers of the day — but also to hear their first opera or symphony, or to be entertained by a humorist, a magician, or perhaps a forerunner of what not many years later would be called "a song and dance man."

James Redpath had been the first to take the show on the road effectively, by forming a bureau to book speakers out of Chicago. But it was left to entrepreneur Keith Vawter, who took over the Redpatch Bureau at the turn of the century, to reshape chautauqua. At its height in the mid-twenties, the circuit played to at least forty million Americans in eight to ten thousand communities all across the country. That's 40,000,000 in person; in the 1920 census, the total population of the United States was pegged at only 105,710,620.[54]

Those familiar dramatic images of Elmer Gantry outlined in torchlight — which are not complete fabrications — obsure our vision of what chautauqua started out to be. Its founders were as far from emotional evangelism as one can imagine them. Lewis Miller was a quiet, practical man who had been successful in several businesses after having made both fortune and fame on an invention he brought to the market in 1857, the immortal Buckeye Mower and Reaper (some aptitude along this line of inventing was also evidenced by his son-in-law, one Tom Edison). The Reverend John Heyl Vincent was more forceful, a transfixing speaker who had been tangentially involved in political life ever since he had been minister to the Galena, Illiniois, church of young Ulysses Grant. It was an index of this forcefulness that, a few years later, Vincent not only delivered the address welcoming the return of the then-triumphant General Grant; but when the General—as was apparently his wont—was temporarily struck speechless, Vincent cheerfully took it upon himself to deliver Grant's response too.

If anything, Reverend Vincent was even more averse than Miller to the evangelical religion of the camp meeting. Accounts abound of Vincent's firm determination to keep chautauqua on a different path. For a long time he had resisted the idea of holding a program during the summer at all, "fearing that the plan would be thought of as merely another camp meeting with its emotional extravagances." And he never felt comfortable about holding chautauquas in any relationship to a camp meeting, or even on a campground. J. B. Hurlburt, a close associate, recalled that Vincent

> was not in sympathy with the type of religious life manifested and promoted at these gatherings. The fact that they dwelt too deeply in the realm of emotion and excitement, that they stirred the feelings to the neglect of the reasoning and thinking faculties, that the crowd called together on a camp meeting ground would not represent the sober, sane, thoughtful element of church life—all these repelled Dr. Vincent from the camp meeting. . . .

There were times, in fact, that Vincent positively exorcised the camp meeting spirit from Chautauqua. Many who attended the first session had "brought with them . . . exuberant expectations" but were rather sternly informed "that exhortation and a call to sinners to repent had no place on the program, and that voluntary and spontaneous gatherings were not permitted."[55]

Neither Vincent nor Miller, then, had any connection with the revivals with which chautauqua is so frequently identified, or with the heterogeneous programs of entertainment that formed an even larger part of the chautauqua circuit. After thirty placid years, however, chautauqua was transformed into a business just as the lyceum had been; and like the lyceum business, the chautauqua business became dependent on audience approval in a way that brought on and enforced the circuit's intellectual degeneration and degradation.

For several years after Keith Vawter took control of the small speakers' bureau that Redpath had originated, he experimented with ways of systematically taking chautauqua on the road. By 1904 he had struck upon the two policies that, it was said, made the circuit the kind of success that it was. What kind of success was it? Its nature is revealed in the nature of Vawter's two brainstorms. They were not in any sense policies directed toward improving the educational quality of the circuit. They were instead shrewd business practices: the unique chautauqua contract and the practice he called "tight booking."

The noteworthy feature of the contract was the guarantee. Each community that bid for a chautauqua had to form a committee that would be responsible to raise a stipulated amount, the guarantee, by selling season tickets. The "hook" was that each member of the committee agreed to be legally liable for the amount of the guarantee. It was of course an unimpeachable sign of eminence in one's community to be a sponsor of culture, and those who saw themselves as their community's leading citizens contended zealously for the honor of membership in the chautauqua committee. In binding this caliber of citizen the guarantee gave the most prominent and responsible citizens, at each stop along the circuit, a personal stake – in terms of the loss of money and also the loss of personal face – in the chautauqua's success in their town.

"Tight booking" required a particular chautauqua company to book towns in fairly compact strings, within one day's travel of each other. This entailed an elaborate logistical scheme for moving people and baggage. Most of a company's "talent" – except site superintendents, the work crew, and sometimes a host or "morning hour lecturer" – was divided into teams according to the number of days its program was to run. Thus a seven-day chautauqua would require seven distinct teams. "First-day talent" would appear on the first day at each stop, then proceed to the next town up the line to open the show there. "Second-day talent" would follow them, and so on. The repertoire of a good many chautauqua acts had formerly been too limited to carry a program for more than one or two performances; after that, performances were often judged to have "sunk progressively."[56] Under tight booking, each act only had to be able to produce one good evening's entertainment per audience. Like the lyceum orators who crisscrossed the country delivering and redelivering the same speech, many chautauqua acts staged the same performance night after night, town after town. And it must be frankly admitted that often even these performances were lacking in cultural content. What began with Vincent and Miller's attempt to blend popularized education, religion, and entertainment grew increasingly variable in intellectual quality. A sample chautauqua bill serves to illustrate.

PULASKI, TENNESSEE CHAUTAUQUA
June 15 to 21, 1912 A.D.[57]

($2 season ticket)

Superintendent:	C. W. Thomas
Morning Hour Lecturer:	C. E. Varney
Boy Scout Master:	R. C. Coonradt

Programs Begin Promptly!

Boy Scouts – 9:00 A.M.	Morning Lecture – 10:00 A.M.
Afternoon Music – 2:30	Afternoon Lecture – 3:00
Night Music – 7:30	Night Entertainment – 8:15

Saturday

Afternoon	Concert — Ladies Spanish Orchestra
	Lecture — "A Lesson to the Nation" — Judge A. Z. Blair
Night	Concert — Ladies Spanish Orchestra
	Character Studies — John B. Ratto

Sunday

Afternoon	Concert — Carroll Glee Club
	Lecture — "The Monday Mormon Kingdom" — Sen. F. J. Cannon
Night	Vesper Service
	Concert — Carroll Glee Club
	Reading — "The Dawn of Tomorrow" — Mary Agnes Doyle

Monday

Morning	Boy Scouts
	Lecture — "Man's Search for God" — C. E. Varney
Afternoon	Song Recital — Artists from Le Brun Grand Opera Co.
	Lecture — "The Man Against the Mass" — Frank Dixon
Night	Grand Opera — Le Brun Grand Opera Co.

Tuesday

Morning	Boy Scouts
	Lecture — "Safe and Sane Faith" — C. E. Varney
Afternoon	Concert-Musical Favorites
	Lecture — "A Message from Kansas" — Gov. E. W. Hoch
Night	Concert — Musical Favorites
	Indian Lecture in Costume
	"Things I Did as a Savage" — Tahan

Wednesday

Morning	Boy Scouts
	Lecture — "Philosophy of Habit" — C. E. Varney
Afternoon	Concert — Bohimir Kryl and Band
	Entertainer — J. Walter Wilson
Night	Concert — Bohimir Kryl and Band
	Entertainer — J. Walter Wilson

Thursday

Morning	Boy Scouts
	Lecture — "The Value of Imagination" — C. E. Varney
Afternoon	Concert — Mendelssohn's Quartette
	Lecture — "Traitors to Justice" — Judge M. A. Kavanaugh
Night	Concert — Mendelssohn's Quartette
	Magician — Reno

Friday

Morning	Boy Scouts
	Lecture — "The Use of the Will" C. E. Varney
Afternoon	Concert — Anitas Ladies Orchestra
	Author and Humorist — Opie Read

Night   Concert — Anitas Ladies Orchestra
             Entertainer — Ellsworth Plumstead

So the modern image of chautauqua, or at least of the circuit chautauquas, is not entirely inaccurate when it includes the preachers whose earnestness exceeded their profundity, the pedestrian commonsense philosophers, and the unreconstructed apologists for big business — not to mention the numerous practitioners of such exotic art forms as bell ringing, yodeling, and zither playing. This was the sort of material that circuit chautauquas featured ever more frequently. A number of factors contributed to this decline, not the least of which was the sheer sprawling success of the circuit; there simply were not enough John Heyl Vincents, Thomas Edisons, William Jennings Bryans, Mark Twains, William Rainey Harpers, Robert Ingersolls, William Jameses, George Norrises, Eugene Debses, and "Fighting Bob" La Follettes to go all the way around.[58] But an even more degenerative influence was exerted by the commercial nature that chautauqua acquired when Vawter put it on the circuit to stay. The purposes of the original chautauqua, like those of the original lyceum, were primarily political: to tell truths, to open a public forum to new perspectives, in short to educate and thereby serve the community. But the ultimate purpose of a business — what today might be called "the bottom line" — is to indulge customers with what they want.

Vawter the businessman figured out how to do that. He introduced a system of what he called "quality control." Local managers were to gauge the audience reaction to each part of the program, and after every performance they were to report to the central office. More than one performer who "was doing something that was not entirely 'safe' " was greeted at the next stop by "a more or less strongly worded 'suggestion' from the central office." By the early 1920s the years of the circuit's biggest profits and broadest exposure, the net effect of this policy on the intellectual quality of chautauqua was unmistakable:

> surveillance by local managers made crowd-pleasers rather than agents of culture out of too many performers. For the men and women who seriously advocated a program of action, there was no place at all; they might offend somebody in the audience. The inspirational speakers took over, and the once-vigorous Chautauqua movement was drowned in a flood of pap.[59]

This surrender to mass opinion, to commerical standards of what was the kind of material proper for public speech in America, bears obvious similarities to the intellectual concessions that the lyceum made. Once again, the lecture circuit was being forced to change its nature: what had been essentially an educational vehicle had become essentially a business venture based on the indulgence, not the intellectual reconstitution, of audiences.

But its tawdry reputation and insipid end should not obscure the political and intellectual contributions that chautauqua made to American life. These contributions closely paralleled the contributions made by the lyceum circuit a few decades earlier. First of all, chautauqua probably did more than any other factor to make the expanding America of the late nineteenth and early twentieth centuries *one* nation culturally, in narrowing the "gap between a rural Midwestern population and that of the more advantageously situated East." The fledgling towns of the West "were lacking in the most rudimentary amenities . . . the Chautauqua movement offered the discouraged settlers of the new West a link with the heritage they felt they had lost."[60]

Another public virtue of circuit chautauqua resulted, unexpectedly enough, from the guarantee. Not only did its prominent citizens have a special stake in a chautauqua's success in their home town; the townspeople themselves began to feel an interest in having the chautauqua succeed. Community pride expressed itself in many useful ways besides merely buying the tickets, as one of the circuit's most successful bureau directors, Charles Horner, took pains to point out:

> the people would work in zeal for the coming chautauqua. Often they would unite to cut the weeds, mow the grass, trim the trees, decorate the windows and even paint some buildings so that the town would be neat and handsome for the inspection of visitors. Many businessmen would organize booster trips to visit the countryside and neighbor towns to advertise the coming event, and to promise a welcome to prospective guests from far and near. Preachers would often make the Chautauqua a subject for their sermons weeks in advance, and Sunday evening services and mid-week prayer meetings were usually cancelled or held at an early hour so that their congregations could feel free to go to the tent. Strange to relate, many stores and other business houses would lock their doors during the afternoon and evening hours. The mothers would bake and cook in advance, and freely welcome to their homes the itinerant chautauquans. The long hot trail blossomed with a never-ending series of good cheer plentifully embellished with fried chicken.

The visit of the chautauqua caravan, in other words, acted as an occasion to unify the community in a common effort — the object of which effort was, reflexively, chautauqua itself. Horner describes the reflexivity from the opposite angle. "Not the least of its attributes," Horner said of chautauqua, "was its peculiar talent to foster Community unity and action, and these in turn were its chief benefactors." Either way, in its community involvement the circuit reached further and more actively into community life than its successors, the comparatively isolated media of radio and television, seem able to do. In the words of then-President Harding, chautauqua "served to reveal the individual American community to itself at its best."[61]

But in addition to this unifying public effect, chautauqua stirred the community's interrelation in another way, a way that actually enhanced public understanding. One of the observations frequently and accurately made about chautauqua audiences was that often "people went to a Chautauqua to be stimulated," that "instead of the content of a lecture . . . [they] were interested in effect." But "to laugh with the humorists or thrill to the pyrotechnics . . . of oratory" were not the only effects in which chautauqua audiences were interested. Because chautauqua was a community experience, part of its interest lay in those effects that held special meaning for the community. When people attended chautauqua, "they saw their neighbors there. They watched the color creep up the neck of the local banker when Debs castigated the financial interests, and they planned to be present when the banker got his next shave from the barber, an unreconstructed Populist. If Debs had spoken at a political rally, the banker would not have gone, and there would have been no argument to anticipate. But everyone went to Chautauqua . . . ideas presented during Chautauqua Week were argued and discussed in these communities a hundred times in the ensuing year."[62]

The interest and stimulation of a community's personal relations enabled people to come to clearer and more concrete understandings of the new ideas and issues that were presented. Part of the fun was to know what would anger the banker, and what would anger the barber, and why. Listeners, by identifying with people with whom they felt familiar, came to perceive the consequences of the new ideas—how those new ideas worked in the world and how they related to other ideas. The people of a community knew each other and that made the new ideas more interesting to listen to and to talk about. It provided terms that actually made the new ideas more graspable, more *possible* to think and talk about. Put more generally, the circuit enjoyed a special access, for instructing and persuading Americans. When it used that access, the circuit's rhetoric made its characteristic intellectual contribution.

Moreover, as Gould observed, the interest and stimulation of a community drew people to hear speakers like Debs, people who otherwise would never have heard such speakers. It exposed new ideas, yes. But it exposed these ideas *publicly,* made those ideas part of what the community had in common; it gave the barber and the banker something of real intellectual and political value—and, moreover, of mutual value—to talk about. And the hot-stove conversations of the ensuing winter had obvious and continuing effects on the way such a town came to their decisions of self-government, their decisions about how they would shape their future together.

Chautauqua's contributions to democratic community life were widely acknowledged. "The average Chautauquan, wrote Rebecca Richmond, "may be classed as a most desirable citizen. He is the mainstay of democ-

Overleaf: SUMMER CHAUTAUQUA, NEW YORK, CA. 1900–1910.
Library of Congress.

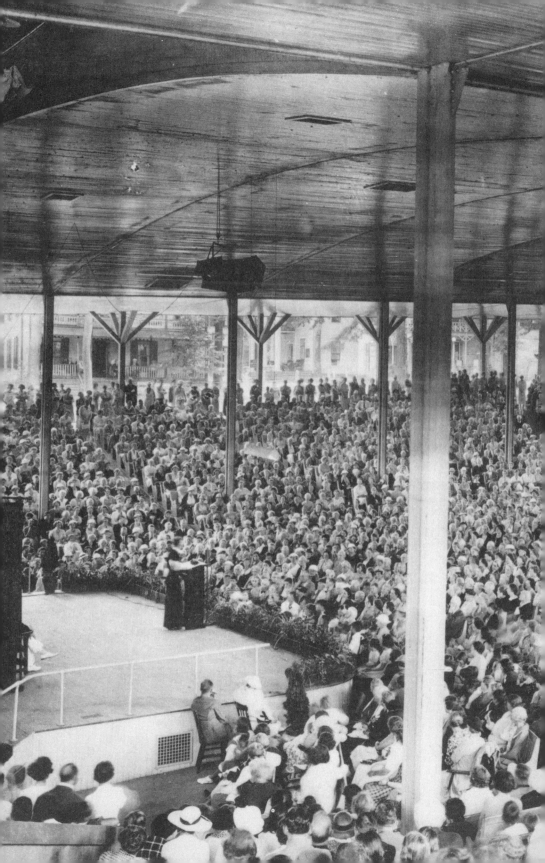

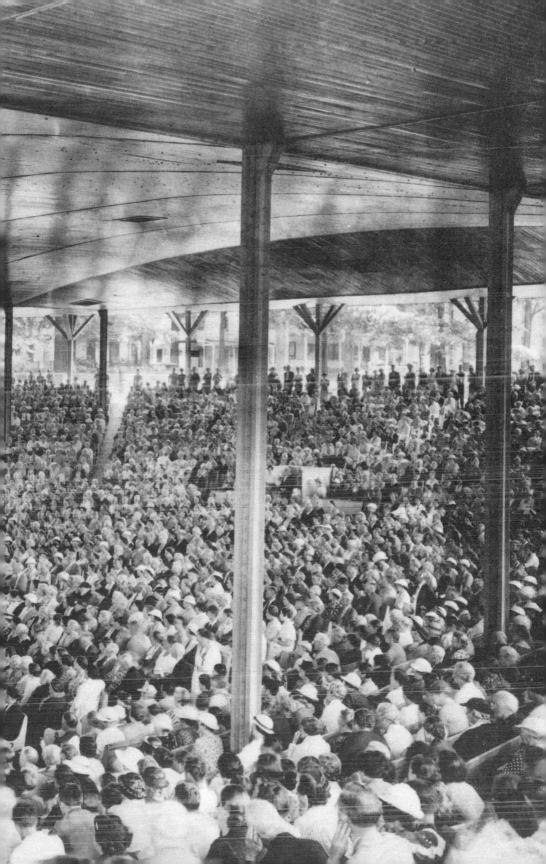

racy." At every stage of its development, people did regard the circuit as more than an opportunity for entertainment, Richmond argues; at least some of them consciously used it as a means to fulfill public duty. "People saw clearly that their new democratic government would require an intelligent and literate electorate to perpetuate it," and so "there was never any getting away from the great responsibilities of American citizenship and the discussion of their extent."[63]

The circuit served as a vehicle for public speech by which and in which the American community maintained itself through some of the most troubled times in its history. Chautauqua appeared in its original form in the 1870s, and

> the American of the 1870's faced . . . a bewildering number of complex problems. There was the arrogance of the railroads and the trusts, a prolonged and severe economic depression, political corruption in city, state, and federal government, a "stolen" Presidential election (Hayes-Tilden), and a wave of bitter strikes which shocked the nation and created widespread fear for the safety of democratic institutions.[64]

Circuit chautauqua developed at the turn of the century,

> that moment in history precisely half-way between Pickett's cavalry charge at Gettysburg and the bomb run over Hiroshima. The frontier had moved; railroads spanned the continent. But there still remained in the southwest a few blank spaces on the maps. Horsepower still meant horses. The America that watched the first Chautauqua tent rise in an Iowa meadow in 1904 and the America that saw the last tent come down twenty-nine years later in a little Illinois village, were separated by a period that marked swift changes in a people's thinking, in concepts of both humor and morality, in public and private manners. Early Lyceum had induced a Civil War; tent chautauqua survived the Argonne and Belleau Wood. The movement had reached from T. R. to F. D. R., from the Surrey with the fringe on top to a speedometer that could register seventy miles an hour.[65]

Educational movements in the United States have thrived on community crises, and none more than the public speech circuit. Conversely, chautauqua began to exhaust itself after the Great War, in the placid, isolationist twenties when there were fewer, less serious crises and less concern with public questions. But before it ran out its string, chautauqua made serious and tangible contributions to American life. Although it was afflicted and ultimately despoiled by magicians, yodelers, zither-wielders and bell ringers, chautauqua had still found time to influence public policy concretely on a number of matters of real public import: the eight-hour day, the conservation of natural resources, the establishment of national forests and parks, pure food and drug legislation, the regulation of inter-state commerce, city planning, slum clearance, Prohibition, the establish-ment of the Federal Reserve, the direct election of United States senators, and women's suffrage. But ultimately an even more significant contribution of chautauqua to the democracy was a broadening, a diversification of the American intellect. The exposure of those intellects to different disciplines provided alternative ways to see and talk about and act on their world — a world that, because it was democratic, was theirs in a uniquely powerful way.

It's one thing to claim that the lyceum and chautauqua circuits made significant, serious, and tangible contributions to American life; it's quite another to claim that they succeeded in reconstituting the democratic au-dience in any permanent way. Their degraded, tarnished ends testify per-suasively to the contrary. Both circuits changed from educational vehicles to business ventures, striving to give the people what they wanted. The democratic audience — notwithstanding any lessons that educators of the caliber of Emerson, Twain, or James had taught them — unmistakably chose indulgence over intellectual reconstitution.[66]

The overall degeneration of the circuits does nothing to diminish the particular rhetorical accomplishments of individual educators; if anything, these achievements are enhanced by a fair appreciation of how difficult reconstituting this democratic audience could be. Change was a kind of constant in democratic America; there was no accomplishment that was permanently safe from being overturned. All its proponents claimed for the circuit was that it was "an episode in continuing American revolution," one episode with presumably more, of different sorts, to follow.[67] The price of democracy, to paraphrase George Washington, seems to be eternal rhetori-cal vigilance. In a democracy's process of constant self-renewal, it is the duty of democratic education to play a constantly innovative role. This, at least, was the conclusion of the democratic educators; it is similarly the conclusion — perhaps even the admonition — implicit in the rhetorical possi-bilities of the American character as reflected in the circuit of public speech.

II

The Rhetoric of Democratic Education

Let me repeat once more that a man's vision is the great fact about him. A philosophy is the expression of a man's intimate character, and all definitions of the Universe are but the deliberately adopted reactions of human characters upon it.

— William James

But do your thing, and I shall know you. Do your work and you shall reinforce yourself.

— Ralph Waldo Emerson

CHAPTER 5

Ralph Waldo Emerson as Democratic Educator: Man Thinking

God has granted to every people a prophet in its own tongue.
— *The Koran*

God, when he made the prophet, did not unmake the man.
— JOHN LOCKE

I count him a great man who inhabits a higher sphere of thought, into which other men rise with labor and difficulty; he has but to open his eyes to see things in a true light and in large relations, whilst they must make painful corrections and keep a vigilant eye on many sources of error.
— RALPH WALDO EMERSON

What we ardently love,
we learn to imitate.

— RALPH WALDO EMERSON

T H E single most troublesome consideration in evaluating the rhetoric of the American circuit of public speech, especially given the character of the democratic audience, is formulating an appropriate notion of success.

Some observers insist that the best indicator of a medium's successful use is, quite simply, public response. The circuit had its share of popular rhetoricians, perennial favorites who took their share of the circuit's material rewards and "F.A.M.E.": Bayard Taylor, John Gough, especially Henry Ward Beecher made very comfortable livings indeed from lecturing; Davy Crockett made himself a living legend and a congressman in the bargain; Daniel Webster very nearly made himself president. In this measure, such speakers have been considered—and clearly considered themselves—rhetorical successes, even though at least some of these successes involved pandering forms of indulgence of democratic audience in preference to making some effort to reconstitute that audience.[1]

But another kind of observer defines rhetorical success less as a measure of receipts than as a quality of thought and character and demands something like "moral stature" or "greatness"—the general sorts of qualification that distinguished democratic education from indulgence. This kind of observer also had ready examples of "success." For there were on the circuit some lecturers who unquestionably achieved moral stature, even greatness. Abolitionists like Wendell Phillips and William Lloyd Garrison, suffragettes like Anna Dickinson and Fanny Wright, and a whole crew of Transcendentalists including Orestes Brownson, Bronson Alcott, and Henry David Thoreau spoke artfully and provocatively for their causes. Their problem was that, very often, they spoke so provocatively as to leave the audience not only unpersuaded by their arguments, but perhaps more adamantly opposed.

There were many examples of this sort of unsuccessful rhetoric, but perhaps the most consistent and spectacular failure was the contentious Fanny Wright. She gave a lecture in Philadelphia entitled "A Geographical and Historical Sketch of the North American United States" and the mayor forbade her to speak there again! It was still worse when she turned to politics. In New York she spoke for Jackson and versus the bank. The lecture platform was, it seems, almost torn away beneath her. Recall that New York was the home state of Martin Van Buren, Jackson's own vice-president and heir apparent; to have evoked this response from that audience was an amazing rhetorical accomplishment.[2]

While "successful" rhetoric may well involve moral standards, by definition it involves persuading the audience too. High-minded rhetoricians who aimed simply and uncompromisingly to state their case with intellectual rigor and elegance could succeed in being admirable logicians, occasionally even exalted poets. But in the measure that they failed to share the force of the logic or the power of the poetry, to make it identifiable to their listeners, they failed as rhetoricians. It is not too strong even to claim that insofar as they did not recognize or could not animate all of what was humanly moving in their message, they did not completely understand the message itself and its ethical possibilities for the democratic audience.

Neither of the simple notions of success seemed to have the sheer dimensions of fully successful rhetoric. The rhetoric of Beecher, of Crockett, even of Daniel Webster clearly suffered from shallowness; but the morally and intellectually more ambitious efforts of a Garrison or a Wright often suffered just as severely from narrowness of appeal. Since neither notion of rhetorical success will suffice, part of our enterprise must be to develop a more adequate notion of rhetorical success and a form of criticism to go along with it. But for the moment these two standards, however crude, are all we have; and in fact there appeared some few speakers on the circuit who achieved success by both definitions. Speakers like Wendell Phillips, Anna Dickinson, Robert Ingersoll, Robert LaFollette and — for the first few years of his career, at least — the elder Oliver Wendell Holmes all achieved some such success. In later chapters, I shall argue that some of the great successes the circuit ever knew were achieved by two American popularizers not primarily remembered for their lecturing, Mark Twain and William James. But of all the speakers who ever "pounded the boards," from the first quiet lyceum meetings till the last chautauqua company folded its tents, the circuit's most successful rhetorician, its greatest and its most enduringly popular democratic educator, was Ralph Waldo Emerson.

> In any study of the lyceum there is bound to be much talk about popularity but little about greatness. Emerson is perhaps the only lecturer in the movement who could unhesitatingly be called great. The amazing thing is that he was also enormously popular.[3]

His was an extraordinary career. In 1829 he ascended to the pulpit as assistant pastor of Boston's prestigious Second Church at the callow age of 26; his first lyceum appearance occurred in 1835; but he really made his rhetorical mark with two controversial speeches. The first was the oration he gave as a last-minute substitute speaker at the Harvard Phi Beta Kappa convocation in 1837. This was the celebrated "American Scholar" speech, a digest of his earlier work in *Nature* in which he urged his countrymen to throw off the limits of tradition in their intellectual life and become purely Man Thinking. Oliver Wendell Holmes regarded this oration as nothing less than "our intellectual Declaration of Independence." The "Harvard Divinity School Address" the next year was so unorthodox, even for his liberalizing times, that his alma mater banned him from speaking on campus. This injunction lasted upwards of thirty years; yet from that time on, Emerson never wanted for bookings. The fairly substantial records which survive demonstrate that through the lyceum's golden age in the 1840s and 1850s, he delivered "more speeches than any other American of his time."[4] The Civil War vastly curtailed lyceum activities; but by the end of the war, when circuit activity picked up again, the aging Emerson's faculties had already begun to fade. From this time on, he produced almost no new works, but instead contented himself with reshuffling old journal material and reprising old platform favorites. Even so, Emerson prospered. He grew *more* popular as audiences seemed finally to recognize him as a distinctively American genius: they literally rushed to honor him, however belatedly. Emerson lectured tirelessly to them well into the 1870s. More and more often, however, he was only able to get through his speeches with the aid of his daughter Ellen, who had to become his regular traveling companion and apparently something like his guardian. His vast audiences remained faithful to the end — and even beyond — in their massive purchases of the works that grew out of his lectures.

In this chapter I propose to examine the principles of Emerson's distinctive rhetorical success. Popularity and greatness had seemed to pull in different directions before Emerson appeared (and, candidly, they continued to do so for the most part). In one respect, however, his achievement was seminal, multiplying the possibilities for democratic education, for successful rhetoric on the circuit. Emerson's approach was, in ways we shall examine, peculiarly suited to the requirements of the democratic audience; through this peculiarly fit way of arguing, the sources of greatness could become sources for his popularity. The reconstitution thereby effected is best described in his own words; Emerson's success was in making the lecture "a new literature, which leaves aside all tradition, time, place, circumstance, and addresses an assembly as mere human beings."[5] Emerson's own authority was no more complicated and exotic, and no less persuasive, than that of Man Thinking.

Fully appreciating Emerson's success requires some understanding of the staggering rhetorical problems he successfully confronted. Many of the problems, as we shall see, were of his own making, functions of his character; but others, which confronted all the circuit's rhetoricians, issued from the audience's democratic character.

Emerson fostered no giddily sentimental illusions about the unreconstituted democratic audience.

> Leave this hypocritical prating about the masses. Masses are rude, lame, unmade, pernicious in their demands, and need not to be flattered, but schooled. I wish not to concede anything to them, but to tame, drill, divide, and break them up and draw individuals out of them![6]

This audience's character at the time of Emerson's appearance on the circuit did not promise much for educational enterprises. At least it did not unless this audience could be reconstituted from an undisciplined mass into an audience of individuals — each an instantiation of man thinking. The "mind of the multitude" Emerson found "sluggish and perverted," "slow to open to the incursions of reason." Thus "I like man, but not men."[7]

In the terms developed in Chapter 3, the unreconstituted democratic listeners saw themselves represented directly in the character of Andrew Jackson: confident heroes against odds, outsiders ambitiously taking advantage of their prized new equality of opportunity to "enter the scramble." This distinctively democratic confidence and ambition made them peculiarly shifty and shallow listeners; and for the rhetorician's practice, this cut both ways. On the one hand, democratic audiences were more willing to listen, to be attentive to the introduction of new ideas. On the other, it required that new ideas show identifiable and desirable results — "cash value," as William James later called it — almost immediately, and that they continue to "produce" in this vein. Democratic audiences could be more easily drawn to listen unhampered by traditional, conventional presuppositions; but their commitment to listening was never much better than fearfully shallow and undisciplined. Practically, this meant an especially powerful resistance to intellectual specialties that seemed unnecessarily difficult or obscure. "Seeing that they are successful in resolving unaided all the little difficulties they encounter in practical affairs," says Tocqueville, "they are easily led to the conclusion that . . . nothing passes beyond the limits of their intelligence. Thus they are ready to deny anything which they cannot understand."[8]

These problems bedeviled every speaker who approached democratic audiences with intent to do anything intellectually and morally more ambitious than gross pandering. With such difficulties attending democratic education, and with considerable material rewards involved in indulging, the temptation to succumb must have seemed compelling. Emerson himself felt the pressure of "what *must* be said" more than once, and several times he had to admonish himself to "remember that you are not to say what must be said in a Lyceum," and not to speak merely "what they will expect to hear, but what is fit for me to say." But these difficult problems and alluring temptations were common to every lecturer; in addition, Emerson found others that were peculiar to him.[9]

Perhaps the most immediately obvious of Emerson's special problems was the difficulty, the obscurity, the sheer depth that his message seemed to have — or at least the obscurity with which it often came out. In this respect, the task of democratic education Emerson undertook for himself was difficult indeed. He was armed only with disconcertingly lofty propositions like

> Time and space are but physiological colors which the eye maketh; but the soul is light.

> All my willful actions and acquisitions are but roving; — the most trivial reverie, the faintest emotion are domestic and divine.

> Vast spaces of nature, the Atlantic Ocean, the South Sea, vast intervals of time, years, centuries are of no account.

and finally, perhaps appropriately,

> To be great is to be misunderstood.[10]

Emerson went boldly forth to try to make them coherent and convincing to even the most hard-headed and down-to-earth of the circuit's audiences: slick, sceptical entrepreneurs from rough-and-tumble western boom towns like Cincinnati, Detroit, Chicago, St. Louis, and later even bawdy San Francisco; and no-nonsense truck farmers of places like "the show-me-state" of Missouri and downstate Illinois, listeners who were not reluctant to express their evaluation of a lecturer's performance by giving wing to some of their own produce.[11]

Nor is it clear whether Emerson's audiences were disposed more or less receptively by the advance work of his energetic but perhaps somewhat intellectually overmatched promoters. Often Emerson arrived at a new booking to find that he had been modestly touted as the "sage of Concord" and "the celebrated metaphysician of the East."[12] It could not have made for very comforting conjecture to guess what those audiences thought they were coming to see. Sometimes the expectations were damagingly inaccurate. One tradition, ostensibly tracing back to Emerson's nephew, has it that Emerson came to address an audience that was expecting, by some mistake, to hear comic Petroleum Vesuvius Nasby. Emerson gave a characteristic performance and was received politely, but auditors later allowed that the quiet man who had spoken to them was at best only a tolerable humorist. But whatever they might have been expecting, what they got was a mild, shy, quiet man whose own temperament and personality, as represented in his speaking character or "ethos," posed still further problems.

The one way Emerson seems most to have unsettled the conventional expectations of his audience was by his speaking style. The circuit's equivalents of matinee idols — Taylor, Gough, Beecher — were strikingly handsome men and spoke with great animation and demonstration. The conventional expectations that audiences developed from such oratory could not be rewarded by Emerson, whose style reflected his reserved character; and so sometimes — usually on his first appearance in a town — the audience response did not necessarily include the serious attention he hoped for.

> His audiences found more amusement in looking at Emerson than in listening to his discourses. His platform manner was novel and amusing. He began his lectures without preliminaries and continued them without flourishes. He spoke without gestures, except for an occasional angular movement of his forearm and a slight tremble in body and voice when he came to a moving passage. His hesitations and difficulty in bridging the gaps between paragraphs appeared to them like a man crossing a brook on stepping-stones. His voice was clear and penetrating, but did not appear to be musical until listeners had become accustomed to his slight nasal twang.[13]

The mannerly Emerson managed to entangle himself in activities not often seen on the podium — activities that hardly characterized him as just another hero of the hustings.

> He shuffled them [the pages of his speech] and rummaged through his pockets also, as if he expected to find something more there; he lost his

place, omitted passages, and skipped inadvertently. Once he is supposed to have stopped in the middle of a sentence, searched vainly among his papers, and then left the platform. He twirled his glasses when he had them, but once he came without them and could not see to read until he had borrowed a pair from a member of the audience. Once he upset a vase, descended from the platform, gathered up the scattered flowers, and replaced them, all without any sign of perturbation. When he read the second Phi Beta Kappa Address at Harvard, he kept losing his papers until putting a cushion under them, and when he read his famous "Boston Hymn," some of his leaves escaped into the audience and had to be retrieved before he could go on. His delivery was, generally speaking, monotonous; he rocked his body and took a hasty backward step after reading a striking passage. His endings were always abrupt, and he left the platform without giving the audience a chance to applaud.[14]

As Emerson himself allowed, "a man cannot speak but he judges himself. With his will or against his will he draws his portrait to the eye of his companions by every word. Every opinion reacts on him who utters it."[15] By personal manner as well as by subject matter, the audience was moved to think about the character of the man addressing them; and it seemed impossible to avoid the conclusion that this speaker was a character altogether different from the lecturing lions they were used to. And to a significant extent, that conclusion was biographically true: Emerson's public behavior was in large measure an extension, a projection of his private character. That private character was hardly of the ebullient sort that had natural affinities with a rowdy house in Zanesville or Kalamazoo. On the contrary, Emerson had a certain asocial reserve that made it difficult for anyone—for even his closest associates, let alone his audiences—to feel very familiar with him. "My doom and my strength is to be solitary" he told himself.[16] And so he could without compunction break off the approaches of Margaret Fuller this way: "I do then with my friends as I do with my books. I would have them where I can find them, but I seldom use them."[17] He would put off meeting people, reasoning blandly, "whom God has put asunder, why should man join together?"[18] Although Emerson never really reformed his reticence, the period during which it posed him the most painful public problems was probably his youthful ministry.

> Called to the deathbed of Captain Green, a rough-and-ready old Revolutionary officer who lived next door to the church, Waldo was diffident and embarrassed, fumbled among the clutter of things on the sick man's table, and began to talk about glassmaking. The captain was angry and told him that if he knew nothing to do at a deathbed but to lecture about glass bottles he had better go. Another story told how Waldo, getting stuck in the middle of a prayer he was making at a funeral, took his hat and left without further ado.[19]

"There was always the appearance of a certain bloodlessness about him,"

Carl Bode records. "He himself . . . admitted that he lacked warmth."[20] And in the practice of addressing the breezy, unreserved, familiar, not to forget worldly democratic audience, this sort of appearance created another difficult problem for Emerson to solve—in rhetorical language, an "ethical" problem. As Aristotle was only the first to point out, the "ethos" or projected character of the speaker could be an important source of the persuasiveness of his speech. Conversely, if it was mismanaged and misrepresented, the speaker's ethos could actually subvert his own persuasiveness. In Emerson's situation, the threat loomed particularly large: for the democratic audience had been distinctively sensitive to considerations of character—"ethical" considerations since their original constitution.

The fundamental political truths, "self-evident" to all fair observers, had been flouted by the king of Britain: "*he* has refused his assent to laws the most wholesome and necessary for the public good," "*he* has dissolved representative houses repeatedly," "*he* has obstructed the administration of justice," and so on. These offenses were serious enough to justify the absolution of allegiance to the crown, the severing of political connection with Britain, the declaration of independence itself; and what constituted offense in the king's behavior involved the invocation of a special personal "ethical" authority to overrule common truths and common rights. Thus from their beginning as a people, Americans resisted the claims of special ethical authority—a resistance that could only grow as the culture became more thoroughly democratized, as it did in the nineteenth century.[21]

On the other hand, as Tocqueville puts it, some "authority is always bound to play a part in intellectual life." For those who wanted to engage in popular education—for each of those who, like Emerson, "aspired to be a public teacher"—some kind of usable authority had to be found. Normally the educator already enjoys this rhetorical advantage: in formulating his argument, he can use what Aristotle calls "didactic premises." The validity of such premises need not be formally established before their use can begin, but can be flatly assumed on the special ethical authority, "on the word of the master." These premises can be used to guide the discussion according to the "given discipline's rules, techniques, specific ideas and presuppositions, as well as the method of criticism and its findings in terms of a discipline's own requirements"—that is, to begin to transform, to reconstitute an unspecialized, undisciplined mass audience into a specialized, disciplined audience of students.[22]

Since such an invocation of special ethical authority, far from being persuasive, would actually evoke resistance from democratic audiences, the problem for aspiring popularizers was to invent an alternative kind of authority to which that audience would respond receptively. Such an alternative was in fact evolving from that audience's democratic character: given their equalitarian notions, Tocqueville observed, Americans were coming to feel that they could equally well "look into themselves and their fellows for the sources of truth."[23] If Americans put up a distinctive resistance to claims of special ethical authority, they responded distinctively well to claims of common ethical authority. More simply, they listened to speakers who, they sensed, were like them. By virtue of their democratic character, American audiences were inclined to grant—at least provisionally—some persuasive authority to speakers with whom they could identify.

What distinguished Emerson's rhetoric on the circuit—what was essential to his greatness and productive of his popularity—was his ingenious solution to his problems of ethical authority. Emerson's success was in bringing to popular education a new, democratic kind of rhetoric: a rhetoric of representation and identification.

Although Emerson honestly believed that, somewhere down deep, "every man is a lover of truth," it cannot be emphasized strongly enough that his optimism and his empathy for his democratic audience never clouded his vision of them.[24]

> Altogether independent of the intellectual force in each is the pride of opinion, the security that we are right. Not the feeblest granddame, not a mowing idiot but uses what spark of perception and faculty is left, to chuckle and triumph in his or her opinion over the absurdities of all the rest. Difference from me is the measure of absurdity. Not one has a misgiving of being wrong.[25]

Besides viewing his audiences with uncompromising honesty, Emerson was also an active observer and critic of the rhetoric of his times. He may have been, as Vivian Hopkins contends, actually the most active observer; but any serious listener, especially one instructed in classical rhetoric as Emerson had been, would have noticed a change in the way rhetoric was directed toward and was working with this audience. Appeals were being addressed to the common man by virtue of his being common. The orators who were heard most receptively portrayed themselves as characters genuinely representative of the audience—that is, genuinely *like* them—and worth hearing for that reason. "In deference to the popular will of hour," Fenimore Cooper had observed, "there is a simple boldness in the use of personalities." Emerson's innovation was in turning such use of personality, such "ethical argument," to the purposes of democratic education.[26]

In doing so, Emerson was declaring independence from a whole formal tradition, the dominant tradition in which he had been trained at Harvard. Emerson's professor of eloquence there had been one of America's two most elegant practitioners in that tradition, Edward Everett.[27] Biographer Regis Michaud even claims that "whenever he [Everett] spoke, the young Emerson followed him about 'as the hunter follows his quarry,' and that young 'hero-worshiper's' first stated vocational aspiration was to become, like Everett, a professor of eloquence and poetry."[28] But when Emerson began his own career on the platform and tempered his theory with practice, he discarded the tradition's "emphasis upon organization, figures of speech and pronunciation as the keys to successful speaking"; instead, as Hopkins formulated it, Emerson's crucial move was to locate "the orator's power over men chiefly in his depth of idea and strength of character."[29]

The very first critics to credit Emerson with a successful move were his audiences.

> It used to be said of him that he was too much of a transcendentalist, prone to discuss subjects transcending the reach of the senses, and so beyond reach of the average comprehension. Of his ability to grapple and to vanquish each and all of those he attempted there is no lack of proof, while the very fact of his frequent appearance here shows conclusively that he was never beyond our reach, however high he soared . . . and we were never willing to dispense with his teachings.[30]

Since the democratic audience paid such peculiar attention to the "use of personalities," perhaps what was most important in Emerson's new rhetorical approach was his peculiarly adept handling of representation in structuring his ethical arguments. In order to popularize successfully, a speaker had to appear both like and unlike his audience: like enough in character to tap the resources of common ethical authority, yet still sufficiently unlike in order not to compromise his thought (and also in order not to dilute the audience's sense of needing to hear about it). The paradoxes here are sometimes difficult to formulate clearly, but we do have a vocabulary for it, coming from our discussion of representation.[31]

The word "representation" had, even by Emerson's time, already been popularly used to denote the two somewhat different functions in American life — regency and reflection. Representation could mean *acting for*, on the basis of superior competence recognized by the represented constituency to constitute authority. This representation was an activity: in rising so majestically far above his fellows, George Washington was the classic American representative of this sort. Representation on the other hand could mean *acting like;* here, the constituency is understood not merely to recognize superiority and to delegate authority, but somehow actually to create or constitute them in themselves. Thus to be like the constituency, to reflect their character, is the condition of legitimate authority; to depart from that character in any degree (even if to "rise above," whatever that might now mean) is in this definition actually to disqualify oneself from authority to that degree. This representation was less an activity than it was a state of being, a quality of character; Andrew Jackson was the first celebrated representative of this sort. Put in language more popular but in a sense more pertinent, the representative could be identified with the best of his audience, or the rest of his audience; phrased another way, the difference is between the highest common factor and the lowest common denominator ethically.

We should note here that this distinction between the two forms of representation is not simply my own construction onto the situation; Emerson himself understood this distinction. He applied it most famously in his final judgment of Daniel Webster. At first Emerson admired Webster but gradually became disaffected, coming to believe that in trying to appeal to the voting masses, Webster was using his Senate seat—a representative role that Emerson understood as properly a position and a responsibility of leadership—to appeal to the ethically lowest common denominator. The one incident that probably disillusioned Emerson most was Webster's compromise in favor of the Fugitive Slave Bill, to which Emerson promptly responded, "the word *liberty* in the mouth of Mr. Webster sounds like the word *love* in the mouth of a courtezan. . . ."[32] In the light of longer reflection, Emerson diagnosed the offense more explicitly as an impoverishment of, a *mis*representation.

> Webster truly represents the American people just as they are, with their vast material interests, materialized intellect and low morals. Heretofore, their great men who have led them have been better than they, as Washington, Hamilton, and Madison. But Webster's absence of moral faculty is degrading to the country.[33]

It is perhaps obvious which sort of representation applied in indulgent rhetoric: rhetoricians who merely indulged their audience used the merely reflecting kind of representation, simply appealed to and confirmed commonplace expectations and ideas. They made no effort to draw individuals out of the mass, to free them for independent thinking, or for that matter any kind of thinking at all. Indulgers made themselves seem ethically like their audiences in order to cash in on the rewards of unchallenged, unthinking, unreconstituting approval.

Happily, indulgence was not the most ambitious form of democratic education attempted on the circuit. Some lectures aimed at the full-scale intellectual reconstitution that is the central subject of this study; but others struck a less ambitious balance that is worth at least a mention here.

This latter approach—call it "vulgarization"—was far from pure indulgence; it genuinely aimed its persuasive force at changing the audience's mind. But this was attempted by limiting discussion to the immediate issue, by focusing persuasive force behind one particular conclusion—not by addressing the fundamental assumptions generating not only this conclusion, but potentially others, too. It argued in order to convey to the audience a particular thought, but never quite to initiate the audience into a comprehensive discipline that could equip listeners to think out answers and even formulate new questions for themselves.

Perhaps the most familiar, and likely the most distinguished illustrations were provided by the moderate abolitionists. These men and women were moved to speak by intelligently elaborated and deeply felt moral objections against slavery. But judging their audience's commonplaces to be unshakable (or assaying the task as not worth the Herculean effort), they argued their case on other grounds: though thinking to themselves that slavery was morally wrong, they swallowed hard and tried merely to convince their audiences that it was inexpedient. Arguing their case this way unavoidably changed, vulgarized, its nature: such an argument invariably would wind up founded on premises and building toward conclusions less serious than the orators themselves held and might have hoped to induce.[34]

Such an approach depends elementally on commonplace beliefs, no matter how crude, and it "must fit its discipline or doctrine into the framework of common knowledge,"—no matter how common, how narrow, how rickety, and even how misshapen that framework may be.[35] It can acquaint audiences with particular new opinions or interesting results, but it does not enable them to use the special method or discipline that made it possible to reach these opinions or results and would make it impossible to test and evaluate them critically. Fully independent understanding of a proposition—a complete taking it on and taking it in, an internalization—is only available through the discipline that generated it. But this rhetorical approach presents propositions independent of their discipline.

So long as listeners are allowed to conceive and conduct themselves as the everyday, unreconstituted public-at-large, the criteria they will ultimately invoke for judgment will be their everyday standards—a difficult situation for the speaker who wishes to question some of those very standards and replace them with less commonplace, more appropriately reconstituted ones.

There were also democratic educators who, in making arguments for new conclusions also sought to expound the fundamental premises of those conclusions—premises which constituted to some extent a distinct intellectual specialty, a whole different *way* of thinking and talking. Such a rhetorician aimed even beyond gaining assent to particular conclusions, toward actually equipping the audience to use this way of thinking. Such use was not restricted to a given conclusion on a given issue but could be applied in handling any issue that might arise in an increasingly pluralistic society— that is, to persuade each listener to think independently in one or other disciplined way.

But even to undertake so radical a reconstitutive enterprise, popularizers did not present themselves as radically unlike their audience. In most ways they were not; and perhaps, as Emerson suggested, they could not be. Rhetoric, even the rhetoric of education, is a two-way street, and to some extent "also the constituency determines the vote of the representative. He is not only representative, but participant. Like can only be known by like.

The reason why he knows about them is that he is of them."[36] Popularizers, as practicing rhetoricians, had to know that every effective form of persuasion moves from previously held beliefs to new ones that seem somehow more satisfying extensions or conclusions of the original beliefs. And in the case of the democratic audience, as we've seen, the deepest and most intractable of their beliefs concerned their own identity.

The problem for popularizers was to find a rhetoric for making this move while retaining the intellectual integrity of the kind of thought being popularized. The basis of the solution, as Emerson articulates it, was an insight into human nature.

> What does every earnest man seek in the deep instinct of society, from his first fellowship—a child with children at play—up to the heroic cravings of friendship and love—what but to find himself in another's mind: because such is the law of his being that only can he find out his own secret through the instrumentality of another mind. We hail with gladness this new acquisition of ourselves. That man I must follow, for he has a part of me; and I follow him that I may acquire myself.
>
> The great are our better selves, ourselves with advantages.[37]

What makes an orator successful with an audience, then, is "that he speaks that which they recognize as part of them but which they were not yet ready to say."[38]

The solution was to represent one's thought in one's character so that the audience could find their better selves there. In his virtues, the character would seem representatively like them; but in the discipline his thought had given him, he would seem somehow more so. The suggestion was that in becoming more like the popularizer intellectually and ethically, the democratic auditor could become more himself—literally find himself in the popularizer's mind. Put more formally, the new rhetoric of democratic education centered its appeal on ethical argument. It used the "ethos," the identity of the speaker as it was presented in the speech, to represent his intellectual specialty to his audience. Appealing to an audience preoccupied with the relation of character and authority, it used the speaker's distinctive virtues to represent his kind of thought as an actually truer, richer, more authoritative fulfillment of the audience's own essential character. The virtues that the specialty brings were of course represented as the audience's own virtues—only in an advanced, advantaged state, far more complete and compelling.

Thus the educator also "represented" his audience—represented the achievable best in his audience. He represented what his audience could become if they were educated to the deepest meanings and richest possibilities of their identity. Since "what we admire, we learn to imitate," the speaker's admirable virtues evoked from listeners the wish to emulate the ethical principles that made him admirable, all in order to become more like the speaker and thus paradoxically more like themselves — for he was like them, only more so.

For the best sort of democratic educator, the virtues of his character were directly related to the principles of the special kind of thought that he was expounding. These principles were the sorts of didactic premises that could not be established for the democratic audience "on the word of the master" but were nonetheless necessary for initiation into the intellectual specialty to begin. In representation, in identification and ethical imitation, the democratic audience quite literally found itself in the mind of the educator. Through a rhetoric of representation and identification, thought and character could be brought into an ethically authoritative relation for the democratic audience.

In this chapter and the succeeding two, we shall examine how three different rhetorics of education reconstituted the thought and character of the democratic audience. But for Emerson, rhetoric lifts both "him that speaks and them that hear, above the dust and smoke of life, searching out every noble purpose, every sublime hope that lurks in the soul."[39] Thus we must not overlook the very real ways rhetoric was also reconstitutive for the speakers themselves. Here, in fact, is precisely where the rhetorical art came in. The rhetoric, of course, was to some extent determined by the subject matter: the virtues of the popularizer's projected character had in some representable sense to be functions of the intellectual specialty popularized. But this account alone would imply far too deterministic a view of the relation between an educator and his very subject matter, of the possibilities of relation between thought and character.

If intellectual specialties completely determined their representative characters, then obviously there would be no *art* of constructing such representative characters for books like this one to study. But as we shall see for each of our three rhetoricians, the popularization of intellectual specialties — and this goes for specialties so different in character as those of Emerson, Twain, and James — involves both analysis and synthesis. The process is not only passively absorptive, but actively creative; in the process of synthesis the intellectual specialty becomes the product of a human being who has a particular character. Thus he becomes responsible for it, becomes blame- or praiseworthy for it as his artifact; for even the essentials of these popularized intellectual specialties could not be made sharable and persuasive in the same way by a different proponent. This is demonstrated by one striking historical fact about the circuit and about each of the rhetorical situations in which these educators put themselves: other rhetoricians tried to popularize substantially similar kinds of thought without anything near comparable measures of success — either of greatness or of popularity.

A considerable number of other transcendentalists, most of them associates of Emerson, went out on the circuit to preach their good news. They included talented and accomplished men and women like Bronson Alcott and Margaret Fuller. The most articulate of them, Thoreau, eventually did achieve considerable success in the medium of print. But none of them had any real success reaching the audiences of the circuit through the spoken word, least of all Thoreau. With due respect to the philosophical differences between Thoreau and Emerson, it seems clear that their very different degrees of success on the circuit owed less to their differences of philosophy—differences too subtle, I suggest, for the decidedly unsubtle democratic audience to discern at their first cursory hearing and to cause such great differences in response—than to their differences in character.

Carl Bode reports, "as a rule Thoreau thought little of his audiences, and as a rule they retaliated." As we've already seen, Emerson didn't entertain any illusions about his audiences' foibles either; he did not differ from Thoreau on this point. But it was his character to react differently to it, to behave differently about it. Thoreau was a naturally contentious person, "a man whose independence was so rooted in his nature that he cooly set up his private opinion against the average opinion of the human race, and contrived so to incorporate his opinion into his daily life that he came out in the end a victor in the contest." But as we shall see, it was an integral characteristic of Emerson to avoid contention and argument, to do nothing but affirm. The democratic audience could not be counted on to pick up any differences in shading of doctrine here, but they obviously did pick up the difference in behavior and character; and it made a difference for them in the persuasiveness of the popularization.[40]

But this is not to say that contentiousness—or any other given characteristic—*of itself* could directly determine the reaction of the audience.[41] The contentiousness that grated so annoyingly in the context of the rest of Thoreau's character wore wonderfully well for Mark Twain. Moreover, it could even be used in different ways to mean different things: William James's contentiousness is of a humbler, more provisional order and consequently had a rhetorical effect quite different from Twain's more polemic subversions.

The art of our democratic educators consisted in constructing and communicating an authoritative character of one sort or another, in each case the character most appropriate to his subject matter. That is to say, each tried to represent himself as the particular sort of man who would do his particular sort of intellectual thing with the most authority for this particular audience. Our inquiries into these popularizations will begin by examining individual characteristics, for they are the basic terms in which (and in the interrelation of which) we get to know a character. But we must move to a larger perception; a perception of the whole character in which those individual characteristics were persuasive, the character with whom the audience was to identify. I wish to be explicit about the reasons behind this methodology of ethical criticism: praise and criticism leveled at democratic educators are most useful when they concern the sense we have of the speaker as the right person to articulate the particular message, our sense of his or her ethical authority over the democratic audience.

But again, as we proceed to examine the character of each rhetorician as popularizer, we must also stress another influential way in which democratic education was ethical education: this time, ethical education *for the speaker himself.* The circuit played a crucial role in the intellectual biography of each popularizer. It was on the circuit that Twain found a voice in which he could speak with characteristic humor about serious matters. Almost all of James's books—works of professional philosophy, mind you—are collections of essays that in some form or other started out as lectures. And this is even more categorically true of Emerson's published essays. In fact, of the three—perhaps of all the circuit's figures—no character is more essentially a lecturer than Emerson. The most famous achievements of Twain and James were primarily not their speeches; Emerson was "best known to his own generation and throughout life" as a lecturer.[42] Further, as I shall argue, nothing is more characteristically Emerson, nothing has a richer feel of both his thought and his character, than his speeches. If the other speakers found their voices in popularizing on the circuit, Emerson found himself.

For all of our three popularizers, however, the projected character was in some important sense his real character; and in the processes of rhetoric, in working out how to communicate the intellectual specialty that his character was to represent, each discovered truths about that character which made them themselves, only somehow more so—more fully and deeply and richly, more authoritatively so. The rhetorical processes of their popularization reconstituted both the character of their audiences and, in the bargain, their own characters as well. Samuel McChord Crothers points to this relation of thought and character when he tells us "the only way to know Emerson is to join him in his intellectual exercises." This is what Emerson himself articulates when he says "but do your thing and I shall know you. Do your work and you shall reinforce yourself." The specific character we get to know as Emerson does his thing, the character he reinforces in doing his work is best identified in his own words. In his rhetoric, Emerson has assumed precisely the identity he urged on the democratic audience: most simply, Man Thinking; most powerfully, the democratic visionary; and always as elusive as life, the "man without a handle."[43]

Man Thinking as Common American

Whatever audiences might have been expecting from "the celebrated metaphysician of the East," they found him acquainted with their familiar

reality and making conscious appeals to everyday values and commonplaces. Hardworking (if not always spectacularly prosperous) farmers must
have been gratified and buoyed by the notion that "a man is relieved and
gay when he has put his heart into his work and done his best." Such
listeners certainly shared the fundamental assumptions about life and human worth implicit in a comment like "kingdom and lordship, power and
estate, are a gaudier vocabulary than private John and Edward in a small
house and a common day's work: but the things of life are the same to
both; the sum total of both is the same." Again, bonds of identification are
formed and ethical authority is earned by this sort of evaluation:

> If the first genius studies at one of our colleges, and is not installed in
> an office within one year afterwards in the cities or suburbs of Boston
> or New York, it seems to his friends and to himself that he is right in
> being disheartened and in complaining the rest of his life. A sturdy lad
> who in turn tries all the professions, *who teams it, farms it, peddles,*
> keeps a school, preaches, edits a newspaper, goes to Congress, buys a
> township, and so forth, and all in successive years, and always, like a
> cat, falls on his feet, is worth a hundred of these city dolls. He walks
> abreast with his days, and feels no shame in not "Studying a profes-
> sion," for he does not postpone his life, but lives already."

Many different levels of communication are at work here, different
kinds of information being communicated; but perhaps the most influential
kinds of information are the messages, conveyed implicitly but unmistakably, about the character of the speaker. Made explicit (as it could never
convincingly be), it would come out something like this:

> I, Emerson, am from the East. Yet I see how it falls short of the simpler
> and purer way of life that *you know* I know you live. It is a life that I
> understand. What is more, it is a life that I sympathize with and side
> with and *prize* so deeply and insightfully that I am able to make il-
> luminating observations about it. They are evidences of a bond we
> share. We meet as well in our criticism of that other way of life—effete,
> whining, over-complicated, literally sophisticated; and what we both
> feel, I can articulate for us. We are one in our common valuing of the
> self-reliant way, *your* self-reliant way. My articulation of this value
> amounts to praising you, of course. I know that, and it is a good thing,
> if not really a coincidence. But every phenomenon teaches, and the
> lesson of this one belongs to all. The grand doctrine of self-reliance—
> what I have already spoken of it, and what is to come—is not in any
> way the exotic rumbling of a crank. It is the word of your own heart
> said aloud. It does not depart from the way you live now, except to give
> your life voice, exaltingly. I invite you to stay, to hear its whole song, to
> join in singing those verses you discover you know.

At least one regular listener thought that Emerson's sense of identification with the audience was the characteristic most worthy of note and
praise in his rhetoric. "I find he has impressed truths to which I always

assented, in such a manner as to make them appear new, like a clearer revelation." But the power of these truths had a distinctive flavor worth an additional comment: "their effect was immediate and personal, not to be detached from his presence."[45]

But Emerson was careful to avoid claiming any personal authority; he asserted that his eloquence, so full of moral resonance, was at least of common stuff. "In every work of genius we recognise our own rejected thoughts: they come back to us with a certain alienated majesty." Moreover, the highest eloquence, genius, was within the reach of any individual who shut off the noise of the world, and listened in quiet confidence to the music of his own heart. "To believe your own thought, to believe that what is true for you in your private heart, is true for all men, — that is genius."[46] The key was for the listener to emerge from the mass as an individual, that he might listen to his private heart. It was to that individual, to his individualization, his achievement of his own individual identity, that Emerson dedicated — and constantly, publicly rededicated — himself. "In all my lectures I have taught one doctrine, namely the infinitude of the private man." "I cannot find language of sufficient energy to convey my sense of the sacredness of private integrity."[47]

Emerson's dedication to the individual was so emphatic that he made articulating it his calling — a calling of real importance and not a little grandeur, for it was "the only way to make the world better . . . to make better the individuals in it."[48] And, for him at least, the issue of success in his calling was a simple one: "I gain my point, I gain all points, if I can reach my companion with any statement which teaches him his own worth."[49]

This standard of success departs in several ways from traditional rhetorical assessments. It eschews the simple turnstile counts by which Emerson's preeminence was unquestionable, for mass measures registered nothing important. But it also dismisses as off the point a standard convention for scholars by which Emerson fares less well. Irving Rein, for example, judges unsuccessful the efforts of all the New England Transcendentalists prominently including Emerson, on the ground that few new converts were persuaded into the Transcendental faith.[50] But this standard is based on the conventional view of rhetoric as persuasion, and Emerson was formulating his rhetorical purposes not in terms of persuasion, but in something explicitly more like modern notions concerning the identification of speakers and audiences.[51]

By that different standard, Emerson enjoyed frequent and profound successes. One resident of a small town that had invited Emerson back again and again explained, "We are very simple people here, and don't understand anybody but Mr. Emerson." A somewhat more loquacious auditor declared, "Listening to his incantations, his oracular symphonies, it seemed as if one could sin no more." And even what might be regarded as failures seemed to have a bracing ethical effect.

> "Do you understand Mr. Emerson?" a washwoman was asked as she was eagerly making ready to attend his lecture. "Not a word, but I like to go and see him stand up there and look as though he thought everyone was as good as he was."[52]

Emerson would not have considered reactions like this—of which he seemed to evoke more than his share—as betokening failure; for he believed that always "men are wiser or better than they know."[53] Emerson would have thought it altogether possible that this, or any other common American, unknowingly, might be his ethical equal—or superior.

This projected ethos of the democrat was not deceptive rhetoric, not dishonest or disingenuous with respect to his private life and character, but rather, in a powerful sense, his "real" identity. In the humblest details of everyday life, Emerson seemed to consider himself a common American. For instance, "his wife told a correspondent that Emerson never used the term 'lower classes,' and that it was wholly objectionable to him." Edward Wagenknecht comments that Emerson

> disliked being waited on—when he went on his lecture tours, he would even insist upon carrying his heavy luggage to the railroad station himself—and once he developed a plan for having the servants eat with the family, but they refused the invitation.

And he documents that Emerson "greatly enjoyed . . . the society of the humble. 'I much prefer the company of plough-boys and tin peddlers,' he said, 'to the silken and perfumed.' "[54]

Two more common American characteristics in Emerson's character— public and private alike—are often overlooked. We tend to think of this quiet Concordian as mild and mannerly; but one of the intellectual virtues most characteristic of him—just as it was characteristic of his audience— was bluntness. "He never hesitated to tell the poets, prose writers, reformers, 'fanatics' who were his friends and acquaintances, exactly what he thought of them, and there was never a doubt of his mental and moral honesty in their reception of his criticism." J. Arthur Hill suggests that "in spite of his serenity, he did not suffer fools gladly," and there is substantial evidence—most of whose unforeshadowed apparitions tend to strike us as delightful surprises—to prove him right. In many public remarks, Emerson pulled no more punches than the common American would.[55]

> Now and then an amiable parson, like Jung Stilling or Robert Huntington, believes in a pistareen-Providence, which, whenever the good man wants a dinner, makes that somebody shall knock at this door and leave a half-dollar.[56]

Then there is the wonderful story of the "literary lady" of Chicago who interrupted Emerson to ask point-blank whether he believed in immortality. Emerson is said to have paused, looked searchingly at her for a moment, and then in a sweet and confidential tone said, "Madam, are we swill?" But perhaps the best and probably the most famous example of the common American's bluntness in Emerson is recounted by Newton Dillaway. Emerson, it seems,

> was once introduced to a man who had just delivered a lecture full of obvious hypocrisy . . . the story has it that he said to the notorious hypocrite: "Sir, what you are thunders so loud, I cannot hear what you say."[57]

One of the mainstays of the common American is humor. Emerson is not much renowned for his, and surely humor was a far less important part of his appeal than of William James's, and especially of Mark Twain's. Still he was far from bereft of wit; even in the unlikely virtue of humor, Emerson's "real" character was related to his projected character.

Emerson liked to tweak the clergy with this story: three bishops were aboard a ship that was foundering in rough seas. At the height of the storm, they rushed to the captain to ask if there was any hope. "At his answer, 'None but in God,' they turned pale, and one said to the others: 'And it has come to that!' " In fact, the solemn, serious character of Emerson in some circumstances could, as Hill perceptively notes, actually enhance his humor. In the midst of one of his loftier meditations, he began

> if we could only make up our minds always to tell the truth, the whole truth, and nothing but the truth . . . (the audience waited eagerly for the culminating phrase) to what embarrassing situations it would give rise![58]

But perhaps the one characteristic in which Emerson most faithfully reflected the common Americans of his time was his unfailing, unflagging, almost exhausting optimism.

> It is rank blasphemy . . . to doubt anything in the universe; everything in life makes for good. The moral element in man is supreme, is progressive. Man is always better than himself. The world is all for happiness, and is meant for the happy. It is always improving. Pain and sorrow are of no account as compared with the joy of living; if a man be overcome by them he violates the moral order.
>
> The universe is not a cheat; the beauty and the order of the external world are sufficient proof that the spiritual world is in accord with the hopes and instincts of man and nature for their own perfection.

Order, goodness, God are the one everlasting, self-existent fact. For Emerson, "Life is an ecstacy."[59]

The only rhetorical trouble that such radiant optimism caused Emerson was with a somewhat specialized audience. There is a certain kind of auditor, apparently in the minority in Emerson's audiences, who suspects that such singular lightheartedness in a fallen world can only be maintained by ignoring the facts of that world. But Emerson, to his credit, never does lose sight of those facts, nor does he betray his faithfulness to them.

> We must see that the world is rough and surly, and will not mind drowning a man or a woman, but swallows your ship like a grain of dust. The cold, inconsiderate of persons, tingles your blood, benumbs your feet, freezes a man like an apple. The diseases, the elements, fortune, gravity, lightning, respect no persons. . . .[60]

Quite the contrary, optimism consists for Emerson not in turning away from harsh facts of existence in studied ignorance as though, if once seen, they could undermine human hope; instead, optimism consists in rejoicing in the bounteous order at the heart of the world. It is in contrast with the glories of the order in being that Emerson mildly concludes "the ways of Providence are [merely] a little rude."[61]

Emerson's persistent optimism reflected the mood of common Americans in a time of unchecked growth and the apparently more equitable spread of economic abundance; it was, as well, the age of Manifest Destiny. His optimism, his notions of self-reliance, his boundless regard for the individual (Stephen Whicher even claims that "Emerson believed in the dignity of human life more unreservedly, almost, than anyone who has ever written") caught the character of the period and the people compellingly.[62] Even James Truslow Adams, who found a very great deal to criticize in Emerson, nonetheless had to concede that "in no other author can we get so close to the whole of the American spirit." The whole of it, but also the best of it: from the perspective of a century's remove, the contemporary critic Leonard Neufeldt makes the historical argument that Emerson was nothing less than "the Progenitor of the truest and most vital legacy in American literature." That moral and intellectual eminence translated into political virtue. For not only did Emerson reflect the whole of the American spirit; not only was he the progenitor of the best in American literature; for John Dewey, he is "the prophet and herald of *any* system which democracy may henceforth construct and hold by." Or as Edward Wagenknecht put it,

> Nobody, whatever he may have thought of Emerson's thinking, has ever doubted that he was a good man, but it is more important here to realize that he exemplifies the *kind* of good men we must breed in increasing numbers if democracy, whose long-run success in this world is still far from being assured, is to survive.[63]

But in Emerson's close identification with common Americans, he came in contact with their characteristic need for something uncommon: "people who had been bearing the heat and burden of the day, and whose

RALPH WALDO EMERSON. *Library of Congress.*

souls were parched, came for refreshment. In their arid lives, it was wonderful to meet a man who was thinking aloud." And what magnificent thoughts he *was* thinking aloud! Emerson came to be regarded as "the voice of the highest aspirations of his people"; in other words, precisely by representing so powerfully and appealingly what was common among Americans, Emerson had assumed the role that Dillaway called "the prophet of America," had represented the character that John Dewey lionized as "the philosopher of Democracy."[64]

Man Thinking as Democratic Visionary

The paradox of Emerson's rhetorical enterprise is nowhere sharper than in his function as democratic visionary.[65] In his democratic character, he identifies with his audience, mirrors their virtues. But a seer must rise far above his fellows in order that his vision not be obstructed with matters of the day. The paradox was crystallized in an image of Bliss Perry's; for Perry, Emerson seemed almost to have two different faces.

> Seen from one side, it was the face of a Yankee of the old school, shrewd, serious, practical; the sort of face that may still be observed in the quiet country churches of New England or at the village store. Seen from the other side, it was the face of a dreamer, a seer, a soul brooding on things to come, things as yet very far away.[66]

No visionary of his time dreamed deeper or saw further. He foresaw the phonograph and the radio and predicted that someday wars would be fought in the air. Edward Wagenknecht adds that "as early as 1838 Emerson suggested a Congress of Nations; he also anticipated William James in pointing out the need to establish some moral equivalent for war, some means of releasing peacefully and constructively the energies which war released horribly and destructively."[67]

And in the shorter run also, Emerson anticipated the issues of his time and the trends in contemporary opinion. Moncure D. Conway called him "the first American scholar to cast a dart at slavery": on Sunday, 29 May 1831 he admitted an abolitionist into his pulpit at Boston's Second Church to lecture on the subject. Similarly, in his second Phi Beta Kappa address, Emerson openly upheld as evidence of progress "women's claim to suffrage" and "the search for just rules affecting labor." But Emerson was always more than a child of his time. As Santayana put it, "he belonged very little to the past, very little to the present, and almost wholly to that abstract sphere into which mystical or philosophic aspiration has carried a few men in all ages." The contemporary issues that most deeply engaged Emerson probably were those that led up to the Civil War. Yet the book he published in 1860 was *The Conduct of Life,* the message of which was

precisely to look beyond immediate concerns to consider transcending issues like "Fate," "Power," "Culture," "Behavior," "Worship," "Beauty," "Illusions," and "Considerations by the Way." On another occasion, pestered
to deliver a temperance speech, Emerson agreed — and serenely proceeded
to exasperate his hosts, for

> it was temperate living, not merely temperate drinking, that he praised.
> Temperance pledges, he warned, would not win the victory. Souls were
> not saved in bundles, he was sure. If he bowed for the moment to
> organized reform, it was only to reissue his declaration for self-re-
> liance.[68]

Emerson discounted any need to try to be topical; but of course the democratic visionary never would have that need.

> What is the use of telegraphs? What of newspapers? To know in each
> social crisis how men feel in Kansas, in California, the wise man waits
> for no mails, reads no telegrams. He asks his own heart. If they are
> made as he is, if they breathe the like air, eat of the same wheat, have
> wives and children, he knows that their joy or resentment rises to the
> same point as his own. The inviolate soul who is in perpetual tele-
> graphic communication with the Source of events has earlier informa-
> tion, a private despatch, which relieves him of the terror which presses
> on the rest of the community.[69]

The peculiarly triumphant qualities of the despatches to which Emerson's inviolate soul was privy manifested themselves in several ways.
Perhaps the kind of manifestation most disarming to the modern reader of
Emerson is his capacity to stretch, a moral colossus, across the decades to
illuminate our own day. He can speak insightfully to our particular experience because, we are made to see, the real content of experience is not in
the contemporary particulars, but in the always timely, ever-fresh, transcending essentials, the essentials that all men share equally — democratically.

What could be more timely than his assessment of the moral situation
of "The Times"?

> Our forefathers walked in the world and went to their graves tormented
> with the fear of Sin and the terror of the Day of Judgment. These
> terrors have lost their force, and our torment is Unbelief, the Uncer-
> tainty as to what we ought to do; the distrust of the value of what we
> do.

In what I find an even more satisfying instance, with a few words Emerson
encapsules a modern theory of behavior, an ethics, a whole anthropology —
and answers it, devastatingly. "You think me the child of my circumstances:
I *make* my circumstance."[70]

This sort of prophecy is related to another of the Concord seer's most distinctive characteristics: his uncanny capacity to make the comments that we all wish we had made; he somehow knows how to catch and crystallize the experiences we all feel we have had—all sorts of experiences.

> Infancy conforms to nobody: all conform to it so that one babe commonly makes four or five out of the adults who prattle and play to it. . . .

> You will always find those who think they know what is your duty better than you know it.

> There is a mortifying experience in particular which does not fail to wreak itself also in the general history; I mean "the foolish face of praise," the forced smile which we put on in company where we do not feel at ease in answer to conversation moved, but moved by a law usurping willfullness, grow tight about the outline of the face, and make the most disagreeable sensation—a sensation of rebuke and warning which no brave young man will suffer twice.[71]

To make one such comment, to crystallize one glimpse of common experience is to gain some amount of authority; to manage to do so a few times is to consolidate that authority. Listeners gradually become willing to grant rhetorical credit to a speaker who has demonstrated acquaintance with a familiar reality. As long as he sees and speaks from our perspective, what is the risk? But his insights are so overwhelmingly frequent and lucid; even so cosmopolitan an observer as Horace Mann allowed that "it was almost impossible to catch the great beauty and proportion of one truth before another was presented."[72] Thus the cumulative effect is that Emerson assumes an authority of a higher order. Anyone who can see so often and so deeply into reality eventually begins to be credited with having a qualitatively better perspective. We learn from him, for his visions are great.

Great they were. Edwin Percy Whipple claims that a few of Emerson's words, originally from a lecture on Shakespeare, constitute "the best prose sentence ever written on this side of the Atlantic":

> The recitation begins; one golden word leaps out immortal from all this painted pedantry and sweetly torments us with invitations to its own inaccessible home.[73]

So beyond Emerson's ability to transfigure the proximate, common particular is this almost mantic capacity to conjure the uncommon, the great thought or perception, the distantly transcending truth, yet to put it in a manner we can understand and share. At the former level, some of his listeners even by this time might feel "I could have done that." But the special inflation and emphasis Emerson applies to the latter kind of observation tends to arouse very different, yet not begrudging feelings. Emerson's suggestion, if made explicit, might sound like this: you know that I

can see the realities you do: but because I am a master of my distinctive
intellectual specialty, my characteristic way of looking at things, I am able
to speak these majestic truths, I am able to see more — as you could if you
learned to see this way. If you did, your new vision could exceed your old
myopia in power of insight by as much as my words surpass common
speech in depth and beauty.

> A foolish consistency is the hobgoblin of little minds.

> Character teaches above our wills.

> Greatness always appeals to the future.

> My life is not an apology, but a life. It is for itself, and not for a
> spectacle.

> These roses under my window make no reference to former roses or to
> better ones; they are for what are; they exist with God today. There is
> no time to them. There is simply the rose. . . .

> We lie in the lap of immense intelligence, which makes us organs of its
> activity and receivers of its truth.

This ability is Emerson's most distinctive identifying characteristic: he is the
most quotable — and in fact the most quoted — American literary figure.[74]

"Man Without a Handle"

But if the ethos of the democratic visionary was an important source
of Emerson's persuasiveness in popularization, it actually caused him problems, undermined his persuasiveness, too. The objections seem mainly of
two sorts: objections to Emerson's chaotic, transitionless style, and objections to an impoverishment, a certain detached soullessness, in the character of Emerson himself.

Although Emerson had been trained in classical rhetoric by a man he
admired, he was nonetheless a revolutionary in the matter of style. We get a
scent of that even in our own self-consciously nonconformist times.

> The disjointedness of Emerson's style would be more marked in his
> own day than it is now. Literature was still suffering from the pon-
> derosity of the eighteenth century, and the rounded periods of Gibbon
> and Johnson were the standard of comparison. Addison, Dryden,
> Goldsmith, DeQuincy — all wrote ponderously, according to modern
> standards. Emerson was one of the first to break away. "Refuse the
> good models" was one of his maxims, and he followed it out. Other
> writers are good; but "I am also a man." The result is a distinctive style
> which reads, moreover, with an astonishing modernity and is perhaps
> even yet a little ahead of us.[75]

Emerson's style set off howls from conventionally inclined critics right from the beginning. As the *Ohio Register* put it,

> The lecturer could begin in the middle, and work forward or backward; or go to the end first, and take his beginning last; or strike this paragraph, or that one, this or that sentence — go through or between or above or below — and the Lecture would be as complete in any case, even though half were left out, or more patched on.[76]

Morse Peckham complains, "He does not build us bridges; he makes us leap. And the matter is made worse by his fusion of capriciousness greater than Lamb's with the philosophical earnestness and moral seriousness of Plato. . . . With the air of one bent on absolute lucidity, he devotes himself to eluding us." She adds, it seems aptly, that "almost any sentence could appear in almost any essay." J. Arthur Hill finds he must use the same image: "There is often a chasm between sentences, which the reader must get across as best he can." Emerson's problem was so widely known that even fictional characters complain of it: in Augusta Jane Evans's *Beulah,* even Beulah carps: "His writings are, to me, like heaps of broken glass, beautiful in the individual crystal, sparkling, and often dazzling; but gather them, and try to fit them into a whole, and the jagged edges refuse to unite." But perhaps the most pungent criticism of Emerson's lack of transition was leveled against him in parodies. A surprising number were published, but the best, contributed by a certain "S. Phynx." appeared in the *Ohio State Journal,* 21 January 1857. I reproduce it in its entirety here both because it makes its objection so well, and because it so accurately echoes the characteristic in Emerson to which it objects.[77]

HOW TO LIVE PROPERLY

Mankind are like oysters — of little value till rightly seasoned. Pepper comes from India, salt from the Hockhocking, mustard and vinegar are cheap and homebred. He who uses only mustard on his natives, will water at the eyes, and perhaps be choked. He whose intellectual powers know only common and indigenous culture, will wear stoga boots, and go to church twice on Sunday.

It is one of the maxims of Burram pooter Bog, the Hindoo Mounshee, that truth is frequently the opposite of falsehood — and Lord Bacon says, "if you wish to make me angry, don't strike my nose with a brickbat, but tweak it gently with thumb and forefinger." And Schiller says that the invention of gun-powder is hidden in the silence of the Dark Ages — yet nothing has made more noise in the world. Two and two make four, and a right angle may be produced as well by a perpendicular and horizontal, as by a horizontal and perpendicular.

France is finished with a blacking-brush. The empire, the monarchy, the republic, the noble, the bourgeois, the peasant. Louis Le Grand, Tallyrand, Jean Baptiste, Sansculotte, all bear the same polish. Thus a Frenchman implies your ability to ride in his every day salutation, and will never kick you before your face.

A wise man has no more ears than a fool; and in those of both are the same parts; — tympanum, auricle, mucous membrane, clavicle, and pax-wax; yet where the one hears only the discourse of many geese or the pandemonium cries of swine, the other discerns heavenly harmonies. For nature is a *maquignon* — a horse jockey, who often sells splints and spavins for health and strength and bottom. Yet it was Al. Bowler, the idiot, says the Zandavesta, who puts heads on both ends of his pins, that he might not prick himself.

Life is a wheel within a wheel. Thought, feeling, sensation, emotion, desire, are all necessary to him who would enjoy a buttered parsnip; — how much more to him who would feast on stars and sunsets. Zoroaster says that when the gods created man, they gave him an arm on each side, instead of two on his back, which they might have done. Zoroaster was right.

Great men can better afford to be small, than small to be great. The fact that Alfred once burnt cakes in a neat-herd's cottage, is fixed in history forever. How often the neat-herd himself burnt cakes, we know not, nor would know, if for a single day he had ruled Essex, Sussex and Wessex.

The Bhagoat Veda says — All men are tarred with the same stick, yet it does not follow, that if you burn the stick, the tar will necessarily have come from North Carolina. It is easier to say one thing twice at different times than two things once at the same time. Hence, if a man is wise, he will not run his head against a gatepost, he will strike it if he goes forward, unless he passes round it, or escapes it in some other way. Even the tenth commandment and the rule of three are not inseparable.

If a man has three friends, he will have four by counting himself one, and the same rule of addition would hold good if he had half a dozen. I called on a distinguished chemist the other day, and found him in the act of converting chicken salad into oyster patties. He told me it may easily be done by means of a leather retort and a guttapercha gridiron. Yet there are not more than sixty men in a century, or maybe sixty-five, who are seven feet nine, and half of those live in Boston.

The true test of a great woman is the speed with which she will run from a bull in a meadow, yet how few there are who have done more than scream at a spider in a cupboard. "Various and changeable," said the poet, and well does the Shaster say, because a woman with fine teeth is always laughing, it does not follow that one with beautiful eyes will lay awake o'nights.

"Allah il Allah," says the Arabic philosopher, Mohammed Ben Frangelin. Carlyle is Carlyle, and Emerson is his most discouraging symptom.[78]

The relationship between speaker and listener is a personal one, peculiar to their specific characters; what is distracting for some auditors can be tolerable, even persuasive, for others depending on just who they are. It is of course the rhetorician's responsibility to adjust as best he can to his audience. Emerson did adapt somewhat, Ralph Rusk asserts, in moving toward a "plainer, less poetic style" as the years went on. But it would be misleading to give much emphasis to this relatively mild shift; Emerson for the most part remained Emerson, and his audiences for the most part seem to have adapted to him. In the consistent attentiveness with which they listened to him, they may even have been in agreement with Edward Wagenknecht's response to Emerson the apparently transitionless speaker.

> It was chaos come again, but it was a chaos full of shooting-stars, a jumble of creative forces! . . . Since the style is the man, Emerson's style was exactly right for him, a fitting body for his soul, indeed, the inevitable style for a man who believed that matter is significant only as an expression of spirit and that art is not craftsmanship but inspiration, since such a writer must testify to the faith that is in him not only by what he says but by the way he says it.[79]

The force of this response might be more apparent if stood on its head. Every character has certain internal limitations. This doesn't mean that by transgressing them one creates a *bad* version of that character, but that in the act of transgressing them one becomes *another kind* of character, or at least less identifiably himself. The character of visionary had these sorts of limitations too. If, for example, a speaker bothered too much with transitions, he would be taking his eye off those visions that are to come. It would be difficult indeed for him suddenly to straighten up and speak with the timeless, impassive voice of a seer again — at least, difficult to do plausibly and persuasively.

But I do not mean to discount all validity in the objections. For listeners who wish to know precise connections between point-A and point-B in an argument, Emerson is less convincing on this account. And, frankly, almost every listener and reader of Emerson gets exasperated at some time. It has been my suggestion that this exasperation is an unavoidable consequent of the identity Emerson represents. But for a great many people — both listeners then and readers now — he more than made up for the exasperation by realizing that identity so well; the engagement we feel refers to the whole man we are coming to know. We read on, even when bewildered, because knowing Emerson we have good reason to believe he will reward our effort in all these other ways. After all, as Phillips Russell argued, Emerson's rhetoric was not primarily directed to propound a formal dogma, with all the connections precise and tidy: "he did not wish to direct, but to instigate." In that case, connections might actually get in the way, in doing the listener's work for him. It may be precisely because of this alleged flaw, Rusk indicates, that "more than almost any other public speaker, he makes an intelligent hearer think for himself."[80]

Other critics argue, however, that Emerson's projected identity undercut his rhetoric in a more fundamental way. As we have seen, Emerson put a particularly great demand on ethos argument for his authority: "Men do not convince by their argument, but by their personality, by who they are. . . . " Such a demand created a palpable strain for Emerson, these critics assert, insofar as we are never really allowed to know who he is, to know the identity of the man thinking. Maurice Gonnaud grumbles,

> What I find characteristic of him, almost to the point of fatigue, is a mercurial ability to shift his ground and assault variety from a kaleidoscope variety of angles. Except for a few occasional stretches of exalted language, or on the contrary — and even more rarely — of commonplace prosiness, Emerson never stays put.

Stephen Whicher frets,

> We hear his grand, assuming words, but where is the man who speaks them? We know the part he played so well; we feel his powerful charm; we do not know the player. He is, finally, impenetrable.

Or as Henry James senior (father of William James and one of Emerson's longtime friends) exclaimed, "Oh, you man without a handle!" For critics of this persuasion, the absence of an engagingly personal ethos was a profound problem in Emerson's rhetoric.[81]

The most obvious way in which Emerson presented this problem to his audience was his refusal to argue. "Emerson's eloquence . . . was affirmative rather than demonstrative. He refused to be drawn into argument, or even to answer questions; and the more he eluded, the more he exasperated." This is also the most obvious difference separating the rebellious Twain and the pluralistic James. Even for a listener sympathetically inclined, this characteristic lack of individuality, this apparent diffidence could be subversive of authority. In the words of a contemporary and associate, Henry James, Sr.,

> On the whole I may say that at first I was greatly disappointed in him, because his intellect never kept the promise which his lovely face and manners held out to me. He was to my sense a literal divine presence in the house with me; and we cannot recognize literal divine presences in our houses without feeling sure that they will be able to say something of critical importance to one's intellect. It turned out that any average old dame in a horse-car would have satisfied my intellectual rapacity just as well as Emerson. . . . No man could look at him speaking (or when he was silent either, for that matter) without having a vision of the divinest beauty. But when you went to him to hold discourse about the wondrous phenomenon you found him absolutely destitute of reflective power.[82]

"He would do nothing more than make affirmations regarding the deep things of the spirit, which were to be accepted or rejected as they happened to strike or miss the point of inlet into the other intellects he addressed," Whipple reports. "He went on, year after year, in affirming certain spiritual facts which had been revealed to him when the soul was on the heights of spiritual contemplation; and if he differed from other minds, he thought it ridiculous to attempt to convert them to his individual insight and experience by *arguments* against their individual insights and their individual experiences." And Whipple shows Emerson was not always immensely tactful in turning questions and arguments away:

> I shall never forget his curt answer to a superficial auditor of one of his lectures. The critic was the intellectual busybody of the place, dipping into everything, knowing nothing, but contributing by his immense loquacity to lead the opinion of the town. "Now, Mr. Emerson," he said, "I appreciated much of your lecture, but I should like to speak to you of certain things in it which did not command my assent and approbation." Emerson turned to him, gave him one of his piercing looks, and replied, "Mr. — — —, if anything I have spoken this evening met your mood, it is well; if it did not, I must tell you that I never argue on these high questions."[83]

Even replying to his copastor at Boston's Second Church, Henry Ware, Emerson was uncompromising: "I do not know what arguments mean in reference to any expression of a thought. I delight in telling what I think; but if you ask me why I dare say so, or why it is so, I am the most helpless of mortal men." Emerson was so extreme in this tendency that, according to one listener, he hardly seemed to be speaking to the audience at all.

> Often his interest seemed more of one looking at his own thought than of one who has to impress thought upon others. . . . In so far as he spoke to the audience, he was curt, aphoristic, oracular. There was no arguing, no explaining, no bridging the gaps for little feet or unaccustomed limbs: the giant hurled his stepping-stones into the river-bed and strode across, seldom looking back to see if others could follow.[84]

Why didn't Emerson deign to debate? "He felt that argument is mean," explains Hill; "the reasoners have no vision—the two things are incompatible. 'Argument burns up perception.' It makes the mind busy and fussy, and destroys the placidity which is a condition of inspiration. Also, by introducing passions, bias, desire to convince, joy of victory, anger at defeat, it contracts the visual field—as in a hysteric's eyes—and disables the disputants for seeing all round the question."[85]

Emerson's explicit reply to this controversy was characteristic: inimitably put, and aimed not directly at, but "all round the question."

> The spirit is not helpless or needful of mediate organs. It has plentiful powers and direct effects. I am explained without explaining, I am felt

> without acting, and where I am not. Therefore all just persons are
> satisfied with their own praise. They refuse to explain themselves and
> are content that new actions should do them that office. They believe
> that we communicate without speech and above speech.[86]

Perhaps he spoke more to the point when in another connection he said,
"My doom and my strength is to be solitary." Whatever the cost, whatever
the "doom," Emerson's power lay in his sense of distance from the typical
concerns of individuals. "One who would tame the Holy Ghost must first
put aside his individuality." Put another way, a sage is not readily identifiable as just one of the guys. To speak timeless truth, audiences would
expect an oracle *to draw himself up* somehow in order to sing his holy song;
if a prophet is a conduit for messages of a higher wisdom, it helps keep
things straight if he is empty of his own.[87]

The rhetorical requirements of his role limit him from too much familiar activity, too much individual personality. Prophets just don't *do* that
sort of thing, can't do it, at least not in their prophetic character — which is,
as we've seen, an important part of his ethical appeal. Thus one critic
argues that "Emerson undermines himself when he makes his speaker more
personal." Thus another, calling Emerson's deliberately impersonal relation
to his audience "solitariness," claimed quite simply that this "solitariness
was a condition of his power." Insofar as it is necessary to play the role, to
make the appeals of the visionary, the "solitariness" was a rhetorical condition of Emerson's persuasive power.[88]

We should not pass this point without catching a hint of something
important about the function of rhetoric in the formulation of an identity.
It is perhaps obvious that to play the role of visionary to an audience
requires the distinct semblance of distance from that audience. But to say
that Emerson used rhetoric to play the role of visionary may mislead in
suggesting that the role was somehow put on, acted out. Yet even in his
personal life, Emerson was faithful to the visionary role. Believing that
"though I prize my friends, I cannot afford to talk with them and study
their visions, lest I lose my own," Emerson made this mantic solitariness a
principle of his private behavior for the rest of his life. As Hill concludes,
"It is significant that even his intimates called him *Mr.* Emerson."[89]

This function to which Emerson was so personally dedicated was in a
number of ways a rhetorical function of course; but that it was rhetorical
made it no less binding, no less real for him. And in the process of working
out his speaking ethos — that is, in doing rhetoric — Emerson was also working out his "real ethos," his own character. This was as it should be, for
Emerson, "the speaker is affected by his speech as much as the audience,"
and good rhetoric elevates "him that speaks and them that hear, above the
dust and smoke of life, searching out every noble purpose, every sublime
hope that lurks in the soul." In helping to make character, rhetoric actually

helps make reality, even the most influential sort of reality. There is more to say about the relation of rhetoric to the constitution of character in this chapter, in the chapters on Twain and James, and in the concluding chapter. It is enough for the moment to see that, for Emerson, rhetoric established another influential connection between thought and character.[90]

None of this is to discount or disregard all the criticism leveled at Emerson's solitariness. When I am engaged in his rhetoric, I find his lack of personal warmth a serious ethical shortcoming, undermining his authority. It limits how and how much I am willing to identify with him. That identification, after all, would involve me with him in ethical education, in identifying with, and so becoming like him in both thought and character. And, very simply, with respect to *this* characteristic I must join the critics who do not choose to identify with him: Jeffrey Duncan calls Emerson's lack of a personal vitality a "complacency that can be irritating." Steven Whicher is moved openly to "wonder if he paid anything at all for his peace. The only coin in which we can discharge our debt to suffering is attention to it, but Emerson seems to evade this obligation." Morse Peckham even begins to doubt the value of another of Emerson's representative characteristics, wondering whether "what is often called the optimism of Emerson is closer to a sunny and cheerful indifference."[91]

"Compensation": Emerson Does His Thing, and We Know Him

The best way to examine this characteristic, and to see how it tends to subvert Emerson's other ethical appeals, is to see them all functioning together. A work that like most of Emerson's works was tried out first in lectures and combines some of Emerson's most persuasive ethical appeals with a numbing lack of personal warmth is "Compensation."[92]

He offers a few very down-to-earth sorts of appeal there. Emerson chooses as one allegory of compensation "the theory of the mechanic forces" of which his practical audience would have working knowledge, and common magnets as another. He understands that his listeners would consider an unpunished wrongdoer the hard case for his notion of compensation and address it explicitly, arguing "you cannot do wrong without suffering wrong." He describes a situation we all have been in and a reaction we all have had in his opening story about the preacher who advises us to be good in this life so that we can literally make out like bandits in the next.[93]

It is from the voice of the oracle that we hear of the compensating polarity in every part of nature. "An inevitable dualism bisects nature so that each thing is a half, and suggests another thing to make it whole, as spirit, matter; man, woman; subjective, objective; in, out; upper, under;

motion, rest; yea, nay." Only a prophet could claim the authority plausibly to intone, "This Law writes the laws of cities and nations." Moreover, he interjects a few of those formidable lines:

> He that loveth maketh his own the grandeur he loves.

> A man cannot speak but he judges himself.

> The dice of God are always loaded.

Another of his distinctive characteristics is optimism, and what could be more optimistic than a statement like "every man in his lifetime needs to thank his faults"? Well, how about Emerson's sunny praise of calamity?

> The compensations of calamity are made apparent to the understanding also, after long intervals of time. A fever, a mutilation, a cruel disappointment, a loss of wealth, a loss of friends seems at the moment unpaid loss, and unpayable. But the sure years reveal the deep remedial force that underlies all facts.[94]

There is also here the characteristically Emersonian appearance of sprawling disorder. An attempt at transition from examples of the law of compensation in nature and history to applications of the law to individuals flounders pitiably. It is not clear what determines this order, or why the world's fables and proverbs appear next, succeeded by another argument against doing wrong. The argument lurches bewilderingly to the application of the law to human labor and then its meaning for the issue of human weakness. There is at least some tenuous connection between all this and Emerson's next move, an argument for doing good: if all good is paid equally with bad and all bad with good, it is not unreasonable to wonder "why bother?" But the reason why he chooses to close with "the natural history of calamity" is not so clear; for all we can tell, he may simply wish to go out with a bang. It seems hopeless to find a unified logical structure in all this; he has, as one critic put it, somewhat ill-naturedly, "replaced logic with endless repetitions, by sublime tautologies."[95] The closest thing to structure is a kind of circling—Vivian Hopkins calls it "spiraling"—around from restatements of the law to its manifestation and back again and from individual applications to the most encompassing that he can manage: "history," "nature," "the universe."

So far, the appeal is vintage Emerson—for all its peculiarity, characteristically impressive and attractive. But there are limitations to that appeal, subversions of its authority.

It seems that Emerson has sacrificed his characteristic commitment to the worth, the sacredness of the individual. Emerson's best attempt is a limp one: "There is a deeper fact in the soul than compensation, to wit, its own nature." Very well, "the soul *is*."[96] But the rest of the essay argues that the law of compensation also *is,* and the grandeur in the catalogue of its applications — while necessary to prove its status as Law with a capital L — transcends any individual soul. Actually, introducing the individual only causes Emerson a problem. Either the individual soul is better off for incorporating "Jesus and Shakespeare," or it is not. If not, then why put out the effort? If so, then what happens to the law of compensation? Is Emerson willing to equate morally the effort and rewards of such an enterprise with any other activity that might have been done instead: bank robbery, for instance? Well, no. But the reasons why not cannot be explained in much detail in a work on "Compensation." The appearance of the individual creates an embarrassment that Emerson does not, perhaps cannot, handle without awkwardness. That is doubtless why the soul must disappear with disconcerting abruptness, and we must be hurried along.

Nor can we find any humor; there are no ingredients for it. Humor depends on incongruity and surprise for many of its effects; but in a world that is "mathematically just," there is no incongruity, there can be no surprises.

An even more serious ethical problem seems to arise from a gift gone haywire. There is the echo of prophecy, Emerson's characteristic gift of expression, in statements like "all love is mathematically just, as much as the two sides of an algebraic equation."[97] There are at least some people to whom this sentiment, however prophetic it may sound, rings false — even painfully false. There is, moreover, a whole realm of common human nobility being shrugged off almost callously here: the experience of unrequited yet unstinting, faithful love.

Emerson, I take it, is asserting either that this sort of experience does not exist — in that, he would seem factually wrong — or that it only seems to exist but is really an illusion. Such faithfulness, then, no matter how sincerely given, would not be the moral abundance of generous heart, but rather at best a sentimental self-deception.

The resolution of such issues, Emerson himself would insist, ultimately depends on one's own interior experience. Compensation, after all, is a theory, and Emerson would be the last to worry more about the embarrassments of a theory than about a truth of the heart. Thus even Emerson's *alleged* fault moves us to work with our own truths, to become Men Thinking ourselves.

Still, I think the fault is not merely alleged, but real and damaging to Emerson's authority. To discount this sort of unrequited faithfulness seems to me ethically diminishing, for it is to close doors to one kind of human virtue, as well as to listeners who identify with that virtue. And it was Emerson who delivered — to the rest of us Men Thinking, to be sure, but first of all to himself — an injunction against just such beggaring of the human heart: "Be an opener of doors for such as come after thee, and do not try to make the Universe a blind alley."[98] I find him—and for any critic of Emerson who engages him in his own terms, the question is always how she or he, as a Woman or Man Thinking, finds him—speaking with much more authority in this injunction to enrich the world than in his pontifications about the world's tidy justice. That is, this Man Thinking seems more authoritatively a Man; we would be more manly identifying with this Emerson than with the Emerson of "Compensation."

This most substantive of Emerson's ethical problems in "Compensation" arises even more objectionably, more cold-heartedly in the conclusion.

> The death of a dear friend, wife, brother, lover, which seemed nothing but privation, somewhat later assumes the aspect of a guide or genius; for it commonly operates revolutions in our way of life, terminates an epoch of infancy or of youth which was waiting to be closed, breaks up a wonted occupation, or household, or style of living, and allows the formation of new ones more friendly to the growth of character. It permits or constrains the formation of new acquaintances, and the reception of new influences, that prove of the first importance to the next years; and the man or woman who would have remained a sunny garden-flower, with no room for its roots, and too much sunshine for its head, by the falling of the walls and the neglect of the gardener, is made the banian of the forest, yielding shade and fruit to wide neighborhoods of men.[99]

Indisputably, there is wisdom here: in the darkest situation glints the promise of brighter days. But it is not by any means made clear that all losses are entirely compensated for, that there can be nothing inherently and enduringly tragic in life—for example in the life of Emerson, the man himself.

Emerson had his portion of sorrow. He lost his father in early childhood, which forced his family to live on the margin of poverty, his mother struggling financially to the end of her life. And "if Hawthorne had his Clifford Pyncheon, Emerson had his own brother Bulkeley."[100] What "compensation" did life offer Emerson's retarded brother or those who felt for him? But Bulkeley was only one of Emerson's three brothers; the other two were gifted and full of promise. Both of them died young.

In the fall of 1829 Emerson took Ellen Tucker as his wife—and his life, of a sudden, burst into bloom. "During this period, at any rate, he has no doubt about the warmth of his nature"; and it even seemed that "his writing grows better. In his prose the striking, felicitous images that we now associate with him appear."[101] But the dream was quickly shattered. His adored young wife died after only a year and a half of marriage—precisely at the most uncertain moment of his young career, as he was resigning his position at the Second Church and finding himself without a profession.

Emerson recovered, of course, to live a richly productive life. The doctrine of compensation itself was part of that recovery. In my own manifest admiration for the work that he continued to do, I find Emerson a banian of my forest, and I am grateful for the shade and the fruit he provides. I do not begrudge him his recovery; insofar as it makes him more authoritative, I celebrate it.

My criticism is not of compensation as a personal solution to a grief that I, a younger man, have no way of quite knowing; rather it is criticism of his way of representing it to the democratic audience (and, in an important sense, to himself).[102] As we have seen, representations of any intellectual specialty to the democratic audience are inescapably matters of character, and persuasion is to some extent the personal response of the listener to the speaker's character—the decision whether the speaker is worthy of being identified with. Where a speaker seems less than abundantly in possession of his own life and manhood, where his character does not represent his message in a way with which the listener is made to wish to identify, where he is not "me with advantages," the rhetoric does not work, his rhetoric is not persuasive. In this characteristic Emerson scanted his grief as a resource for manhood; he shrugged off the dignity that accrues to a man who in his mortal life suffers irreparable losses, losses that themselves became precious and essential to his humanity.

What sort of compensation was there for Emerson as a man? In explaining away his sadness, he sometimes seems to be explaining away part of himself, his manhood. Could the unique place that Ellen earned in his heart have been utterly filled up, leaving no ethical trace? Emerson insists on it: "The parted water," he says, "reunites behind our hand."[103] Well, perhaps it does. But am I not to wonder then whether Emerson seems the more authentic, the more authoritative man for it? And for the very purposes of democratic education that Emerson was trying to serve, must I not question whether I would be the better man for joining him? This is precisely the question that the democratic audience did in fact ask—and answer—inevitably, in deciding whether to be persuaded by his popularization, whether to identify with and be drawn into his intellectual specialty.

Emerson suffered another loss that he felt was more profound even than the loss of Ellen—the tragic death of his young son Waldo. The extreme tenderness that Emerson felt for his son during his five precious years, Evelyn Greenberger remarks, "was greater than that for any other person"; thus it was only human "that Emerson's grief should have taken the form of a sense of inner disunion and failure of energy. . . . " Greenberger argues that "for Emerson to have a son was in some sense to heal the wound left by his own loss of his father; it was, in a way, a chance to replay the scene as it should have been."[104] Now the first wound was torn open again, uncompensated for; and it was joined by an even deeper one. Yet it was not long after little Waldo's passing that Emerson, while admitting it was a blow, was publicly saying that nonetheless it "in the long run counted for little."[105]

Little, perhaps, in the transcending terms exclusively in which the universe achieves its balances and compensations; but can he mean little in individual human terms? To say this is, for the moment at least, to take his discussion beyond that human realm, to flee from its unsupportable emotion. This is an understandable and in the short run perhaps a healthy thing to do. But to flee too far risks losing touch altogether—surely no attractive characteristic:

> The only thing grief has taught me is to know how shallow it is. . . . In
> the death of my son, now more than two years ago, I seem to have lost
> a beautiful estate—no more. I cannot get it nearer to me.[106]

This inability to get even so deep and precious a personal moment nearer makes him seem less a man, thus less appealing a representative of his message, in this respect. It is an ethical loss that diminishes his authority as Man Thinking. For he could not, on his word alone, convince all his listeners that losing a son is no more than losing an estate. I suggest that Emerson would have seemed more authoritatively a man if he at least had shown himself to be struggling with his sorrow—a sort of Jacob, grappling with a force ultimately beyond his ken but earning the special dignity of manful defeat. And in not inhabiting all dimensions of his own heart, in not using all the resources of his manhood, Emerson's rhetoric came up short. Put another way, Emerson's rhetoric failed where he did not use all his available means of persuasion—that is, all the virtues of his own character—in effecting his identification.

Thought, Character, Identity, Rhetoric

The key to Emerson's success in democratic education was a rhetoric of identification, a rhetoric that persuaded his listeners to identify with the character he projected and the thought it represented, and a rhetoric in which he established an identity between his thought and his own character. "As I am," he said, "so I see." Thus he could claim that eloquence in the expression of thought bespoke an analogous soundness in character, and vice versa: "No act indicates more universal health than eloquence," he once remarked; and again, "If I should make the shortest list of the qualifications of the orator, I should begin with manliness." Shortcomings in the persuasiveness of his character, therefore, represented shortcomings in the persuasiveness of his thought. On the other hand, we have also seen how the authoritative virtues of his character made his thought the more persuasive. Indeed, the same truth applies in a different way to other democratic educators. The success of Mark Twain was of another, distinctly different character, in that of William James still another; they were, after all, different characters themselves. But what is true for Emerson will turn out to be true in different ways for them too. Quite literally: as they were, so they saw and spoke. There was an identity in their rhetoric between their thought as they projected in their character, and their character as they lived it in their lives.[107]

The identity between Emerson's thought and character affects the way we approach him critically, just as it affected the way his audiences listened to him. It determines what we expect and how we evaluate it and even limits what Emerson plausibly may do. The straightforward Man Thinking could no more intelligibly or persuasively deliver Twain's ironic subversions than could the humorist Twain have delivered "Compensation" with the sort of authority necessary to its meanings. And in neither case could James have stopped there, with the articulation of only one side. In this chapter we have seen how popularizing authority is established in rhetoric; in the succeeding ones we shall see how there can be different kinds of authority, how they can do different persuasive things.

And to be clear: the identity between thought and character that issued in Emerson's authority was established in his rhetoric — quite literally in the practical rhetorical processes involved in his lectures. That process directly generated most of his thought; as Bode points out, "fully three-quarters of his published writing began as lectures." And the rhetorical processes he applied on the platform always remained an integral part of his thought: "As soon as you read aloud, you will find what sentences drag. Blot them out and read again, you will find the words that drag. ['Tis'] like a pebble inserted in a mosaic. Resolute blotting rids you of all those phrases that sound like something and mean nothing."[108]

The part that the rhetorical processes of lecturing played in the development of Emerson into Man Thinking is a central theme in Rusk's excellent life of Emerson: for example,

> As his struggle in early life for self-trust was finally rounded out by his essay "Self-Reliance," so his incessant endeavor to adjust himself to the tragedy of his own losses came to a fitting climax in "Compensation."[109]

But just as thought became essential to the character, the character became essential to the thought:

> His lecture is not to be reported — without his own language, his manner, his delivery, it would be little — to essay to reproduce it would be like carrying sodawater to a friend the morning after it was drawn, and asking him how he relished it.[110]

The identification of thought and character through rhetoric was the key to the success Emerson achieved: it made him great *because* it made him himself, Man Thinking; and it made him popular because it evoked from his listeners an identification toward him that, they were persuaded, made them more themselves.

Henry Nash Smith points out that Emerson was virtually the democratic audience's first glimpse of Man Thinking outside the college classroom or the pulpit. Shortcomings notwithstanding, it was a powerfully authoritative glimpse. Even in the midst of the tremendous uproar over the Divinity School Address, a firmly orthodox minister named Father Taylor said, "I am sure of one thing: if Emerson goes to hell, he will change the climate there, and emigration will set that way." But perhaps the best measure of the success of Emerson's rhetoric is suggested in Stephen Whicher's remark: "To reject Emerson utterly is to reject mankind." Such is the identification evoked by Man Thinking.[111]

Mark Twain as Democratic Educator: Rebel with an Innocent Eye

So the world thought that there was a vast matter at stake here, and the world was right, but it was not the one they had in their minds. . . . I was a champion, it was true, but not the champion of the frivolous black arts. I was the champion of hard unsentimental common-sense and reason. I was entering the lists to either destroy knight-errantry or be its victim.

— HANK MORGAN, in *A
Connecticut Yankee in
King Arthur's Court*

Humor makes me reflect. . . . Always, when I am thinking, there comes suggestions of what I am, and what we all are, and what we are coming to.

— MARK TWAIN, in a
speech on "Theoretical
and Practical Morals"
to the New Vagabonds'
Club, 8 July 1899

The Dead Loss

IT looked like trouble. The town hall in the tough little mining community of Red Dog was packed to the rafters. The audience was made up mainly of prospectors who as a group were probably not the most decorous folks in California and not much noted for their patience, either. They had come to hear the up-and-coming newspaper columnist from San Francisco who was making quite a stir for himself in those parts as a lecturer, a young fellow who called himself "Mark Twain." But the program was now late in getting started, and the audience was growing restless. The problem was caused by one of the customs of the California circuit: the evening's speaker was usually introduced by a member of the audience. But the harried lecture hall manager was having difficulty finding anyone to "do the honors." Finally, somehow, he managed to wheedle one of the miners into performing the task. Twain, writing his *Autobiography* forty years later, still remembered — and still savored — the somewhat unconventional introduction that followed. "It was gravely made by a slouching and awkward big miner," Twain recollected. The man stood puzzling a moment, then said,

> I don't know anything about this man. At least I know only two things: one is, he hasn't been in the penitentiary; and the other is (after a pause, and almost sadly), *I don't know why.*[1]

To our sensibilities and expectations — which might after all be a tad more delicate than those of the representative citizen of Red Dog — this may seem a little harsh. It surely would have seemed that way to the cultural establishment of the day, which may help explain why Twain recalled it — or perhaps invented it — with such obvious relish. But whatever outsiders might think, to that audience the miner's judgment must have seemed appropriate. For the man who shuffled up to the Red Dog podium that night projected a character like no circuit personality they had ever seen.

> With the exception of an occasional curious trot, as when recounting his buck-jumping experiences, Mark Twain stands perfectly still in one place during the whole time he is talking to the audience. He rarely moves his arms, unless it is to adjust his spectacles or to show by action how a certain thing was done. His characteristic attitude is to stand quite still, with the right arm across the abdomen and the left resting on it and supporting his chin. In this way he talks on. . . .[2]

This fellow acted nothing like the roaring cultural lions who stalked the platforms of the day — nothing like the powerful John Gough, nor the sensational DeWitt Talmadge, nor the princely Bayard Taylor, nor the thundering, compelling, almost Jovian Henry Ward Beecher (whom one impertinent observer described as looking just like "a Pre-Raphaelite version of a Congressman"). Instead, this Mark Twain looked — well, he looked *funny.* To the bemused correspondent for the *Fort Wayne Daily News,* he even looked "half-scared . . . as though he hadn't the least idea what he was there for, and would give more money than he ever saw to get out of the scrape without serious trouble."[3]

He acted funny too — that is, he seemed to have a natural gift for violating the conventions of delivery in exactly those ways that made the spectacle most irresistibly laughable:

> he shuffled on stage with stiff-legged awkwardness — "like a ready-made cripple," one reporter said — pretended to be scared, assumed an expression of solemn imbecility, vacantly looked around, behaved like a be-

wildered bumpkin, or, as one observer said, 'like a small boy who had forgotten his 'piece.' "

From such appearances, the miners of Red Dog might have judged Twain an unpromising feature for the evening; in this, they would have been pleasantly surprised. From such descriptions we might judge him an unpromising hero for grave scholarly dissertations on democratic education (and, after all, Twain had openly assured his listeners that they were unlikely to be much afflicted by "constant attacks of my wisdom and learning"). It surely seems that, at first blush, to grant this strangely humorous figure the full-fledged status of popularizer might just be what Huck Finn would call a "stretcher." Twain's looks and manner indeed counted against him, but they were only the first, and far from the worst, of his oratorical offenses.[4]

The graver indictment was that Twain played sometimes to his audiences' lowest preferences, really got down and pandered to them. Far from trying to educate them, he sought desperately to give them what they wanted. For Hamlin Hill, *no* American literary figure in the nineteenth century "demeaned himself more to his various audiences." "He was a dead loss to anybody who expected a message or a moral lesson," declares Paul Fatout. "He was not at home in the realm of ideas. In the formal sense he was not a lecturer at all. He was a story-teller, a yarn-spinner. What he called a lecture was a series of anecdotes interspersed with descriptive passages, the whole loosely held together, and sometimes revolving vaguely about a central theme, sometimes not." In the final analysis, Fatout concluded, "on the platform he was primarily, if not almost entirely a joker." V. L. Parrington concurs: "he loved to make a splurge, to be talked of, to be in the public eye, to live on an ample scale; he accepted the world's standards and wished to be measured by them."[5]

This sounds like quite the reverse of democratic education. In this view, he did not popularize any new discipline or set of values *to* his listeners; instead he was supposed to have filched his standards *from* them. Twain, his accusers assert, was not trying to lead intellectually, but to follow. Thus his rhetorical ethos was "representative" in the meanest sense — representative not of the best in his audiences and subject matters, but rather of the most impoverishingly common in each.

Roughly at this point in my argument, it is incumbent upon me to spring to Twain's defense. I am after all putting him forward as a genuine full-blooded democratic educator in some sense — though as we saw with Emerson, how one earns that status can be a complicated matter. The trained reader is by now consoling himself that I shall doubtless adduce some startling evidence to show how Hill, Fatout, Parrington, and the whole mangy gang of such critics — a rather large gang, actually — interpreted him incorrectly, read Twain all wrong.

Problem is, in many cases I'm not sure they did. As in his writing, the quality in Twain's oratory is terribly uneven. In the first stage of his lecturing career (from his debut in 1866 until, say, the publishing of *The Innocents Abroad* and *Roughing It*), Twain essentially contented himself with scrounging laughs. In our terms, he indulged his audiences (even some of his best work in his mature period still shows traces of this sort of straining for effect). "There is nothing in his lectures," the *Chicago Tribune* scolded the young Twain; he "sacrifices everything to make his audience roar." In the late period of his oratorical career (dating approximately from the death of Mrs. Clemens in 1904), most of his speeches were impromptu responses to toasts, and while some (including several we shall examine) are nonetheless of real substance, most are simply exercises in witty self-ingratiation and self-aggrandizement (a certain amount of which is also present, damagingly, in the middle period too). This again is indulgence — but indulgence less of his audiences than of himself.[6]

When the young Twain played to the lower inclinations of his audiences, he did so with no apparent concern for intellectual quality; nor did he seem to think of what he was doing in the context of any conceivable process of democratic education. As certain commentators seem to take a special delight in noting, the grandstanding began even before the lecture did. "Like Walt Whitman, he was not a man to stand by modestly while waiting for attention to wander his way," notes Paul Fatout. "He went after it with great energy"; "he was never reluctant to propagandize . . . and when he found that one of his lectures had been poorly advertised, somebody was sure to be singed by his displeasure." Often he took over the publicity — what in the argot of his day was sometimes called "humbugging" — entirely; and as Justin Kaplan remarks, "he went at his publicity with the hand of a master of ballyhoo and self-promotion. Like Artemus Ward, who once publicized a lecture on the Mormons by printing up tickets that read 'Admit the Bearer and ONE Wife,' he wooed his audiences through crude nonsense." He would offer outrageous and perfectly illusory prizes "for the best conundrum, for the best poem on summer or summer complaint, and for a plausible essay on female suffrage."[7]

Commentators of this inclination seem to have something of a case. Twain's methods of self-advertisement appear to constitute in themselves a subversion of claims for the profundity of his popularizing. Looking at representative samples (originally employed in the promotion of his 11 October 1866 appearance at the Metropolitan Theater in San Francisco), it's difficult to find much evidence of any concern for democratic education and easy to find evidence supporting the claims that Twain on the platform really *was* a dead loss intellectually; that he was, essentially, only a joker:

For Only One Night!
And Only a Portion of That!

THE CELEBRATED BEARDED WOMAN
Is not with this Circus

THE WONDERFUL COW WITH SIX LEGS!
Is not attached to this Menagerie.

THE IRISH GIANT!
Who stands 9 feet 6 inches . . .
and who has been the pet of kings . . .
will not be present, and need not be expected.

The public are privileged to expect whatever they please!!![8]

For another San Francisco appearance, "he had teased his prospects with promises of a splendid orchestra, a menagerie of ferocious animals, a fireworks display, and a grand torchlight procession"; later on, in St. Louis, in order to illustrate a particularly interesting custom of the Sandwich Islands, he offered "to devour a child in the presence of the audience, if some lady will kindly volunteer an infant for the occasion." But he promised to understand if no one volunteered, the women's rights movement having made children a scarce commodity thereabouts.[9]

We even have Twain's own confession of such humbugging in his youth. Reflecting on the ephemeral quality of speakers and writers who have no ideal higher than "that of merely being funny," he admitted, a little ruefully it seems, to Archibald Henderson:

> when I first began to lecture and in my earlier writings my sole idea was to make comic capital out of everything . . . I treated my readers as unfairly as I treated everybody else—eager to betray them at the end with some monstrous absurdity or extravagant anti-climax.[10]

One example may serve to illustrate how Twain would "betray" his serious material and his engaged listeners. In almost all of the variations of his "Sandwich Islands" speech (the most fluid and adaptable in his repertoire), Twain included a peculiarly evocative and even touching passage on some of the breathtaking natural beauty of his tropical paradise. Hardly allowing his audience any time to appreciate the real lyric quality of the passage, Twain would deflate it abruptly with a stage whisper: "there, I'm glad I've got that volcano off my mind." It brought an easy laugh, but at least one critic, from the *Springfield Republican,* complained of having been "misused," and this fairly cheap trick undoubtedly confused others, making

them wonder what to trust, where to stop in their reconstructions of ironies. Twain knew it, but for his first few years on the circuit was always
willing to sacrifice beauty and continuity for a laugh.[11]

Late in life, too, Twain explicitly admitted that he fell short of maintaining his moral and intellectual position. Twain was an old man, ravaged
by a succession of bitter personal tragedies; he was already "completely lost
to the world," as Hill puts it. In washing his hands of any responsibility to
follow up his scathing essay "King Leopold's Soliloquy," Twain gave this
estimation of his intellectual concerns: "I scatter from one interest to
another, lingering nowhere." The wild, tortured old man was shrugging off
forever the burden of disciplined commitment to any consistent doctrine or
coherent set of values; he would content himself now with the mere
"vulgarization" of the particular points that happened to snare, however
momentarily, his attention and interest.[12]

In short, some of the criticism leveled at Twain pertains very aptly to
his lesser platform performances. Twain probably would not take this criticism too kindly; in response to a similar analysis he once said that he "felt
like using a gun on anybody who treated me that way . . . I don't mind
slanders. The facts are what I object to."[13] But the facts are that sometimes
he was merely a vulgarizer; and other times, particularly at the beginning
and at the end of his career at the podium, he was merely an indulger—
either of his audience or of himself.

Professor of Moral Culture

Of course, it's different opinions that make a horse race, and a very
different opinion of Twain on the platform was maintained by an equally
vocal and probably larger group of critics—an opinion that would surely
have astonished our Red Dog miner. Whatever Mark Twain might have
been at his worst, these critics say, at his best he was a moralist.

In fact, Twain himself made this assertion in a letter purportedly in
application for an editorship. "What you want is a good Moral tone to the
paper," he wrote. "If I have got a strong suit, that is it. If I am a wild
enthusiast in any subject, that is the one. . . . What the people are suffering
for is Morality. Turn them over to me . . . when I play my hand in the high
moral line, I take the trick every time." The letter was signed "Mark Twain,
Surnamed the Moral Phenomenon."[14]

But Twain could not laugh off the indictment of first-degree, premedi-
tated seriousness entirely. In the words of "R.C.B.," the reviewer for the
Critic magazine, "every story he tells serves the purpose of illustrating a
moral." Phillip Foner, in his *Mark Twain: Social Critic,* makes this case
more fully, undertaking the formidable task of tracing nothing less than
"Mark Twain's emergence as a champion of the oppressed of all races,

colors, and religions." He attempts to isolate the one "strain" organizing and "dominating" Twain's social criticism; and he finds it, quite simply, in "a burning hatred of all forms of intolerance, tyranny, and injustice, an abhorrence of cant and pretension, a passion for human freedom, a fierce pride in human dignity, a love for people and for life, a frank and open contempt for the mean, the cruel, the selfish, the small and petty. Despite all hesitations and contradictions, he was true to the precept that the man of letters must with all his force oppose every form of tyranny."[15]

Foner may not succeed in explaining how, or if, a passion for human freedom and fierce pride in human dignity squares with the sour determinism into which Twain lapsed at the end of his life, culminating in his one-sided, bitter dialogue "What is Man?" Foner may not attempt to explain how, or if, Twain's love for people squares with his attitudes toward "the damned human race," expressed both privately as in his 9 April 1900 letter to his sister Pamela ("I cannot think why God, in a moment of idle and unintelligent fooling, invented this bastard human race; and why, after inventing it, he chose to make each individual of it a nest of disgusting and unnecessary diseases, a tub of rotten offal"), and in frequent public statements like this one:

> I am the only living man who understands human nature; God has put me in charge of this branch office; when I retire there will be no one to take my place. I shall keep on doing my duty, for when I get over on the other side, I shall use my influence to have the human race drowned again, and this time drowned good, no omissions, no Ark.[16]

Nor may Foner succeed in explaining how in the world all these different and at least potentially conflicting aspects of Twain's character could constitute ONE strain in his social thought. In his admiration, Foner may never succeed in generating a single principle by which to understand all of Mark Twain or a single evaluation which adequately covers all of Twain's work; but for all these somewhat unsettling shortcomings, Foner does accomplish something of distinct importance. He does uncover another character in Twain and document it carefully. It is a character very different from the sly, genial buffoon documented by Hill, Fatout, and Parrington. The author of "King Leopold's Soliloquy" or, say, "To the Person Sitting in Darkness" may be many things, but Foner is surely correct in asserting that in *these* sorts of lectures Twain is NOT merely an intellectual and moral "dead loss," not merely a joker. Nor perhaps is the author who, in times of the highest tide for the spirit of imperialism, dared to confront his audience with "The War Prayer."

> . . . O Lord our Father, our young patriots, idols of our hearts, go forth to battle—be Thou near them. With them—in spirit—we also go forth from the sweet peace of our beloved firesides to smite the foe. O Lord our God, help us to tear their soldiers to bloody shreds with our

shells; help us cover their smiling fields with the pale forms of their patriot dead; help us drown the thunder of the guns with the shrieks of their wounded, writhing in pain; help us lay waste their humble homes with a hurricane of fire; help us to wring the hearts of their unoffending widows with unavailing grief; help us to turn them out roofless with their little children to wander unfriended the wastes of their desolated land in rags and hunger and thirst, sports of the sun flames of summer and the icy winds of winter, broken in spirit, worn with travail, imploring Thee for the refuge of the grave and denied it — for our sakes who adore Thee, Lord, blast their hopes, blight their lives, protract their bitter pilgrimage, make heavy their steps, water their way with their tears, stain the white snow with the blood of their wounded feet! We ask it, in the spirit of love, of Him Who is the Source of Love, and Who is the ever-faithful refuge and friend of all that are sore beset and seek His aid with humble and contrite hearts. Amen. . . .[17]

No reading of "The War Prayer" has left room for doubt that Twain had *some* moral and intellectual dimensions to him. Although Foner is perhaps the most ambitious in his claims for Twain, many other critics share his general assessment.

Maxwell Geismar judged Twain "an American prophet" and "the poet of human feeling." Robert Regan called him "above all, a moralist, whether hurling a sober phillipic at the persecutors of the Chinese or delivering an offhand sarcasm against the . . . Railroad. Gladys Bellamy even claimed for Twain a "sense of being responsible in some way for all his fellow beings," a sense that in her view ultimately spelled his disillusionment. "He always expected too much of life, too much of himself, and too much of mankind. Essentially a perfectionist, he was too bitterly disappointed to be able to make ready adjustments when life and mankind failed to measure up to his expectations."[18]

These critics saw Twain as somehow popularizing a coherent doctrine, an explicit formal body of principles that constituted his intellectual or moral contribution as a democratic educator in the way transcendentalism did for Emerson, or pragmatism did for William James. Yet, strangely enough, they cannot agree among themselves about just what that doctrine might be. In fact, no one of them offers a formulation of the doctrine that comes even close to embracing the very different contents of works as disparate as *Joan of Arc* and "What is Man?" No one offers a formulation that makes compatible the very different positions that Mark Twain advocated at one time or another — sometimes within the same week.

So if it makes any sense to call Twain a democratic educator, it seems a shaky proposition to grant him that status on the basis of any formal doctrine he may have explicitly taught. The formal doctrine he explicitly taught was — well, actually it was quite a mess. This was not the case simply because Twain changed his mind at some point in his life (although his proclivity in this line does make the task of tracing his thought rather more of a challenge). Instead Twain's explicit doctrine was an intellectual mess because of fundamental conflicts in Twain's thinking, conflicts among opinions he advocated off and on alternately, all through his life, and never fully reconciled. He was often spectacularly effective in "vulgarizing" specific points and positions, of course. But true democratic education equips its students to employ the *principles* of its doctrine, not merely to nod an almost dumb assent to its conclusions. Twain never articulated a formal body of values that was ultimately coherent — that is, a doctrine with coordinated and genuinely usable principles. If inculcating his confused explicit doctrine truly had been the extent of his popularizing, then his contribution to democratic education would have been insignificant, even negligible. For what Twain built with one hand, he tore down — sometimes, it seemed, gleefully — with the other.

Let's have a closer look at the mire of conflicting principles in which even the most insistent attempts at explicating a formal Twainian doctrine in his writing bog down: the freedom and dignity of the individual human being (which is expressed directly in *Joan of Arc* and in the characterizations of Huck and Jim in *Huckleberry Finn* and which informs his equalitarian and antimonarchical social thinking, as in *The Prince and the Pauper* and *A Connecticut Yankee in King Arthur's Court*); his indignation and rage at how people used their freedom (as perhaps most powerfully expressed in the darker passages of *Huckleberry Finn*); his beloved "doctrine of mechanism," a loose sort of determinism of conditioning (which Twain thought that he had put forward definitively and triumphantly in "What is Man?" but which in a more palatable and persuasive way also invaded his social books like *The Prince and the Pauper* and *A Connecticut Yankee* in his insights on "training"); and his inclination to use all of this as fodder for a satire he did not always control. As Gladys Bellamy, perhaps a little too simply, puts it.

> his work was set too much at cross purposes: as a moralist he tries to save mankind for a life which he often shows as not worth the living; as a satirist, he expends his scorn on men whom he makes too contemptible to be worth the trouble.

Bellamy goes to some pains to show that the "mess" the conflicts made affected Twain's art as well as his philosophy. "The urgency of the reform drive within him, coupled with his impatience toward mankind, caused him to strike through the short circuit of rampant humor, eliminating the aesthetic distance necessary for artistic effect." "He was a sensitive creative artist," she amplifies, "and he needed the human race as the material for his art. But frequently, when he looked at that race, his ideas fell off into mere rages . . . he was led into shattering outbursts of hatred against human evil in which the whole idea — if there had been a literary idea — came to naught." In short, "his stylistic weaknesses appear to arise not from carelessness or indifference, but sometimes from the larger structural failure contingent upon a clash of unreconciled ideas and sometimes from the smaller but more immediate obstacle of his indignation."[19]

The ambitious Foner concurs, albeit reluctantly; and he admits, in the bargain, a greater variety of problems: "Mark Twain had his serious weakness as a social satirist. He was often superficial, slapdash, and inaccurate. He himself conceded that he lacked stability in pursuing a cause. . . . He was wrongheaded on many issues, and at times his prejudices made his interpretations absurd. He could be amazingly bad at predicting. He contradicted himself many times. . . . His faith in the correctness of his thinking was sometimes overbearing. No one can deny that pot-boiling tarnished, and hasty conclusions blemished, his astonishing gift."[20]

But Charles Neider seems to suggest that the conflicts in Twain's "doctrine" are irrelevant to his real intellectual virtue: "as for intellectual consistency, Clemens is often without it. There are passages in 'Saint Joan of Arc,' for example, which can be used to confute the chief arguments in 'What is Man?' "; no, "for deep thinking in an orderly, intellectual way I do not go to Mark Twain."[21] But even with conflict, contradiction, and lack of consistency noted, Neider still *does* "go to Mark Twain," goes avidly, and even tries to bring us along. The democratic audiences of the time did go, and I propose that we should too. Critics may never untangle the mess of his formal doctrine, but that doesn't really matter. Mark Twain's most important achievement in democratic education — his lectures as well as the writings that grew out of them — was his popularization of an *informal* set of values. These values constituted an intellectual and moral rebellion against what the Connecticut Yankee called the "knight-errantry" of the dominant culture, an intellectual and moral rebellion for hard common sense — for seeing things through an "innocent eye."

Rebel with an Innocent Eye

Both kinds of critics from whom we've heard — those critics who characterize Twain as a dead loss intellectually (Hill, Fatout, Parrington et al.), and those critics who in one way or another find Twain an explicit professor of some formal body of values (Foner, Geismar, Regan, Bellamy) — might find this assertion about Twain's contribution to democratic education strange. And it may even seem to *us* a "stretcher" to assert that true popularization goes on in, say, a speech like Twain's "Advice to Youth."

> Being told I would be expected to talk here, I inquired what sort of a talk I ought to make. They said it should be something suitable to youth — something didactic, instructive, or something in the nature of good advice. Very well, I have a few things in my mind which I have often longed to say for the instruction of the young; for it is in one's

tender early years that such things will best take root and be most enduring and most valuable. First, then, I will say to you, my young friends — and I say it beseechingly, urgingly —

Always obey your parents, when they are present. This is the best policy in the long run, because if you don't they will make you. Most parents think they know better than you do, and you can generally make more by humoring that superstition than you can by acting on your own better judgment.

Be respectful to your superiors, if you have any, also to strangers, and sometimes to others. If a person offend you, and you are in doubt as to whether it was intentional or not, do not resort to extreme measures; simply watch your chance and hit him with a brick. That will be sufficient. If you shall find that he had not intended any offense, come out frankly and confess yourself in the wrong when you struck him; acknowledge it like a man and say you didn't mean to. Yes, always avoid violence; in this age of charity and kindliness, the time has gone by for such things. Leave dynamite to the low and unrefined.

Go to bed early, get up early — this is wise. Some authorities say get up with the sun; some others say get up with one thing, some with another. But a lark is really the best thing to get up with. It gives you a splendid reputation with everybody to know that you get up with the lark; and if you get the right kind of lark, and work him right, you can easily train him to get up at half past nine, every time — it is no trick at all.

Now as to the matter of lying. You want to be very careful about lying; otherwise you are nearly sure to get caught. Once caught, you can never again be, in the eyes of the good and the pure, what you were before. Many a young person has injured himself permanently through a single clumsy and ill-finished lie, the result of carelessness born of incomplete training. Some authorities hold that the young ought not to lie at all. That, of course, is putting it rather stronger than necessary; still, while I cannot go quite so far as that, I do maintain, and I believe I am right, that the young ought to be temperate in the use of this great art until practice and experience shall give them that confidence, elegance, and precision which alone can make the accomplishment graceful and profitable. Patience, diligence, painstaking attention to detail — these are the requirements; these, in time, will make the student perfect; upon these, and upon these only, may we rely as the sure foundation for future eminence. Think what tedious years of study, thought, practice, experience, went to the equipment of that peerless old master who was able to impose upon the whole world the lofty and sounding maxim that "truth is mighty and will prevail" — the most majestic compound fracture of fact which any of woman born has yet achieved. For the history of our race, and each individual's experience, are sown thick with evidence that a truth is not hard to kill and that a lie told well is immortal. There is in Boston a monument of the man who discovered anaesthesia; many people are aware, in these latter days, that the man didn't discover it at all, but stole the discovery from another man. Is this truth mighty, and will it prevail? Ah no, my hearers, the monument is made of hardy material, but the lie it tells will outlast it a million years. An awkward, feeble, leaky lie is a thing which

you ought to make it your unceasing study to avoid; such a lie as that
has no more real permanence that an average truth. Why, you might as
well tell the truth at once and be done with it. A feeble, stupid, preposterous lie will not live two years — except it be a slander upon somebody.
It is indestructible, then, of course, but that is no merit of yours. A
final word: begin your practice of this gracious and beautiful art
early — begin now. If I had begun earlier, I could have learned how.
Never handle firearms carelessly. The sorrow and suffering that have
been caused through the innocent but heedless handling of firearms by
the young! Only four days ago, right in the next farmhouse to the one
where I am spending the summer, a grandmother, old and gray and
sweet, one of the loveliest spirits in the land, was sitting at her work,
when her young grandson crept in and got down an old, battered, rusty
gun which had not been touched for many years and was supposed not
to be loaded, and pointed it at her, laughing and threatening to shoot.
In her fright she ran screaming and pleading toward the door on the
other side of the room; but as she passed him he placed the gun almost
against her very breast and pulled the trigger! He had supposed it was
not loaded. And he was right — it wasn't. So there wasn't any harm
done. It is the only case of that kind I ever heard of. Therefore, just the
same, don't you meddle with old unloaded firearms; they are the most
deadly and unerring things that have ever been created by man. You
don't have to take any pains at all with them; you don't have to have a
rest, you don't have to have any sights on the gun, you don't have to
take aim, even. No, you just pick out a relative and bang away, and you
are sure to get him. A youth who can't hit a cathedral at thirty yards
with a Gatling gun in three-quarters of an hour, can take up an old
empty musket and bag his grandmother every time, at a hundred.
Think what Waterloo would have been if one of the armies had been
boys armed with old muskets supposed not to be loaded, and the other
army had been composed of their female relations. The very thought of
it makes one shudder.

   There are many sorts of books; but good ones are the sort for the
young to read. Remember that. They are a great, an inestimable, an
unspeakable means of improvement. Therefore be careful in your selection, my young friends; be very careful; confine yourselves exclusively
to Robertson's *Sermons,* Baster's *Saint's Rest, The Innocents Abroad,*
and works of that kind.

   But I have said enough. I hope you will treasure up the instructions
which I have given you, and make them a guide to your feet and a light
to your understanding. Build your character thoughtfully and painstak-
ingly upon these precepts, and by and by, when you have got it built,
you will be surprised and gratified to see how nicely and sharply it
resembles everybody else's.[22]

   Both sorts of critics would find reasons to find fault with this speech
for the purposes of democratic education. The "dead loss" critics could find
it in an example of what would be judged moral bankruptcy by conventional standards. The speaker, after all, is attacking parental authority, the
canons of etiquette, and the work ethic. He virtually advocates lying; and
when he tries to resolve the issue, he does so by principles repugnant to the

expectations of polite society. Then he proceeds to make a thoroughly taste-less joke out of the human tragedy of accidents with firearms! Finally, after managing to plug his own book, he states that the moral regimen he advo-cates leads to a character like "everybody else's." Even the breathtaking abruptness of transition — between the paragraph on lying and that on fire-arms or between the paragraph on firearms and that on good books — betrays a lack of a really coherent doctrine undergirding and uniting Twain's thinking here. In short, Twain violates — indeed, he positively flouts — almost every tradition and convention that makes society what it is, every one that he can get his hands on.

For many of the same reasons, the "professor" critics could be hard-pressed to find any positive morality explicitly stated here, to patch to-gether any formal doctrine that can account for the selections of topics that constitute Twain's advice, or for the sprawling disorder in which they ap-pear. Twain, far from attempting anything primly systematic, simply seems to be talking in a common sense way about what he sees.

But to Henry Nash Smith there is something of genuine intellectual substance at work precisely in this mode of seeing things — seeing as if through an eye unobstructed by any of society's conventional standards, canons, expectations, and customs. This "vernacular perspective" is itself a substantial form of rebellion: "vernacular values were at odds with the values cherished by accredited spokesmen for American society. The ver-nacular perspective was potentially subversive." Smith sees Twain's efforts as being aimed "to find an alternative to the prevailing cult of gentility and to define his own role in society." Twain's work thus was a kind of rebellion, a "vernacular protest against the dominant culture."[23]

Smith's notion is an interesting one, but it can be pushed much farther than he chose to take it. I propose that Twain, at least sometimes, was a full-fledged democratic educator. The intellectual speciality he taught con-sists precisely in his rebellion against the real moral hollowness of dominant culture. There are values implicit in the rebellion, "vernacular" values that make Twain's humor work for his audience. Where Twain and his audience share such values — and our own reading will show that they do so fre-quently — then they can share in the ironic fun. I understand these values to constitute the substance of Twain's popularizing. And we shall find, not coincidentally, that these values correspond to the virtues in the projected character of Twain the speaker.

With these possibilities in mind, let's give a closer listen to Twain's "Advice to Youth" and see how it accomplishes what it does. Paragraph one is almost conventional in form. So many such "seeds of advice" had been solemnly strewn from lyceum platforms across the country that listeners almost automatically summoned up a whole set of expectations at this introduction. And their expectations are satisfied to a preliminary extent:

the audience *is* to be pelted with tarnished old nuggets like "always obey your parents," "be respectful to your superiors," "go to bed early, get up early." The traditional good-advice monger never told his audience anything they hadn't heard before with such old chestnuts, and Twain very apparently wasn't trying to introduce anything novel in consciously rehearsing them. But specifically what these conventions and expectations are to mean here, how their ironies are to be recognized and read, remains to be determined by the large context of what follows. It turns out that Twain has put a new—and wrenching—twist on these sagacious counsels.

Obey your parents *when they are present,* we are advised, because if you don't *they will make you.* It is of course a "superstition" that parents know better, but even so, *you can make more* by humoring it. Thus youth is apparently being counseled to abandon an intellectual and moral activity that, in other contexts, is conventionally applauded: using one's own judgment. The reason behind obeying one's parents is a calculation, not conspicuously uplifting, of relative pain and profit to which, the maxim asserts, one should surrender even his virtues—if the price is right. The reasons behind the advice sound clearly (and comically) baser than the customarily respectable justifications and have the unmistakable ring of familiarity. People really *do* think this way.

Respect your superiors, youth, *if* you have any; and extend this respect to others—*sometimes.* Again, conventional advice is given a twist, like "if you are in doubt about an offense, do not resort to extreme measures"—be moderate and patient, "simply watch your chance and hit him with a brick." Twain even covers the possibility that this decision could be a hasty one. If it turns out, youth, that you've thereby wronged your victim, "acknowledge it like a man"—that is, "say you didn't mean to." Twain subverts the mood with comic deflation again; after having advocated employing a violent tactic to good effect, he gently reminds the youth of this refined age to "leave dynamite to the unrefined." Finally, youth must turn traditional advice like "get up with the lark" to their own advantage and work at the poor bird until a comfortable rising time is drilled in.

Twain is mixing two kinds of humor. Sometimes he raises expectations and then simply hits them with a comic brick. Other times he is a little more subtle. His discourse on lying begins with the most respectable of advice: don't lie. Then the advice goes through a process of qualification (or, from the moralistic perspective of the dominant culture, a process of decay) in which the advice grows less and less pious and respectable and more and more in conformity with everyday concrete reality as that statue in Boston. Don't lie, because you'll get caught; well, more exactly, don't lie *if* you'll get caught. In that case, for what lying will get you, you might as well tell the truth. But—through practice and experience, yet!—you may learn how not to get caught. You may become confident, elegant, and precise in your lying, and then, youth, your mendacity will be *grateful*. And in Twain's shockingly pragmatic aesthetics, grace is inextricably linked with profit. Then Twain, hinting that he is not quite the liar he'd really like to be, baldly recommends the lie-refining practice and experience to begin as soon as possible.

The firearms advice is outrageous humor in full flight. Everybody knows what is *supposed* to happen when the old, gray, sweet, hardworking grandmother pleads unavailingly that the gun not be pointed. Grandson had *supposed* it was not loaded—and bang! Surprise! He was right, it wasn't. Thus all the conventional melodramatic expectations are blown away. Our resulting amusement confirms that this is "probably the only case of this kind" that *we* have ever heard of, too; come to think of it, our common experience (which Twain so manifestly shares) really does suggest that a youth who can't hit a cathedral with a Gatling gun can "bag" his grandmother from across the valley.[24] The reduction (or rather, the expansion) to the absurd dimensions of Waterloo would indeed be a sight to see— and is a delightful, if not particularly moral, instructive sight to envision.

If youth follows Twain's advice, and reads those classics of moral instruction (including of course his *Innocents Abroad* with which everyone is conventionally obligated to be conversant), then he promises that their characters will shape up like everybody else's.[25] In his originality Twain has offered fantastically base new reasons to follow old advice. Still, there is an unmistakable echo of familiarity, perhaps even a ring of truth, to it.[26] Notwithstanding the pieties that one is accustomed to hearing, it is altogether plausible to suppose that children in fact obey less out of filial devotion than almost actuarial cost/benefit calculations, or that people in fact believe that what's bad about lying is the consequence of getting caught. This realism, this common sense lends special credibility to Twain's conclusion—that might be drawn from this advice—that by following this common advice one can become like everybody else. But also, persuasively if indirectly, it spurs the listener to ask himself whether he really *wants* to shape up as base and calculating as everybody else. In satirizing hollow morality, Twain undertakes some real democratic education: simply by repeating these hoary old adages and coupling them with a commonsense rendering of their real justifications, Twain managed to throw into question all of the conventional wisdom about how characters *should* shape up.

Again, I do not mean to suggest that Twain has, or even could have, a coherent doctrine, a formal body of principles to advance (I do not even mean to advance this as the exclusive, preemptive way of reading *all* of Twain's lectures). The "dead loss" and the "professor of moral culture" interpretations each apply to a fair number of speeches. I only suggest that the "rebel with an innocent eye" interpretation accounts more plausibly for Twain's best platform performances). Smith himself admits that "the vernacular perspective . . . is not easy to define. Mark Twain never made fully articulate what he was trying to affirm; any explicit statement would falsify his presentational mode of thought." Whereupon, of course, Smith intrepidly advances such an explicit statement: "his intellectual position approximates . . . 'horse sense.' " What Twain was affirming also seems to me to resist explicit statement as a doctrine; he seems to incline his work in exactly the opposite direction. He rebels against all doctrines that try to tell a man what he sees before he sees it, sees it with his innocent, unobstructed eye. This spirit informs, for some clear instances, his *Alta California* letters which he turned into *The Innocents Abroad* and his fabulously successful "American Vandal" lectures. "Twain wanted to report what he as an individual saw, whether it be in a European art museum, in the Church of the Holy Sepulchre in Jerusalem, or in the pages of the Bible itself." The push of Twain's humor here was in the same direction as in his "Advice to Youth"; the vision of everyday reality in such commonsense, familiar, true-to-life terms that it actually drew his listener into seeing things that way too—therein drawing him out of prior doctrinal commitments, out of anything that might obstruct the innocent eye.[27]

For Allison Ensor, the "notion of the innocent eye" constituted nothing less than "Twain's declaration of independence . . . from all subservience to accepted, time-honored points of view." Ensor even goes so far as to regard this commonsense approach of the *Innocents* and the "American Vandal" lectures as the touchstone of Mark Twain's greatest work. "People generally, he believed . . . deceived themselves," concluded Ensor. "Like the pilgrims in the Holy Land, they do not see what is really there, but only what someone tells them they should see. Secure in their smug piety, they are often less Christian than persons who have little to do with the church and who know scarcely anything about the Bible. Surely Huck Finn and Jim are more obedient to the commands of the gospel than are the conventional Christian Miss Watson, the Grangerfords and Shepherdsons, or Uncle Silas and Aunt Sally Phelps. Twain again and again in his stories showed false piety being punctured by realistic irreverence."[28]

However strong an assertion it may seem, Ensor is not alone in this assessment. Maxwell Geismar writes:

> It was the "unobstructed eye" which Clemens brought to so many shams of life beyond those of European travel and the fashionable taste of the time. This remarkable writer looked at everything with the candid, unblinking, and clear gaze of the "innocent." Even though he may have sometimes clowned up the frontier spirit, though he was full of notions and obsessions which he did not try to hide, the source of everything good in Mark Twain lies in this transparently honest, open, and full human vision.[29]

I propose that it is in this commonsense approach—this "vernacular perspective" that views the world through an innocent eye—that Mark Twain achieved his greatest popularization: the moral and intellectual rebellion against "the dominant culture," or any dogma that prejudices issues, that decides them before they are ever given a clear-eyed, tough-minded look.[30]

A rebellion on so serious a scale as the one Mark Twain popularized requires much to make it convincing, much to win over converts from the other side; for part of the problem is precisely that the other side has, as Smith might say, already prejudicially acculturated—that is, already brainwashed—them. As we shall see, Twain finds some persuasive resources in his commonsense message when laced with a generous dose of the humor with which, in nineteenth-century America at least, it had an intrinsic connection. As Walter Blair put it, "for almost two centuries the best way to make an idea tasty to most of the people of this country has been to serve it up with a sauce of native-grown humor and horse sense. Because they have loved to laugh, and because they thought horse sense was the best kind of truth, Americans everywhere have welcomed an idea served up with such a sauce."[31] There is an especially powerful education possible in simple laughter: in the realization and in the *celebration* of the beliefs shared by both speaker and audience. These beliefs make possible and mutually intelligible the particular interpretation of events the speaker offers his audience—and, in the same breath, the fun in which he involves them. To the extent that the sources of Twain's humor are inherent in matters American, it might very accurately be said that the horse sense of Twain's "message" informs the "rhetoric" of his appeal.

But to at least as significant an extent, other kinds of resources come into play, resources that can turn that causality around—at least some of which are more readily understood as characteristics of Mark Twain the speaker himself. Here my intent is only something like Hill's assertion that "his . . . craft was always basically autobiographical." Hill very persuasively argues that Clemens "never completely disguised his own articulation" through the manipulation of his literary voice; that "he was a literary ventriloquist whose own lips were moving more and more visibly during each performance." My central concern is not historical, not essentially concerned with making Kaplan's increasingly difficult distinction between Mr. Clemens and Mark Twain. It is rhetorical, concerned mainly with the speaking ethos he projected—what Robert Regan portrays as the quintessential Unpromising Hero. That character—which organizes, focuses, makes sense of the diverse appeals of the speeches in the same way that a character like Tom sustains a book like *Tom Sawyer*—is "another creature of Samuel Clemens' imagination, the role he invented, played, and willingly submerged himself in—his alter ego, 'Mark Twain.' "[32]

In the identification of Mark Twain, we encounter what Twain was not the first to call a "chicken-egg" problem. For many of these characteristics, it is far from clear which comes first, ordinally or cardinally: the curious, mischievous, contentious, outrageous, tough-minded, representatively American, yet powerfully worldly "message"; or the curious, mischievous, contentious, outrageous, tough-minded, representatively American "easy man of the world" who spoke and embodied it, with whom it was identified — and with whom his audience was to come to identify.[33] And in at least two ways, a rhetoric of identification can actually be seen to inform the substance of Twain's popularizing: in one, to set some of its limitations, in the other to open up some of its possibilities. Ultimately, no definitive line can be drawn between substance (the "message") and rhetoric in Mark Twain, for no such division exists.

We should take a moment here to note how such discoveries about rhetoric can be of significance for the study of democratic education. It is a modern tendency, as we see in our everyday discourse, to try to draw the line between rhetoric and substance sharply. "Cut the talk and get down to business." We are inclined to try to dispense with the rhetoric, which in this view is really not relevant to democratic education and perhaps is actually deceiving; we are inclined to try to get to the *real* message itself. But how can we indulge that tendency, or even keep that sentiment, if there is no meaningful distinction between the message and the rhetoric? If "rhetoric" is in fact involved in the very development of the "message" itself, and if the product is of enhanced value to democratic education (not only in the *communicating* of the message to a given audience, but actually in the *shaping* of the limits and possibilities of the message itself), then rhetoric is valuable too, and not to be "dispensed with" out of hand. Of course this is not to argue that rhetoric is always productive, that it cannot be abused in a democratic context; rhetoric is among other things an important intellectual tool, but like any tool, it can be well- or ill-used. Certainly we should be careful to perfect our use of it and apply it only to good causes. That's good advice, just like Twain's advice to youth; but like Twain's advice, it only can amount to anything if we understand what is behind it — only by making it an object of study again, by thinking of it as a legitimate area of both knowledge and activity. The potential benefits for democratic education that rhetoric can bring — that it did bring for Twain — suggest grounds for a reconsideration of rhetoric in a democratic society.

But I'm getting a little ahead of myself; this argument will be advanced in more complete form in Chapter 8. At this point we must return to a consideration of Twain's rhetoric in particular — of the distinctive resources of appeal and persuasion he taps. And in most cases, it seems, those resources will ultimately be qualities of the character Mark Twain himself.

MARK TWAIN. *Library of Congress*

Characteristics of the Rebel as Educator

"What finally appeals to you in Mark Twain," wrote William Dean Howells, "is his common sense." Certainly a large part of what is appealing in Twain arises from his commonsense attributes. One natural attribute of his commonsense, "innocent-eye" approach is curiosity. Maxwell Geismar called it "a dominant feature of Twain's temperament": "never was a writer more interested in the whole world around him, or more involved in every detail of it. . . . He could never stop looking at the world."[34] He can see things unblinkingly, with startling and even rebellious frankness — and sometimes he can even see them lyrically.

> The guide showed us a coffee-colored piece of sculpture which he said was considered to have come from the hand of Phidias, since it was not possible that any other man, of any epoch, could have copied nature with such faultless accuracy. The figure was that of a man without a skin, with every vein, artery, muscle, every fiber and tendon and tissue of the human frame represented in minute detail. It looked natural, because it looked somehow *as if it were in pain*. A skinned man *would be likely to look that way* — unless his attention were occupied by some other matter. . . . [35]

> Down there in the islands they have exploded one of our most ancient and trusted maxims. It was a maxim that we have all of us implicitly believed in and revered — and now it turns out to be a swindling humbug. *Be virtuous and you will be happy*. The Kanakas are not virtuous — neither men, women, nor children — and yet they are the happiest creatures the sun shines on. They are as happy as the day is long. They wait and carry on grievously when a friend or a relative dies, but it is all a pretense; they do precisely the same thing when a friend returns from a month's absence. In both instances the tears are manufactured to order and the joy and sorrow counterfeited. A woman returns from a distance and a lot of her female friends will huddle around her on the ground and twine their arms about her and weep and whine and blubber and howl for an hour — and they would cheerfully repeat the same thing the next day if she died, and dance the hula-hula into the bargain. It is rarely that they show any genuine tribulation. Theirs is a state of placid happiness. All they want is unfettered liberty to eat, drink, sleep, sing, dance, swindle, lie, and pray, and then, whether school keeps or not is a matter of no interest to *them*.[36]

> New England weather — no language could do it justice. . . . If we hadn't our bewitching autumn foliage, we should still have to credit the weather with one feature which compensates for all its bullying vagaries — the ice storm: when a leafless tree is clothed with ice from the bottom to the top — ice that is as bright and clear as crystal; when every bough and twig is strung with ice beads, frozen dewdrops, and the whole tree sparkles cold and white like the Shah of Persia's diamond plume. Then the wind waves the branches and the sun comes out and turns all those myriads of beads and drops to prisms that glow and

burn and flash with all manner of colored fires, which change and change again with inconceivable rapidity from blue to red, from red to green, and green to gold—the tree becomes a spraying fountain, a very explosion of dazzling jewels; and it stands there the acme, the climax, the supremest possibility in art or nature, of bewildering, intoxicating, intolerable magnificence. One cannot make the words too strong.[37]

The speaker "Mark Twain" could as easily be playfully mischievous or pointedly contentious, as in his address on "Plymouth Rock and the Pilgrims":

I rise to protest. I have kept still for years, but really I think there is no sufficient justification for this sort of thing. What do you want to celebrate those people for?—those ancestors of yours of 1620—the *Mayflower* tribe, I mean. What do you want to celebrate them for? . . . Celebrate their landing! What was there remarkable about it, I would like to know? What can you be thinking of? Why, those Pilgrims had been at sea three or four months. It was the very middle of winter: it was as cold as death off Cape Cod there. Why shouldn't they come ashore?

My first American ancestor, gentlemen, was an Indian—an early Indian. Your ancestors skinned him alive, and I am an orphan. Later ancestors of mine were the Quakers William Robinson, Marmaduke Stevenson, *et al.* Your tribe chased them out of the country for their religion's sake; promised them death if they came back; for your ancestors had forsaken the homes they loved, and braved the perils of the sea, the implacable climate, and the savage wilderness, to acquire that highest and most precious of boons, freedom for every man on this broad continent to worship according to the dictates of his conscience—and they were not going to allow a lot of pestiferous Quakers to interfere with it.

Your ancestors broke forever the chains of political slavery, and gave the vote to every man in this wide land, excluding none!—none except those who did not belong to the orthodox church. Your ancestors—yes, they were a hard lot; but, nevertheless, they gave us religious liberty to worship as they required us to worship, and political liberty to vote as the church required; and so I the forlorn one, am here to do my best to help you celebrate them right.[38]

Often, he was flatly outrageous—but still insistently in the commonsense mode, insistently seeing things as they were:

As by the fires of experience, so by the commission of crime, you learn real morals. Commit all the crimes, familiarize yourself with all sins, take them in rotation (there are only two or three thousand of them), stick to it, commit two or three every day, and by-and-by you will be proof against them. When you are through you will be proof against all sins and morally perfect. You will be vaccinated against every possible commission of them. This is the only way.[39]

> I am now on my way to my own country to run for the presidency. . . . I propose to go there to purify the political atmosphere. I am in favor of everything everybody is in favor of. What you should do is to satisfy the whole nation, not half of it, for then you would only be half a President. There could not be a broader platform than mine. I am in favor of anything and everything—of temperance and intemperance, morality, and qualified immorality, gold standard and free silver. I have tried all sorts of things, and that is why I want to try the great position of ruler of a country. I have been in turn reporter, editor, publisher, author, lawyer, burglar. I have worked my way up, and wish to continue to do so.[40]

On informal occasions, Twain's runaway favorite among sorts of outrageousness was fractured history—fractured as impertinently as his belief that " 'George Washington was an Irishman who discovered America and was rescued by Pocahontas from an awful death on Plymouth Rock, after a perilous voyage in the Spanish Armada' which he saved 'by cutting down a mast with a little hatchet which had been given him by his father, who perished in the storm, and so could not give his son permission to leave his post which the heroic boy firmly refused to forsake without his father's orders.' "[41]

Twain's fondness for the outrageous sometimes landed him in trouble. The famous Whittier speech of 17 December 1877 caused by far the worst scrape. The *Atlantic Monthly's* staff was honoring John Greenleaf Whittier on his seventieth birthday. Twain spun a preposterous yarn about a miner in the foothills of the Sierras who supposedly had been visited by three "literary men"—the venerated Boston deities, Longfellow, Emerson, and Holmes. The yarn unraveled immediately. Howells, editor of the *Atlantic,* remembered the scene in his biography *My Mark Twain.*

> After the scope of the burlesque made itself clear, there was no one there, including the burlesquer himself, who was not smitten with a desolating dismay. . . . Nobody knew whether to look at the speaker or down at his plate. I chose my plate as the least affliction, and so I do not know how Clemens looked, except when I stole a glance at him, and saw him standing solitary amid his appalled and appalling listeners, with his joke dead on his hands.[42]

Later a distraught Twain wrote to Howells, "my sense of disgrace does not abate. I feel that my misfortune has injured me all over the country; therefore it will be best that I retire from before the public at the present." He also penned gushy letters of apology to Emerson, Holmes, and Longfellow (all of which were received warmly and generously). But Twain's histrionics notwithstanding, the Whittier speech was probably not quite the catastrophe that Twain and Howells made it out to be. "In actuality the speech had been greeted with a fair amount of laughter"; "at least one qualified reader of the speech in the papers (Francis J. Child) had found it delightful." Henry Nash Smith declares flatly that "accounts published in Boston newspapers next day show that Mark Twain and Howells had simply invented the notion of a public scandal . . . Emerson paid little attention to it. Although Whittier, Longfellow and Holmes may have felt uncomfortable, they seemed to observers in the room to be politely amused. The program was not interrupted but continued under Howells's direction along its prearranged course for an hour or more after Mark Twain's speech." What is more important, Twain did not abandon the impulse behind the yarn; two years later, at a huge banquet in Chicago given by the Army of the Tennessee for Ulysses S. Grant, Twain turned that impulse into one of his most spectacular successes.[43]

It must have been quite a scene: "surfeited with claret, champagne, and rum punch with oysters, fillet of beef, and buffalo steaks, five hundred Union veterans settled down with their brandies and whiskeys for six consecutive hours of oratory, applause, and military music, an orgy of the spoken word which increased in passion and intensity as the night wore into morning. 'I doubt if America has ever seen anything quite equal to it,' Clemens told Howells. 'I am well satisfied I shall not live to see its equal again.' "[44] Twain spoke fifteenth on the program, by which time vinous sociability had largely given way to a glutted and possibly somewhat rapturous dullness. But whatever their mood, the audience must have been startled by Twain's toast: "The Babies — As they comfort us in our sorrows, let us not forget them in our festivities."

This was hardly expected fare for a military banquet, and the surprised audience listened with delight as Twain spun out comic variations on his theme. "You soldiers all know that when little fellow arrived at family headquarters you had to hand in your resignation. He took entire command. . . . When the thunders of war were sounding in your ears you set your faces toward the batteries, and advanced with steady tread; but when he turned on the terrors of his war-whoop you advanced in the other direction, and mighty glad of the chance, too. . . . *One* baby can furnish more business than you and your whole Interior Department can attend to. He is enterprising, irrepressible, brimful of lawless activities. Do what you please, you can't make him stay on the reservation. Sufficient unto the day is one baby. As long as you are in your right mind don't you ever pray for twins. Twins amount to a permanent riot. And there ain't any real difference between triplets and an insurrection."[45]

Such improvisations bring Twain to his fundamental image: the famous man glimpsed as comically cuddly child.

> In one of these cradles the unconscious Farragut of the future is at this
> moment teething — think of it! — and putting in a world of dead earnest,
> unarticulated, but perfectly justifiable profanity over it too. In another
> the future renowned astronomer is blinking at the shining Milky Way

with but a languid interest — poor little chap! — and wondering what has become of that other one they call the wet-nurse. . . . And in still one more cradle, somewhere under the flag, the future illustrious commander-in-chief of the American armies is so little burdened with his approaching grandeurs and responsibilities as to be giving his whole strategic mind at this moment to trying to find out some way to get his big toe into his mouth — an achievement which, meaning no disrespect, the illustrious guest of this evening turned *his* entire attention to some fifty-six years ago; and if the child is but a prophecy of the man, there are mighty few who will doubt that he *succeeded*.[46]

The fundamental impulse here, as Smith pointed out, is the same as that of the Whittier speech: the mild burlesque of the famous character used as an ironic form of tribute.[47]

For all his playfulness, however, Twain could be tough-minded in, for example, political lectures like "Turncoats" and "Consistency." In these speeches, Twain explodes what he considers myths of partisan loyalty. "If to turn your coat, at a time when no one can impeach either the sincerity of the act or the cleanliness of your motives in doing it, is held to be a pathetic spectacle, what sort of spectacle is it when such a coat-turner turns his coat again, and this time under quite suggestively different circumstances? — that is to say, *after a nomination*."[48] "What is the most rigorous law of our being? *Growth*. No smallest atom of our moral, mental, or physical structure can stand still a *year*. It grows — it *must* grow; nothing can *prevent* it. It must grow downward *or* upward; it must grow smaller or larger, better or worse — it cannot stand still. In other words, we *change* — and *must* change, constantly, and keep on changing as long as we live. What, then, is the *true* gospel of consistency? *Change*. Who is the *really* consistent man? The man who changes. Since change is the law of his *being,* he cannot be consistent if he stick in a rut."[49]

What is persuasive in so many of these speeches are aspects of the character of the speaker who delivers it — or perhaps more precisely, the variety of characters which that speaker could adopt. Charles Neider suggests that, in this, the listener becomes "aware of the breadth of his [Twain's] experience. He seemed to have a genius for partaking of the world." He could be a part of that world in a variety of ways, as we have already seen: he could be a reporter, moralist, preacher, raconteur, hoaxer, and the warm, wise patriarch. In his rebellion against the dominant culture, Mark Twain may at first seem what Regan has tabbed an "Unpromising Hero" — unpromising, at least, as judged by conventional standards. But as he articulates his rebellion, he shows characteristics which the listener with common sense MUST value, to which that listener is attracted, with which the listener is tempted to identify further. In the persuasiveness of his *self*-portrayal, Twain induced his audience to identify with him. This identification was in effect a reformulation of his audience, which functioned as the kind of persuasion preliminary to their initiation into the values of his rebellion.[50]

His audience of everyday people found identifying with him so easy and so compelling partly because he so obviously identified with them. In the use of his speaking ethos, Twain was adopting and projecting a character that was distinctively American. Quite democratically, Twain considered himself an average — a "representative" — American, "an average 'sinner-at-large,' " in his phrase, and he consciously aimed his popularization specifically at the common American. As he made explicit in a letter to British critic Andrew Lang, "I have not tried in even one single instance to help cultivate the cultivated classes. I was not equipped for it, either by nature, gifts, or training. And I never had any ambition in that direction, but always hunted for bigger game — the masses." Twain had intuited what Blair would point out: the best trap for that game was humor, the humor that characterized Twain even before he committed himself to democratic education. "As a reformer, he has his own ways of administering reform," one reviewer reflected. "He will wrap it in a rollicking joke, sheathe it in bold burlesque, or clothe it in caustic satire. He knows that men will often accept in a jest what they will evade or ignore in a serious medium, and that if the jest is repeated often enough they may even discover the truth at its core."[51] Ironic reconstruction of the kind that Twain coaxed from his listeners depends on shared values and on mutual perception of shared values; as Wayne Booth comments in *A Rhetoric of Irony,* "the whole thing cannot work at all unless both parties to the exchange have confidence that they are moving together in identical patterns."[52] Here, it does work; Twain and his audience do move together. The proof — and it is irrefutable proof — is the listener's delight. That delight is a sort of celebration, a mutual communing in those values. By sharing the celebration, the audience realizes they do share values with Twain — values that are portrayed as precisely those characterizing him as a rebel. Thus the fun Twain stirs up actually does something to him, to the possibilities open to him and his message. It makes him a character with whom it is easier — less of a leap from his own commonsense values — to identify.

Humor did that much for Twain. But it was also a trap for him. Although it was an essential source of his persuasiveness, humor also generated the worst problems that Twain met in his lecturing and actually set limits to the persuasiveness of his rhetoric.

Rhetoric and the Shape of the Message

In moving toward popularization after he had made his reputation as a yarn-spinning backwoods humorist, Mark Twain learned a painful lesson: "the great lesson of my life was the discovery that I had to live down my past," he confided to Archibald Henderson.[53] But his past rhetoric of humor posed problems very much in the present: it actually limited some of the possibilities of his popularization.

The general trend on the circuit when Mark Twain became a regular was away from the "concentrated solemnity of lyceum courses . . . toward lighter fare." The 11 March 1869 *Geneseo Valley Herald* voiced despair at the extent of the trend: "the majority . . . desire humorous lectures, and will not turn out to hear a sound exposition of ideas." Twain, because of his reputation, was faced with even greater demands: an audience who came to see a humorist of Twain's reputation would be disappointed, perhaps angry, in any case resistant to a straight, serious message, whatever its quality might be. So even when Twain was up to something intellectually serious, he was forced to use a certain amount of humor. He put it to what he felt was good use. "I had two chances to help to the teacher's one," Twain concluded to Andrew Lang, explicitly admitting his involvement in democratic education. "For amusement is a good preparation for study and a good healer of fatigue after it."[54]

This is not to suggerst that the humor that audiences demanded of Twain never caused him anguish. The most frequent and exasperating failures of Twain's popularizing rhetoric were his failures—of which he was sometimes conscious—to overcome the humorous expectations of his audience. Once, after a peculiarly well-received lecture on his tour with George Cable, Twain burst out, "Oh Cable . . . I am allowing myself to become a mere buffoon. It's ghastly. I can't endure it any longer." And as Justin Kaplan points out, this "epithet 'buffoon' took on a kind of terror for him. What he liked about the *Atlantic* audience, he was to tell Howells, was that 'it don't require a "humorist" to paint himself striped and stand on his head every fifteen minutes.' When the Duke in *Huckleberry Finn* decides that what the Arkansas lunkheads want is low comedy, the King comes prancing out on stage on all fours, naked, painted with streaks and stripes, the image corresponds to the way Clemens thought of himself during one of his sudden alterations from the buccaneering high spirits of the successful performer to depression, self-hatred, and hatred of the audience."[55]

Sometimes, the rhetorical failure amounted to confusing his audience, having them waiting for a deflating anticlimax where none was forthcoming, where instead some message was being advanced. The *Boston Daily Advertiser* complained:

> The audience gets into a queer state after a while. It knows not what to trust: for while much is meant to be seriously taken, the fun is felt to be the real life of the thing; and yet they never know where the fun will come in.[56]

Sporadically, Twain would try to deliver straight, serious lectures—in favor of James C. Blaine for president, against governmental corruption—but most often humor played an essential part both in his character and in his audiences' expectations for it. Thus humor had to remain part of his rhetoric—when it could be turned to his purposes, an educationally valuable part—too. Thus the rhetoric of Twain's character shaped in some measure what he could convincingly think and say.

Twain explicitly recognized that he had to employ humor even if it caused him pain and resigned himself to it.

> I know it is a difficult thing for a man who has acquired a reputation as a funny man to have a serious thought and put it into words and be listened to respectfully, but I thoroughly believe that any man who's got anything worth while to say will be heard if he only says it often enough. Of course, what I have to say may not be worth saying. I can't tell about that, but if I honestly believe I have an idea worth the attention of thinking people, it's my business to say it with all the sincerity I can muster. They'll listen to it if it really is worth while and I say it often enough. If it isn't worth while it doesn't matter whether I'm heard or not. . . .
>
> My advice to the humorist who has been a slave to his reputation is never to be discouraged. I know it is painful to make an earnest statement of a heartfelt conviction and then observe the puzzled expression of the fatuous soul who is conscientiously searching his brain to see how he can possibly have failed to get the point of the joke. But say it again and maybe he'll understand you. No man need be a humorist all his life. As the patent medicine man says, there is hope for you.[57]

Humor had not only given Mark Twain his start on the circuit of public speech; it was humor that finished him. Mark Twain suffered a succession of profound personal tragedies at the end of his public life, starting with the death of his beloved daughter Susy in 1896; this was followed with rejection by his other daughters Clara and Jean, the death of his wife Olivia, "betrayal" by his housekeeper Isabel Lyon, and finally the death of Jean, a bare four months before his own death in 1910. All this was complicated by his shakey financial situation. Twain brought these troubles on himself by disastrous speculations in get-rich-quick schemes (representative American, indeed!) like a superfood called Plasmon, the claims for which would have done the patent medicine man proud, and the Paige automatic typesetter—with losses amounting to a debt of over $70,000, forcing the fifty-eight-year old Twain onto a worldwide lecture tour, not to mention the liquidation of most of his estate. Oddly, as he adopted more and more radically deterministic attitudes toward man (culminating in "What is Man?"), he tended more and more to anthropomorphize his dearly beloved gadgets. This "tendency to humanize machines and mechanize people," as

Kaplan puts it, expressed itself very obtrusively in the way he talked about machines. One was "an inspired beggar" and "a cunning devil" which, after passing through a "sick child" stage, could become "a magnificent creature" that ranked "second only to man." Seeing another machine—a press which stopped itself and signaled a foreman for maintenance—he was moved to marvel "my God. Can that thing vote, too?"[58]

After his financial troubles, Twain increasingly (although never quite totally, as in his "Pier 70" speech) abandoned popularization. Instead his growing emphasis was on indulging his audience (and himself) in empty displays of wit. Fewer and fewer of his speeches were prepared pieces, rehearsed and rethought with the painstaking care of earlier years.[59] More and more were simply impromptu responses to toasts, which for the most part featured the sheer display of style, mere rhetorical pyrotechnics, largely without involvement in substantial matters. Even at their best, these speeches were likely to consist mainly of reprises from earlier, popular speeches and precious little original material essayed for the sake of reconstituting himself or his audiences.

Humor had made Sam Clemens a celebrity as Mark Twain. In the wreckage of his old age, he decided simply to play the part of the glib, wild-haired, white-suited "M.T." to the hilt, even to its excesses. As he interjected so revealingly in his speech "The Galveston Orphan Bazaar": "I will be frank with you. I have been playing a part."[60]

The net effect of all this was to make him, if far less a popularizer, far more a *celebrity*.

> On the streets and in theaters and restaurants Clemens was so often recognized and applauded that, as Clara said, "it was difficult to realize he was only a man of letters." He had, in fact, become something else. . . . He became a celebrity—in Daniel Boorstin's definition, "a person who is known for his well-knownness." The reporters who dogged his steps were attracted not so much by his literature, which they rarely read or understood, as by his personality, his mane of white hair, his drawl, his astonishing opinions and mannerisms—all of which, having already been the subjects of bales of news clippings, now by the dynamics of celebrity and his own skillful management, made him even better copy.[61]

As we saw, the rhetoric of humor in Twain's popularization had imposed limits on the substance of his popularization; ultimately, he got carried away with it, and it carried him away from the enterprise of democratic education almost entirely. But in another way rhetoric actually opened possibilities for the popularization. Put another way, there was at least one way by which rhetoric was involved in creating possibilities for Twain to popularize an intellectually deeper message.

"Sam Clemens was intoxicated with oratory in an age that adored it," says Justin Kaplan; "he craved affection and admiration, found them in the laughter and astonishment of his lecture audience and they came to be the basic conditions he needed in order to be creative and happy."[62] Given these conditions, he could develop his comic art, his rhetoric of humor; moreover, given these conditions Twain found himself able to push himself farther—to rise out of the mere joking of his early career to his intellectually legitimate rebellion. Crucial to this transformation was what Robert Regan calls a transformation in the narrator's pose. The mere joker laughed—derisively and emptily, says Regan—from a pose of superiority that, from the listener's perspective, was not particularly earned. But the mature speaker, the educator as rebel, began—and continued for the most part—to speak from some ironically assumed pose of *inferiority* (that of the unsophisticated American Vandal, for the earliest example). Behind this pose, of course, his audiences are led inferentially to find the *genuinely* superior Twain—as curious, mischievous, contentious, outrageous, tough-minded, powerfully worldly, and warmly and persuasively wise as we have found him in this chapter—and join him in ironic celebration of that superiority whenever we get the jokes. These "poses of inferiority were accessible to Mark Twain only when his confidence in his acknowledged superiority was high; they exploit that acknowledged superiority in various ways, all of which underscore it. The poses of superiority, on the other hand, are self-defensive; they posit and construct a reputation he does not possess, or fears he does not possess."[63] This rhetorical consideration—one of the speaker's relation to his audience, and vice versa—actually shaped the possibilities for Twain's "substance," his "message," in so basic a way that the message could not have the same substance of cultural rebellion without it.

There develops a pattern of degrees of communion with readers and listeners that constitutes nothing less than intellectual history of Mark Twain. "In his first period of painful insecurity," argues Regan, "the author could not make his audience privy. . . . In the succeeding period of prosperity, he could . . . invite his readers to join him." It was only in this period, says Regan, that Twain could escape his "narrow confines" and "produce, albeit painfully," a *Huckleberry Finn*. "But when ill-fortune followed good, the motif—his solace against despair—resumed its place of primacy. And again, anxious lest he reveal too much of his inner mind and become a laughing stock, he burlesques his dreams. To trace this theme, then, is to chart the current of the mind of Mark Twain."[64]

In sum, rhetoric was involved in determining the shape of Mark Twain's popularization—even of the substance of his message itself—in both negative and positive ways. It set some of its characteristic limits and opened its characteristic possibilities, characteristic both in the sense of "distinctive" and in the sense of being a function of the character who popularized it. For while being involved in shaping the informal body of values Twain popularized — and, as we have seen, in being shaped by it — the rhetoric of Twain's democratic education shaped the character of Mark Twain too. The degree to which Twain was a creature of the circuit, a rhetorician at heart, was revealed in the speech he delivered in Liverpool on his last visit to England to receive an honorary degree from Oxford in the summer of 1907. The speeches he delivered on his visit, as Hamlin Hill remarks, "were in effect personal yet public goodbyes to friends whose comradeship stretched as far back as 1872."[65] The goodbye he said at Liverpool was his most poignant farewell of all.

Twain — who once had written his friend the Reverend Joe Twitchell, "you have seen us go to sea, a cloud of sail, and the flag at the peak; and you see us now, chartless, adrift — derelicts, battered, water-logged, our sails a ruck of rags" — seemed to employ that personal vision again in choosing and elaborating an image borrowed from Richard Henry Dana's *Two Years Before the Mast:*[66]

> There was a presumptuous little self-important skipper in coasting sloop, engaged in the dried-apple and kitchen-furniture trade, and he was always hailing every ship that came in sight. He did it just to hear himself talk and to air his small grandeur. One day a majestic Indiaman came ploughing by with course on course of canvas towering into the sky, her decks and yards swarming with sailors, her hull burdened to the Plimsoll line with a rich freightage of precious spices, lading the breezes with gracious and mysterious odors of the Orient. It was a noble spectacle, a sublime spectacle! Of course, the little skipper popped into the shrouds and squeaked out a hail, "Ship ahoy! What ship is that? And whence? And whither?" In a deep and thunderous bass the answer came back through the speaking trumpet, "The *Begum,* of Bengal, one hundred and forty-two days out from Canton, homeward bound! What ship is that?" Well, it just crushed that poor little creature's vanity flat, and he squeaked back most humbly, "Only the *Mary Ann,* fourteen hours out from Boston, bound for Kittery Point — with nothing to speak of!" Oh, what an eloquent word, that "only," to express the depths of his humbleness! That is just my case. During just one hour in the twenty-four — not more — I pause and reflect in the stillness of the night with the echoes of your English welcome still lingering in my ears, and then I am humble. Then I am properly meek, and for that little while I am only the *Mary Ann,* fourteen hours out, cargoed with vegetables and tinware; but during all the twenty-three hours my vain self-complacency rides high on the white crest of your approval, and then I am a stately Indiaman, ploughing the great seas under a cloud of canvas and laden with the kindest words that have ever been vouchsafed to any wandering alien in this world, I think; then my twenty-six fortunate days on this old mother soil seem to be multiplied by six, and *I* am the *Begum* of Bengal, one hundred and forty-two days out from Canton, homeward bound![67]

It was "an amazing rhetorical *tour de force,* an emotion-packed and exactly appropriate conclusion" in itself.[68] But an audience consideration made it seem even more so. The audience burst into applause too soon, interrupting Twain's conclusion after "*I* am the *Begum* of Bengal, 142 days out from Canton. . . . " *T. P.'s Weekly* reported that "it seemed like an inopportune cheer, and for a moment it upset Mark Twain, and yet it was felicitous in opportuneness. Slowly, after a long pause, came the last two words — like that curious, detached and high note in which a great piece of music sometimes suddenly and abruptly ends — 'Homeward Bound.' "[69]

This chapter itself has nearly reached the end of its course; let us dock at Pier 70. "Pier 70" was the speech Twain delivered at a dinner given to honor his seventieth birthday. Critics regard this speech more than any other as "the finest he ever made"; and this speech more than any other exemplifies the persuasive characteristics of Twain, the rebel with an innocent eye.[70]

Here he is curious to see the world as it is — and engagingly mischievous, contentious, and outrageous in the bargain.

> I have had a great many birthdays in my time. I remember the first one very well. . . . I hadn't any hair, I hadn't any teeth, I hadn't any clothes, I had to go to my first banquet just like that. Well everybody came swarming in. It was the merest little bit of a village — hardly that, just a little hamlet, in the backwoods of Missouri, where nothing ever happened, and the people were all interested, and they all came; they looked me over to see if there was anything fresh in my line.

He could even be (rather precociously if this case is factual) tough-minded.

> Those people came, they came with that frankness which also is so provincial, and they examined all around and gave their opinion. Nobody asked them, and I shouldn't have minded if anybody had paid me a compliment, but nobody did. Their opinions were all just green with prejudice, and I feel those opinions to this day. Well I stood that as long as — you know I was courteous, and I stood it to the limit. I stood it an hour, and then the worm turned. I was the worm; it was my turn to turn and I turned. I knew very well the strength of my position; I knew that I was the only spotlessly pure and innocent person in that whole town, and I came out and said so. And they could not say a word. It was so true. They blushed; they were embarrassed. Well, that was the first after-dinner speech I ever made. I think it was after dinner.[71]

Twain had a commonsense point to make, and it is quite an unconventional point, a point that actually subverts the conventions for such speech. Usually an enshrined — if doddering — old hero was to declaim on the one or two or three directions that helped him find his way and that eventually brought him to success; and he spoke as if everyone who desired similar success in their own lives should follow precisely the same path. Most such passages seemed to be lifted almost verbatim from Ben Franklin's *Autobiography,* with the same industrious virtues. While Twain imitated some of the stock devices of this sort of speech, his message was of a different sort entirely: "I have achieved my seventy years in the usual way: by sticking strictly to a scheme of life which would kill anybody else. . . . I will offer here, as a sound maxim, this: that we can't reach old age by another man's road. I will now teach, offering my way of life to whomsoever desires to commit suicide by the scheme which has enabled me to beat the doctor and the hangman for seventy years."

Twain's unconventional habits included going to bed "when there wasn't anyone left to set up with, and getting up when he had to"; eating whatever didn't agree with him until one or the other "got the best of it"; as for smoking, his rule was only one cigar at a time, and absolutely none at all when he was asleep. He continues by explaining how he kept his morals carefully—for "processions, and Chautauquas, and World's Fairs." He sagely counseled that if you "disinfect it now and then, and give it a fresh coat of white wash once in a while, you will be surprised how well she will last." Alas, after 63 years, his prize moral got to associating with insurance company presidents, and it became no longer "competent for business." Twain mourned—a little. "She was a great loss to me. Yet not all loss. I sold her to Leopold, the pirate King of Belgium; he sold her to our Metropolitan Museum, and it was very glad to get her, for without a rag on, she stands 57 feet long and 16 feet high, and they think she's a brontosaur."

Twain is taking familiar parts of life and making them seem absurdly exaggerated; "then as an afterthought you see sound reason in it, and finally wisdom," says Charles Neider. "His humor often seems to spring from a sense of the incongruity of life, of man's estate, and to rise from the depths. . . ."[72] Twain had used those familiar perceptions to exemplify some solid commonsense advice; that each man must live by his own regime, must make his journey by his own road. His advice is a little rebellion against the "dominant culture," which by its nature is in the business of dictating which regimens are appropriate for the whole society, and which are not. But we are drawn almost irresistibly to identify *with* Twain *against* the dominant culture: for he has arrived at his commonsense message with mutinous ebullience—with the curiosity, the mischief, the contentiousness, the outrageousness, the tough-mindedness, the worldly yet representatively American characteristics of the rebel with an innocent eye.

CHAPTER 7

William James as Democratic Educator: Ambassador of Thought

James's whole thought can be characterized as an attempt to satisfy opposite demands.

— PATRICK KIERNAN DOOLEY, in
*Pragmatism as Humanism: The
Philosophy of William James*

After all is said and done, it is the human aspect that lasts the longest. The scholar, thinker, teacher, is merged at last in the human being. The man is the ultimate and everlasting value.

— REVEREND GEORGE A. GORDON,
in his eulogy of William James

THE last quarter of the nineteenth century was a particularly turbulent time in American thought. The modern American university was being invented by men like Gilman, Hall, King, Eliot, and Harper at places like Johns Hopkins, Clark, Stanford, Harvard, and Chicago.[1] More and more, the controversies of formal philosophy were becoming accessible and even interesting to democratic audiences. These controversies were at once some of the most difficult and some of the most significant intellectually: the argument between the rationalists and the empiricists, the struggle between optimistic idealists and pessimistic materialists, the conflict between freewillists and determinists, the opposition of monists to pluralists. In all these issues the community of thinking people was divided along battle lines; it seemed increasingly willing — even inclined — either to discount the seriousness of its divisions, to abandon discourse about them, or to tear itself apart.

A mediating, reconciling rhetoric was required to give the opposing sides ways of talking to each other — ways of appreciating the different strengths and limitations of opposing arguments without falling into an

161

uncritical, "do your thing" relativism that would merely amount to another way of not paying attention, ways of keeping the conversation going productively. What was needed was a rhetoric that could make settlements — or at least negotiate enough of a truce to start the sides talking to each other again, perhaps enough even to convince them that dichotomies so polarized (and polarizing) were by their nature impoverished choices.

The Making of an Ambassador

William James was born in the busiest hotel in New York, the bustlingest city in America, 11 January 1842 of a most interesting family. His grandfather, after whom he was named, had been a hustling entrepreneur, a materialist of classic proportions. He had arrived in America in 1789 utterly impoverished; in death, after decades of hard work and shrewd investment in tobacco, real estate, and the Erie Canal, he departed the richest man in New York state except, perhaps, the legendary John Jacob Astor.

Besides his determined and rather grim worldiness, William James the senior had one — and apparently only one — other distinguishing characteristic: he was a Calvinist of the sternest, sourest, most orthodox sort. Where his heart lay, there was his treasure also: in his will, William James senior made the regular practice of Calvinism a condition of his children's receiving their bounteous legacy. The children rebelled, of course, all vigorously enough to break the will on this codicil; but none swung further from the solemn materialism of their father than did Henry James the senior.

From our perspective, it seems as if Henry swung as far to the opposite extreme — personally, philosophically, and vocationally — as he possibly could. Henry "was one of those somewhat obscure sages whom early America produced: mystics of independent mind, hermits in the desert of business, and heretics in the churches." He was a bright, happy, friendly man who flirted with Emersonian Transcendentalism before graduating to a bewilderingly arcane sect of Swedenborgianism. His first career was as a preacher. But it was only a short time before his congregation, though themselves Swedenborgians, found Henry's brand of the stuff too ethereal even for them; they put him, apparently rather unceremoniously, out of the pulpit. James turned to writing as a career and to travelling (on his father's seemingly inexhaustible legacy) as an avocation. Evidently he was rather better at the latter than the former: Henry James's writing evoked virtually no popular response before he died. This failure seemed to stem at least partially from his bafflingly allusive and obscure style: as William Dean Howells gently chided the good preacher, Henry had set out to reveal the secret of Swedenborg, and in the process managed to keep it. But his acquaintances thought him a good and saintly man, and he was a beloved father to his children, the eldest of whom was William James.[2]

William's intellectual inheritance manifested the same sort of conflict that he would spend his life trying to reconcile: a conflict between his father's almost inaccessibly spiritual transcendentalism and his grand-father's almost implacably worldly materialism. Thus, long before it was a matter of professional philosophical interest for William, the mediation of such extremes was a matter of personal import, a matter of his own iden-tity. But as serious as were the problems that William's intellectual inherit-ance presented him, his material inheritance endowed him with some re-sources to help him cope with such problems, to mediate between opposing demands, and to find a manner of reconciling them.

The most crucial of these resources turned out to be travel: the James family was almost constantly on the move — to England, through the Conti-nent, and all around the northeastern seaboard of the United States. In his frequent visits to Europe, William attained a mastery of French and Ger-man and learned at least to function in Italian and Latin. But he was also learning what turned out to be a far more useful lesson. William was ex-posed to a richer variety of life-styles and attitudes than almost any Ameri-can of his time; only Henry Adams comes to mind as having enjoyed a comparably diverse education. James benefitted from this exposure by de-veloping a striking versatility of character, a flexible repertoire of personal modes of relation and mediation. It was observed of William even in his young manhood that "he could pass in America for the most cosmopolitan of philosophers, and in Europe for the most American."[3]

Another benefit of travel was that William was able to acquire much of his education at first hand: that is, he learned to learn personally, which seems to have been a crucial factor in his acute appreciation of the interplay of thought and character. From Renouvier and Peirce to Bergson, Schiller, Pillon, Frederick Myers, Benjamin Paul Blood, Santayana, and even Gertrude Stein, William James knew the great and the celebrated thinkers of his time, both comrades and competitors. Indeed, probably the most productive intellectual relationship of his life was his ongoing friendship with a "competitor," his fellow Harvard faculty member, the staunch idealist Josiah Royce. "At the height of his career he knew personally every important European psychologist and philosopher," and his biographer Gay Wilson Allen calls him in this sense an "ambassador of American thought."[4] I allude by my title to different and I think more important "diplomatic" missions: James's mediation of rhetorical and philosophical rather than geographical differences, and his reconciling diplomacy on be-half of thought itself. But it would be an impoverished acquaintance with William James that did not recognize his contributions in bringing Ameri-can thought as such to Europe, and European thought as such to America.

In the tireless popularizing of his later years, the lessons of travel would become a permanent part of his personal repertoire of means for mediation and resources for reconciliation.

William wandered in his formal education for a long time, casting about for something to engage him. In 1857 and .1858 he studied in Boulogne, in 1859 and 1860 in Geneva. But late in 1860 he found an activity that cultivated what was to become one of his essential intellectual characteristics: he virtually threw himself into the study of painting under the prominent American artist William Hunt of Newport. From the beginning, the boy had a passion for Eugene Delacroix that some biographers find revealing.

> Delacroix was almost a scientist in his knowledge of colors, but he used them to give a general effect of vitality and truth rather than accuracy of minute details, and the results were dramatic. . . . Certainly he was a great painter, and William's enthusiasm for him not only indicates the boy's own innate artistic ability but also throws considerable light on his early character. Delacroix's work had a dynamic vitality and conveyed emotion without sentimentality. Even in his teens William had too keen a sense of humor to succumb to sentimentality, but he cared for nothing that did not stir his feelings—all his life he would be interested in *feeling,* later as a psychologist, and finally as a philosopher.[5]

But after more than a year of study, William abruptly abandoned art for science. Deciding that he would never be a truly great painter (and thinking nothing more pitiable than a "tepid" one), he entered Lawrence Scientific School late in 1861 and then the Harvard Medical School in 1863. William took time out for an expedition along the Amazon with the famed biologist Louis Agassiz in 1865 and 1866, and for a period of study in Germany in 1867 and 1868. But in 1869 he finally earned his M.D. from Harvard, his main examiner being by chance another platform favorite, Dr. Oliver Wendell Holmes. But by that time, William felt no interest in actually practicing medicine. He spent most of the next four years (including a year-long period of severe depression) searching for a vocation that would be more personally satisfying. Then in 1873 Charles Eliot offered him the position of instructor in Anatomy and Physiology in Harvard College and he accepted; in 1875 he began to give instruction in psychology.

"What made psychology a uniquely fit involvement was that it seemed to engage both sides of James, both sorts of his intellectual resources. For him, the issues of psychology engaged both the tough, empiricist maker of distinctions, and the tender, deep-feeling artist of emotion. His seminal *Principles of Psychology,* published in 1890, was quickly recognized as a classic in the field. Indeed, in its haphazard way it anticipates most subsequent psychological positions and movements, even the most modern; to a very real extent it seems to have shaped, to have staked out, the field.

But the *Principles* appeared to exhaust what he had to say on the subject: as James's intellectual biographer Ralph Barton Perry pointed out, "he never afterwards produced any considerable article or book on the standard problems of psychology." Instead, psychology carried him, particularly through the issue of free will, towards philosophy. His first explorations along this line were his collection of lectures *The Will to Believe and Other Essays on Popular Philosophy* in 1897 and *The Varieties of Religious Experience,* originally delivered as the Gifford Lectures in 1902. In his practical approach to religious matters — his focus not on theological theory but on personal results — William James was groping towards a philosophical method that could mediate extremes, could reconcile demands as adamantly opposed as materialist science and transcending religion posed themselves to be. Finally, in the Lowell Institute lectures in 1906, he formally articulated such a method for the first time. "Pragmatism," it was declared, "is to be regarded as a method of mediating between the extremes of competing conceptions of reality and truth."[6]

James claimed new philosophical capabilities for his method, a new flexibility that could effect a genuine reconciliation of oppositions. And his popularizing rhetoric reflected that flexibility, embodied it in its unique versatility of appeal. We find in James, within the course of the opening Lowell Institute lecture alone, the capacity to make statements both of broad popular generality and of detailed professional specialization.

> The philosophy which is so important in each of us is not a technical matter; it is our more or less dumb sense of what life honestly and deeply means. It is only partly got from books; it is our individual way of just seeing and feeling the total push and pressure of the cosmos.[7]

> . . . that Rocky Mountain tough of a Haeckel with his materialistic monism, his ether-god and his jest at your God as a "gaseous vertebrate" . . . Spencer, treating the world's history as a redistribution of matter and motion solely and bowing religion politely out the front door: — she may continue to exist, but she must never show her face inside the temple.[8]

James advances his argument both by collapsing and by delineating distinctions, both by attending to the transcending truth and by attending to divisions, parts, distinctions.

> The history of philosophy is to a great extent that of a certain clash of human temperaments.

The Tender-Minded	*The Tough-Minded*
Rationalistic	Empiricist
(going by "principles")	(going by "facts")
Intellectualistic	Sensationalistic
Idealistic	Materialistic

Optimistic	Pessimistic
Religious	Irreligious
Free-willist	Fatalistic
Monistic	Pluralistic
Dogmatic	Sceptical[9]

His relation with his audience ranges nimbly from calculated formality to offhand folksiness.

> Believing in Philosophy myself devoutly, and believing also that a kind of new dawn is breaking upon us as philosophers, I feel impelled, PER FAS AUT NEFAS, to try to impart to you some news of the situation.

> Facts are good, of course, give us lots of facts. Principles too are good; give us plenty of principles.

> At any rate he and we know offhand that such philosophies are out of plumb and out of key and out of "whack."[10]

In this versatility, this ability to range from one sort of appeal to its opposite, James found a rhetoric of democratic education uniquely fit to his philosophy. Ordinarily a modest man, he was willing to make some ambitious claims for pragmatism: it "is absolutely the only philosophy with *no* humbug in it," and, ever the popularizer, he added "I am sure it is *your* philosophy."[11] James intended pragmatism as nothing less than a sort of architectonic philosophical method, and it's easy to see ambition in that. But it will be revealing to take a moment specifically to appreciate more fully and tangibly the corresponding ambition of his rhetoric. James was a transcendently shrewd tactician in his deployment of the appeals of identification; the key to his success was his understanding of the problem of the democratic audience, seemingly in terms quite like those we have used. James's tactical genius consisted in recognizing and addressing the paradoxical task of expounding the conflict in philosophy powerfully enough to convey its significance without making it sound intellectually inaccessible.

The tactics of James's popularization were enriched in obvious ways by his flexibility in thought and character. Transcending generalizations and mantic utterances put the problems simply and memorably. Lists encapsulate details in a way that renders them handleable. The subtitle and an entire chapter specifically on common sense gives pragmatism the feel not of a new and esoteric doctrine, but a familiar and even distinctively American way of thinking. That is, James was doing nothing in his pragmatism that his audience did not do naturally—except, of course, that James did it all better and more appealingly. He was like his audience in his thought and character—except, because of pragmatism, he was somehow more so.

Having built a comfortable rhetorical context for his audience with appeals like this, James can thus get away with quite formal discussions of "the problem of substance," "the problem of materialism," "the notion of design," "the problem of free will," "the notion of truth," and even "the problem of God"—some of the most obscure and intractable problems of philosophy, popularized successfully through James's tactics of identification.

Character and the Screening of Truths

In the preceding chapters we saw that the character projected by a popularizer can help initiate his audience to a specific mode of thinking, can help locate them in a given field of discourse. Emerson drew us to look outward to the grander vista, the transcending whole, the only source of real significance and meaning. In contrast, Twain prompted us to look closely, materially, almost empirically at each bit of reality for its own very particular consequences and meanings. The prophetic nature of Emerson's educational enterprise led him (and through him his audiences) to look for truth—truth of a lyric, resonant sort—in the radiant totality of things. The power of his argument depends on the sublimity of his entire vision. The rebellious nature of Twain's educational enterprise brought him (and through him his audiences) to look at the whole of things merely as an aggregate of parts that must be distinguished and then to eye each distinct thing with due impertinence for itself. The important turns of his arguments proceed from the distinctions he makes. In sum, we learn from Emerson and Twain to attend to things in different ways, to be satisfied by different kinds of truths.

When Emerson gives his audiences numbered paragraphs at the end of "Self-Reliance" preceded by what appears to be a topical list, audiences acquainted with him know enough not to attend to the order too nigglingly; they have been accustomed to operating on the level of generality required by mantic visions of the whole.[12] Thus those listeners would not be disturbed or even much surprised when the paragraphs wandered from the order of the list, then soared cheerfully off the list entirely, leaving the last four topics untouched. To the objection that this (and most of the rest of Emerson) doesn't follow logically, the calm Emersonian answer is "of course not." It doesn't have to. For Emerson, it is incidental "where you start" and "where you come out." That is why, as we saw, the parts of his speeches were literally interchangeable. What is interesting about "where Emerson is moving to" (or, perhaps, "how Emerson is moving") is that everything is ultimately included, all potential points of departure and termination are subsumed. The most transcendent truth is the most interesting sort—and if it happens that Emerson's auditors are drawn to ignore occasional incidences of other sorts of truths (the sorts that need to be distinguished and listed with drudging exactitude), well, no important meaning is lost.

Think of the contrast with Twain! The innocent-eyed rebel accustoms us to a process of ferreting out a wholly different sort of truth; that is, to a different process of interpreting experience. We learn to look at the parts of reality to see what is materially there and to discover what each phenomenon materially means. We learn to ignore any potentially confusing or misleading connotations or resonances it might have acquired; such overarching connotations, wherever they appear, are always fair game for undermining. The quality of the distinctions you make helps determine the quality of the understanding you achieve—at least, the quality of Twainian understanding.

In other words, the character of each popularizer we have examined functions as a kind of intellectual filter: it tends to screen out irrelevant kinds of truths, the kinds of truths allowed to sift through are those involved in the specific intellectual project. And as we have seen, by no means are the same kinds of truths relevant to projects as disparate as, say, Emerson's and Twain's.

To appreciate all this more directly, I propose an exercise. First, let us listen to hear Emerson speaking: and in the words we hear him say, let us pay attention to the specific kind—the *character*—of the truths we share with him.

> I still keep in mind a wonderful sunset which I witnessed. . . . A broad expanse of the river was turned to blood; in the middle distance the red hue brightened to gold, through which a solitary log came floating, black and conspicuous; in one place a long, slanting mark lay sparkling upon the water; in another the surface was broken by boiling, tumbling rings, that were as many-tinted as an opal; where the ruddy flush was faintest was a smooth spot that was covered with graceful circles and radiating lines, ever so delicately traced; the shore on our left was densely wooded, and the somber shadow that fell from this forest was broken in one place by a long ruffled trail that shone like silver; and high above the forest wall a clean-stemmed dead tree waved a single leafy bough that glowed like a flame in the unobstructed splendor that was flowing from the sun. There were graceful curves, reflected images, woody heights, soft distances; and over the whole scene, far and near, the dissolving lights drifted steadily, enriching it, every passing moment, with new marvels of coloring.
>
>   I stood like one bewitched. I drank it in, in a speechless rapture. The world was new to me. . . .

Emerson has taught us to rejoice in such glimpses of the glory of things, to see in them their deeper grace, beauty, and poetry—how this world is ever new. Since we know Emerson, we understand that this passage is no mere narration of some particular sunset over some particular river; surely this is the quintessential sunset, whose truth lies in its prophetic glimpse of the eternal supernatural whole.

But if Twain were to confront us with exactly the same glimpse of nature — even if it were in exactly the same words — our listening would make an enormous adjustment; even though it would be trained on the same phenomena, on the very same words, it would screen out substantially different things.

Just as an experiment, go back now and reread this passage as if we were now hearing Twain.

We know that Mark sometimes would wax lyrical; there's no absolutely sure warrant for suspicion, and perhaps we could be convinced, by the larger context he put it in, to read it solemnly in a poetic light — well, eventually maybe. But Twain has accustomed us to looking at the particulars of life, to disdain yearning foolishly for bewitching, rapturous truth. That is, if Twain were to narrate this vision, we'd be immediately inclined to pay attention to different things in it — and, very probably, we would expect something more, probably something like undermining.

In fact, more is forthcoming. This passage is not Emerson's but taken from Twain's *Life on the Mississippi;* and its point in its context is that this grand view of the river is a childishly tender and misleading one, precisely in how it ignores what the particulars really mean.

> When I had mastered the language of this water and had come to know every trifling feature that bordered the great river as familiarly as I knew the letters of the alphabet, I had made a valuable acquisition. But I had lost something too. I had lost something which could never be restored to me while I lived. All the grace, the beauty, the poetry had gone out of the majestic river . . . a day came when I began to cease from noting the glories and the charms which the moon and the sun and the twilight wrought upon the river's face; another day came when I ceased altogether to note them. Then, if that sunset scene had been repeated, I should have looked upon it without rapture, and should have commented upon it, inwardly, after this fashion: This sun means that we are going to have wind tomorrow; that floating log means that the river is rising, small thanks to it; that slanting mark on the water refers to a bluff reef which is going to kill somebody's steamboat one of these nights, if it keeps stretching out like that; those tumbling "boils" show a dissolving bar and a changing channel there; the lines and circles in the slick water over yonder are a warning that troublesome place is shoaling up dangerously; that silver streak in the shadow of the forest is the "break" from a new snag, and he has located himself in the very best place he could have found to fish for steamboats; that tall dead tree, with a single living branch, is not going to last long, and then how is a body ever going to get through this blind place at night without the friendly old landmark?[13]

We have seen that the rhetoric of each educational enterprise, and most specifically the appeals made through the character of the speaker, teach us to attend to things in different ways, to screen in—and out—different truths; in our readings of this passage we found ourselves applying different standards of evidence and proof, following different lines of argument with different expectations to reach different sorts of intellectual satisfactions. And all these differences in our listening are triggered, and to some extent controlled, by the character of the man we hear speaking.

Towards a Flexible Thought and Character

The rhetorical ambition of James's project emerges more strikingly in this light. There are certain distinctive meanings, certain characteristic kinds of statements that Emerson or Twain can work with more easily and more intelligibly because of who they are; their audiences have already been put on the right track by the character of the speaker. But in the same way a speaker is somewhat limited to his distinctive kinds of statement. He can make other kinds of statements, speak of other kinds of truths only with difficulty because by his character he has already called forth the wrong sorts of expectations from his audience: Twain's serious speeches, for example, encountered great, and understandable, audience resistance.

But James wants to be able to make *all* sorts of statements, construct *all* sorts of arguments, appreciate *all* sorts of meanings and reasons; thus no one sort of statement or argument or meaning or reason can become exclusively, characteristically, identifiably his—at least not so distinctively as Emerson's mantic utterings, and Twain's clear-eyed rebellions. James is willing to risk losing the persuasiveness of the immediately identifiable comment. Instead, he will try to draw his audiences into "chasing [him] all over the intellectual landscape"—into following, in an understanding and engaged way, a diversity of statements. James's pluralistic philosophy aims his rhetoric at leading us into a universe of discourse where various levels of statements and arguments and meanings can coexist—literally, a pluralistic universe.[14] James even seems to think that the plurality of levels is necessary, as necessary for rhetorical success as it is for philosophical success. Put more exactly (if more complexly) James seems to think the plurality of levels to be necessary for philosophical success *as he somewhat idiosyncratically defines it* as it is for the particular kinds of rhetorical success at which he aims.

For aesthetic reasons, for symmetry's sake, it would be nice to be able to report that James was an unqualified success as a democratic educator, that he did achieve a rhetoric entirely flexible enough to mediate between "tender-minded" rhetoric like Emerson's and "tough-minded" rhetoric like Twain's, to reconcile their opposing demands. Such a rhetoric could then be characterized as the ideal rhetoric for the intellectual reconstitution, in that it could be most inclusive, ranging from one end of the spectrum of appeal to the other while escaping the limitations of both extremes. It would make rather a symphonic ending, really; the more uncomfortable question is whether it would, as James would say, "respect the facts." One thing is certain: not to press the question at this juncture would be to disrespect James, whose most consistent identifying characteristic—as a philosopher, as an educator, as a rhetorician, as a man—was a vigorous suspicion of easy solutions, of tidiness in what is decidedly a world of loose ends.

An Ambassador of Thought

William James first adopted the role of a mediator and reconciler of thought explicitly in his lectures at the Lowell Institute in December 1906 and in January 1907 at Columbia University; he later collected these lectures ("without development," he hastened to add) into the book *Pragmatism: A New Name for Some Old Ways of Thinking.* In the very opening lecture, James characterized "The Present Dilemma in Philosophy," a split between two sides, both clearly worth caring about, that was tearing the intellectual world apart. But he also claimed that this split could be mended; he promised that the seven succeeding lectures would unpack a philosophical approach capable of functioning as "a mediating way of thinking," a means of reconciliation.[15] James thus is proposing to fulfill the functions of an ambassador: to mediate the specific claims of sides that are constitutionally opposed, and to reconcile the sides generally, so as to create the conditions for a permanent and promising peace and cooperation.

James did achieve many negotiated settlements, as we shall see. Some were accomplished literally by a kind of intellectual shuttle diplomacy; his relation with the almost unreachably brusque Charles Sanders Peirce, whom James credits as "the founder of pragmatism himself," can be seen as this sort of mission.[16] But all the individual settlements in the world cannot "add up" to a stable peace. No one recognized more clearly than James that particular mediations are temporary and that new issues, new possibilities of conflict constantly arise. An ambassador of thought must, then, function on two levels: he must, of course, work on the level of specifics, mediating particular conflicts of the past and present. But he must also operate on a higher level, creating the conditions for the process of peace making to continue. This chapter proposes to examine how and how well James fulfilled both sorts of functions in his role as an ambassador of thought.

I shall argue that James popularized a mode of thinking that was not always flexible enough to mediate individual conflicts. Not only did it fail to mediate all such conflicts in philosophy; it actually failed to mediate some such conflicts in his own character. Put another way, this ambassador of thought never managed a comprehensive plan for settlement, all of whose specific mediations succeeded. On the other hand, some of his mediations *were* demonstrable successes: James did display a distinctive versatility, distinctive powers. He could do things rhetorically that Twain and Emerson could not manage; yet his mediation had its vulnerabilities and limitations too, vulnerabilities and limitations that themselves became distinctive to James, characteristic of him. But strangely, in the very exercise of these powers and limitations — simply as a man — James accomplished more for the reconciliation of thought than he ever managed to do for its mediation. James's most productive diplomacy, ultimately the more important service James rendered as an ambassador of thought, consisted in popularizing not a particular philosophical method, but rather the desirability for purposes of character of philosophizing itself.

James as Mediator

In "The Present Dilemma in Philosophy," James provides lists of conflicting tender-minded and tough-minded traits representing the conflicts in thought and character that he set out to mediate.[17] And in his own character, at least, he does succeed in mediating them — at least sometimes. James the popularizer is neither dogmatic nor sceptical; his best efforts sometimes notwithstanding, he was neither religious nor irreligious; and in his "melioristic" orientation, he was neither optimistic nor pessimistic.

Nothing was further from James's character than dogmatism. As a student, Dickinson S. Miller, put it,

> The one thing apparently impossible to him was to speak ex cathedra from heights of scientific erudition and attainment. There were not a few "ifs" and "maybe's" in his remarks. Moreover he seldom followed for long an orderly system of argument or unfolding of a theory, but was always apt to puncture such systematic pretensions when in the midst of them with some entirely unaffected doubt or question that put the matter upon a basis of common sense at once.[18]

There is a problem with negative examples: how can one show James clearly in the act of not dogmatizing? Yet perhaps his lifelong interest in "physical phenomena" as a valid area for psychological, philosophical, and even theological investigation provides examples of just this sort. James maintained that "a genuine first-hand religious experience . . . is bound to be a heterodoxy to its witnesses, the prophet appearing as a mere lonely madman."[19] On this ground, James tolerated practically every lonely madman claiming to be a prophet whom he came across, even including some who openly tried to defraud observers.[20] Moreover, he found matters of genuine intellectual interest in mediums, hypnotists, fortune-tellers, spiritualists of the wildest sorts. Indeed, *Varieties of Religious Experience* focused almost without exception on the most extraordinary (some critics said the most bizarre) experiences—the vision-fraught monk or the goriest, willingest martyr—and left virtually unconsidered more conventional and mundane varieties.

James refused to rule out even the strangest alternatives because of what inevitably would be lost by ruling any one dogma in.

> "The great field for new discoveries," said a scientific friend to me the other day, "is always the unclassified residuum." Round about the accredited and orderly facts of every science there ever floats a sort of dust-cloud of exceptional observations, of occurrences minute and irregular and seldom met with, which it always proves more easy to ignore than to attend to. The ideal of every science is that of a closed and completed system of truth . . . and so far from free is most men's fancy that, when a consistent and organized scheme of this sort has once been comprehended and assimilated, a different scheme is unimaginable. No alternative, whether to whole or parts, can any longer be conceived as possible. Phenomena unclassifiable within the system are therefore paradoxical absurdities, and must be held untrue. When, moreover, as so often happens, the reports of them are vague and indirect; when they come as mere marvels and oddities rather than as things of serious moment,—one neglects or denies them with the best of scientific consciences. Only the born geniuses let themselves be worried and fascinated by these outstanding exceptions, and get no peace till they are brought within the fold. Your Galileos, Galvanis, Fresnels, Purkinjes, and Darwins are always getting confounded and troubled by insignificant things. Any one will renovate his science who will steadily look after the irregular phenomena. And when the science is renewed, its new formulas often have more of the voice of the exceptions in them than of what were supposed to be the rules.[21]

Dogma, for James, was a human construct onto realities, an artifice intended to fulfill human purposes, address human needs, respond to human interests. James, himself a professional philosopher, is indiscreet enough to portray philosophies as the results of human temperament, thought as a function of character.

> Of whatever temperament a professional philosopher is, . . . his temperament really gives him a stronger bias than any of his mere strictly objective premises. It loads the evidence for him one way or the other, making for a more sentimental or a more hardhearted view of the universe, just as this fact or that principle would.

Because human purposes, needs, interests, and temperaments differ, dogmas will conflict and even try to exclude one another: the philosopher

> feels men of opposite temper to be out of key with the world's character, and in his heart considers them incompetent and "not in it," in the philosophic business, even though they may far excel him in dialectical ability.[22]

Because dogmas are human constructs, they are inherently limited. Something valuable — James is perfectly willing to say "some *reality*" — will always manage to seep through the cracks or spill over the edges to escape the limits of whatever the dogma may be. James refused the temptations of dogmatism because he valued, more than any system, these seepages and spillings, this unclassified residuum. As a constitutive principle of his thought, James respected and argued for every other man's right to believe in what worked for him.

The "unclassified residuum" is what makes possible the renewal of philosophies; and for James, a shiny new philosophy is a wonderful thing. While he was no exclusive adherent of any one dogma, neither was he a radical sceptic of all dogmas. James seems (as Harvard's President Eliot once threatened to introduce him) a most enthusiastic "willer-to-believe." "We believe as much as we can," James once declared. "We would believe everything if we only could." There is in the human heart adequate warrant to believe at least some things — to believe whatever genuinely satisfies our "sentiment of rationality." This subjective satisfaction, contends James, is a legitimate and inevitable part of even the most "objective" philosophical processes. A thinker determines when he has arrived at the rational conception at which he aimed only "by certain subjective marks with which it affects him," James contended. "When he gets the marks, he may know that he has got the rationality."[23]

Far from being sceptical of these marks of belief, James gloried in them and contended that the satisfactions involved were actually a signal of deeper insight.

> Every Jack sees in his own particular Jill charms and perfections to the enchantment of which we stolid onlookers are stone-cold. . . . Is he in excess, being in this matter a maniac? or are we victims of pathological anesthesia as regards Jill's magical importance? Surely the latter; surely to Jack are the profounder truths revealed; surely poor Jill's palpitating little lifethrobs *are* among the wonders of creation, are worthy of this sympathetic interest; and it is to our shame that the rest of us cannot feel like Jack.[24]

So although James would not allow any one dogma to achieve absolute, preemptive authority, at the same time he was not sceptical of the act of believing. It didn't seem to matter what the belief was, particularly: "a thing is important," he said, "if anyone *think* it important." That is to say, a thing is important if it provide to any human being those "subjective marks" he talked about, if it satisfy the "sentiment of rationality." But believing, whatever the dogma, was in itself healthy for the individual human being: "the believer is the true full man." James was neither single-minded dogmatist nor jaundiced-eyed sceptic; perhaps the key to his mediation was his unwill-

ingness to allow one man's "objective" dogma to preclude any other's subjective fulfillment.[25]

Just as James was neither dogmatic nor sceptical, he was neither religious nor irreligious; at least he was neither in the conventional sense of the
terms. As his excursions into psychical researches suggest, James was always willing to give the devil, God, and every other possible object of
worship that strayed into his attention, his due. Whatever satisfied a believer's religious needs, whatever "worked" for these purposes was to be
respected (indeed, his book *The Will to Believe* claims to be a philosophical
defense of each man's *right* to believe what he must). But the sorts of
experiences that worked never included formal institutional religion. "What
keeps religion going is something else than abstract definitions and systems
of logically concatenated adjectives, and something different from faculties
of theology and their professors"; no, true religious experiences were essentially internal, personal, even emotional: "if you ask what these experiences
are, they are conversations with the unseen, voices and visions, responses to
prayer, changes of heart, deliverances from fear, inflowings of help, assur-
ances of support, whenever certain persons set their own internal attitude in
certain appropriate ways." In fact, these experiences are ultimately private.
"Religion . . . shall mean for us the feelings, acts, and experiences of individual men in their solitude."[26]

Since the nature of religious experience for James is private and individual, he simply did not find himself in a position to comment one way or
the other about its validity; if another man underwent what seemed in his
heart of hearts a religious experience, however idiosyncratic an experience
it might be, James felt he had no more say of questioning that feeling than
he did of validating it for public purposes. There was nothing inherently
public about the content of religious experience, and its grounds were ultimately private too — not a matter, that is, for public discourse or community decision.

Personally, James tried to sympathize with the impulse to religion: "we
long for sympathy, for a purely *personal* communication . . . with the soul
of the world." For all the apparent oddness of its expressions, James respected the role religion played in human lives and thus in human history:
"Although all the special manifestations of religion may have been
absurd . . . yet the life of it as a whole is mankind's most important function." James was even so far from irreligious as to admit to having something like religious yearning himself — even, once, a kind of religious experience.[27]

> I spent a good deal of the night in the woods, where the streaming
> moonlight lit up things in a magical checkered play, and it seemed as if
> the Gods of all the nature-mythologies were holding an indescribable

> meeting in my breast with the moral Gods of the inner life. . . . The
> intense significance of some sort, of the whole scene, if one could only
> *tell* the significance; the intense inhuman remoteness of its inner life,
> and yet the intense *appeal* of it; its everlasting freshness and its imme-
> morial antiquity and decay. . . . It was one of the happiest lonesome
> nights of my existence.

And yet James drew back from professing a conscious, comprehending,
willing, believing religiousness, even at so powerful a moment.

> In point of fact, I can't find a single word for all that significance, and
> don't know what it was significant of, so there it remains, a mere
> boulder of *impression*.[28]

George Santayana pushed it farthest—perhaps too far—in asserting that
for James "all faiths were what they were experienced as being in their
capacity of faiths; these faiths, not their objects, were the hard facts we
must respect. We cannot pass except under the illusion of the moment, to
anything firmer or on a deeper level. There was accordingly no sense of
security, no joy, in James's apology for personal religion. He did not really
believe; he merely believed in the right of believing that you might be right
if you believed."[29]

James's mediation between irreligiousness and religiousness seems
somewhat a mediation by default: he took his position because nothing
more ambitious could be established with authority. If "the evidence for
God lies primarily in inner personal experiences," then no definitive overthrow of religion could be made for all people, at all times, everywhere; for
no one can tell a man what is and what is not in his heart of hearts. The
possibility lives, however bizarre its avowed manifestations might seem.
Still it must be emphasized that James never found for himself "what it was
significant of." He was never more than a social member of any church and
was deeply troubled by a very traditional objection to religion—the problem of evil: "the scale of evil actually in sight defies all human
tolerance . . . a God who can relish such superfluities of horror is no God
for human beings to appeal to. His animal spirits are too high. In other
words the 'Absolute' with his one purpose, is not the manlike God of
common people." While James had a respect for religious experience, he
always thought formal doctrinalizations of it monstrously inadequate and
inappropriately focused; ultimately, his attitude toward religion concerned
not what it conceptualized about the next world, but only where it came out
in this one. "The difference religion makes" for James, interprets critic
Patrick Dooley, "is a difference in the way life is lived." James says so
directly: "if religion be a function by which either God's cause or man's
cause is really to be advanced, then he who lives the life of it, however
narrowly, is a better servant. . . . "[30]

If religion be productive, *then* one is better off living its sort of life.

James will not, cannot venture any dogmatic opinion on the "if"; the "then" displays James's peculiar orientation to the future, for this question remains to be decided by thinking and acting people.

James does not talk about religion being "true" or "not true." He talks instead about present and future results—as if an idea's products and promises in this world are the best indices of its validity. He says this explicitly. "Truth *happens* to an idea. It *becomes* true, is *made* true by events. Its verity *is* in fact an event, a process: the process namely of its verifying itself, its veri-*fication*. Its validity is the process of its vali-*dation*." For religion, this notion of truth means that each man helps determine its truth for himself, actually participates in making the truth—even the truth about God. "I confess that I do not see why the very existence of an invisible world may not in part depend on the personal response which any one of us may make to the religious appeal." And in his personal life, James's uneasy resolution of his powerful ambivalence about God has less to do with the idea of *who* he is than with *what* that idea can do:

> It is a curious thing, this matter of God! I can sympathize perfectly with the most rabid hater of him and the idea of him, when I think of the use that has been made of him in history and philosophy as a *starting point*, or premise for grounding deductions. But as an ideal to attain and make probable, I find myself less and less able to do without him.[31]

The notion of truth (and of man's part in making it) operating here had other effects. James sees man as living in a world not yet completely made—not surely, inherently saved, as his transcendental father confidently maintained. Nor was it already inherently damned, as his Calvinist grandfather staunchly believed. A recurrent theme in James's writings is the notion of a finite God whom man must help along. "God himself . . . may draw vital strength and increase of very being from our fidelity." When James asks "Is Life Worth Living?" his answer can be neither absolutely pessimistic nor absolutely optimistic. All that can be confidently said is that it depends on us: "this life . . . *is what we make it, from the moral point of view*." Thus we are actively responsible for what we think and feel to be true. This conviction is the basis of James's mediation between pessimism and optimism—what he calls the "meliorist" point of view.[32]

Clearly James felt some warrant for pessimism. "I take it," he wrote to his friend Benjamin Paul Blood, "that no man is educated who has never dallied with the thought of suicide." The evil in the world was too real for him, he felt it too poignantly, too personally to overlook it. "I can't bring myself, as so many men seem able to, to blink the evil out of sight, and gloss it over. It's as real as the good, and if it is denied, good must be denied too." No, the evil must be recognized—because this recognition creates the possibility for transformation. "Much of what we call evil is due entirely to

the way men take the phenomenon. It can so often be converted into a
bracing and tonic good by a simple change of the sufferer's inner attitude
from one of fear to one of fight."³³

James developed a "strenuous alternative to both pessimism and optimism, the genuine mediation he called "meliorism." To James, "the world
stands really malleable, waiting to receive its final touches at our hands.
Like the kingdom of heaven, it suffers human violence willingly. Man
engenders truth upon it."³⁴ The obstacles to shaping the world beneficiently,
to engendering humanly valuable truth on it, are formidable, of course.
Not the least of these obstacles are human beings themselves. But all in all
for James, the call to transform the world — to help save it — is both a noble
vocation and a personally healthy and invigorating adventure.

> Suppose that the world's author put the case to you before creation,
> saying: "I am going to make a world not certain to be saved, a world
> the perfection of which shall be conditional merely, the condition being
> that each several agent does its own "level best." I offer you the chance
> of taking part in such a world. Its safety, you see, is unwarranted. It is a
> real adventure, with real danger, yet it may win unwarranted. It is a
> social scheme of cooperative work genuinely to be done. Will you join
> the procession? Will you trust yourself and trust the other agents
> enough to face the risk?
>
> Should you in all seriousness, if participation in such a world were
> proposed to you, feel bound to reject it as not safe enough? Would you
> say that, rather than be part and parcel of so fundamentally pluralistic
> and irrational a universe, you preferred to relapse into the slumber of
> nonentity from which you had been momentarily aroused by the temp-
> ter's voice?
>
> Of course if you are normally constituted, you would do nothing
> of the sort. . . . Most of us, I say, would therefore welcome the propo-
> sition and add our *fiat* to the *fiat* of the creation.³⁵

James clearly did find this strenuous mode of life a personally satisfying alternative to both pessimism and optimism. "He told his wife that he
took his profoundest pleasure, not in guaranteed victories, but in those
ventures where there was an element of active tension."³⁶ But the moral
significance of human striving, as well as the pratical importance of its
consequences, forced James to another stand that was not a mediation at
all. It was instead an open, decisive commitment to a tender-minded characteristic: James was an unabashed free-willist.

James as Tender-minded

After James had received his M.D., he decided that he did not want to
practice. He wandered for a while in Europe — wandered both literally and
figuratively, looking for something to engage him. Young William was
never much good at doing nothing, and he soon fell into the deepest depres-

sion of his life. He felt torn between what he called "the moral business" and the apparently competing claims of his scientific training. The depression grew in intensity; this apparently subjective problem actually caused severe physical symptoms — it had, if you will, verifiable "objective" results. Finally it all came to a head on 1 February 1870. James wrote in his diary:

> Today I about touched bottom, and perceive plainly that I must face the choice with open eyes: shall I *frankly* throw the moral business overboard, as one unsuited to my innate aptitudes, or shall I follow it, and it alone, making everything else merely stuff for it?[37]

More and more desperately, James cast about for a way to salvage a sense of personal responsibility and significance until he happened upon an essay by the French philosopher Charles Renouvier. "In 1870 he was peculiarly attuned to a gospel such as Renouvier offered — the right, namely, to believe what his moral will dictated, or a philosophical justification of the attitude required for his personal salvation." In Renouvier, James had found a justification for free will that satisfied him, and he promptly decided, "My first act of free will shall be to believe in free will."[38]

Renouvier was to be a lifelong influence on James; Perry judges him "the greatest individual influence upon the development of James's thought."[39] Renouvier's phenomenalism, his pluralism, his fideism, his moralism and theism all were reflected in James's thought. But no such contribution ever exceeded in importance the justification of free will, a doctrine James immediately embraced and reaffirmed at every opportunity throughout his life. It was the key, of course, to his "meliorism"; how could a man choose to make things better unless he really could choose? In the same way it was essential to his religious ideas, and, as we shall see, to his pluralism too. Perhaps no one concept is more basic to James's thought or more productive of it. Certainly on none of the other tough- or tender-minded characteristics does James come down more decisively and identifiably on one side. On the issue of free will James did not mediate: here he was consistently and vigorously tender-minded.

But on other issues too — in the bulk of the issues he raises with the list — James did not simply mediate but instead would participate and take a side. As apparently unbecoming as it was for an ambassador trying to reconcile opposing factions, he was often partisan. In terms of his list of characteristics, we find him taking one side or the other as often as not; and although he had his tender-minded moments, James was more often tough-minded.

James as Tough-minded

From the very beginning of his psychological experimentations, James was materialistic, not idealistic; sensationalistic, not intellectualistic; an empiricist, going by "facts," rather than a rationalist, going by "principles." But he was all these things together in a way that "turned around" their usual orientation from the past and present to the future.

"There is no such superstition as the idolatry of the *Whole*," James declared. He regarded "the Whole" as an idea, an intellectual abstraction with its tender-minded uses, but with no necessary authority over particular parts, elements, and individuals. The advantage of a materialist, sensationalist, empiricist approach is precisely that it "lays the explanatory stress upon the part, the element, the individual, and treats the whole as a collection and the universal as an abstraction." In *Pragmatism* and throughout the rest of his work, James gradually unpacked his argument against rationalism, and articulated an alternative that even his old friend Charles Sanders Peirce called "materialistic to the core."[40]

James makes this flip-flop perhaps too quickly. An Emerson can manage without much transition, but for someone tough-minded (or even a mediator) to try it seems confusing and disconcerting. In the lists of characteristics, rationalism is contrasted with empiricism, intellectualism with sensationalism, idealism with materialism; and in all these cases, pragmatism is originally offered as the mediation of the contrast. But as early on as the second lecture and throughout the remaining ones, James hammers away at the contrasts of rationalism, intellectualism, and idealism *not* with empiricism, sensationalism, or materialism, but — explicitly, mind you — with his philosophy of *pragmatism!*

> Pragmatism is uncomfortable away from facts. Rationalism is comfortable only in the presence of abstractions.

> But now, instead of resting in principles, after this stagnant intellectualist fashion, let us apply the pragmatic method to the question.

> In this first vague conviction of the world's unity, there is so little to take hold of that we hardly know what we mean by it. The only way to get forward with out notion is to treat it pragmatically.

> Surely in this field of truth it is the pragmatists and not the rationalists who are the more genuine defenders of the universe's rationality.

> The import of the difference between pragmatism and rationalism is now in sight throughout its whole extent. The essential contrast is that for rationalism reality is ready-made and complete from all eternity, while for pragmatism it is still in making and awaits parts of its complexion from the future. On the one side the universe is absolutely secure, on the other it is still pursuing its adventures.

And privately, James admitted to this tough-mindedness: James told Theodore Flournoy of "my system of tychistic and pluralistic philosophy of pure experience"; more explicitly, James informed Francois Pillon that "my philosophy is what I call a radical empiricism."[41]

The tough-mindedness seems to have issued directly from James's own character—his "temperament," as he would have it. The tough-mindedness made perfect sense to George Santayana, who knew James as teacher, colleague, and friend. "Where one's gift is, there will one's faith be also; and to this poet appearance was the only reality." Ralph Barton Perry also remarked the extraordinary "acuity of his senses—the voluminousness and richness of the experience which he received through them," and emphasized "the prominence of that experience and of its underlying motive in his life as a whole." James indeed frequently took satisfaction from such acuity in his distinctively vivid perceptions.[42]

> Scenery seems to wear in one's consciousness better than any other element in life. . . . I have often been surprised to find what a predominant part in my own spiritual experience it has played, and how it stands out as almost the only thing the memory of which I should like to carry with me beyond the veil, unamended and unaltered.

> Today everything is a-dripping, the earth has a moving smell, and the sky is full of spots of melting blue.[43]

> I have spent all my mornings and afternoons except yesterday morning alone in the woods, fields, and rocks, with the breath of the woods in my lungs, the smell of the laurels in my nose, the surf pounding rhythmically upon my ear, and the beautiful wash of light before my eyes. It takes all the wrinkles and puckers out of you and washes you whole again, filling you with courage and independence of what may happen in the future.

> The steady, heavy roaring of the surf comes through the open window, borne by the delicious salt breeze over the great bank of stooping willows, field and fence. The little horse-chestnut trees are no bigger, the cow with the broad face still crops the grass. The broad sky and sea are whanging with the mellow light. All is as it was and will be.[44]

> The green is of the vividest, splendid trees and acres, and the air itself an *object,* holding watery vapor, tenuous smoke, and ancient sunshine in solution, so as to yield the most exquisite minglings and gradations of silvery brown and blue and pearly gray.

> God bless the American climate, with its transparent, passionate, impulsive variety and headlong fling. There are deeper, slower tones of earnestness and moral gravity here, no doubt, but yours is more like youth and youth's infinite and touching promise.[45]

James believed that there was value to articulating such sensual perceptions, even if on reflection no system could be built up around it. "There is in the living act of perception always something that glimmers and twinkles and will not be caught, and for which reflection comes too late."[46]

Perry, in his editor's preface to *Essays in Radical Empiricism,* even claims that James came to regard his tough-minded empiricism as possibly more fundamental and important than pragmatism itself.[47] Ultimately, James the mediator fell back on his scientific training. He frankly admitted

> the hours I spent with Agassiz taught me the difference between all possible abstractionists and all livers in the light of the world's concrete fullness, that I have never been able to forget it. Both kinds of mind have their place in the infinite design, but there can be no question as to which kind lies the nearer to the divine type of thinking.[48]

Yet it should be noted that James put a peculiar twist on his materialism, sensationalism, and empiricism that was not anticipated or constrained by the simple categories of the tough-tender list; fundamental as it was to his philosophy and to his rhetoric, this was a tough-mindedness of a peculiarly turned-around sort. For James, "truth is what we work *toward,* a terminus, not a starting point . . . the final synthesis which we ourselves help to establish." He declares that "the truth of a thing or idea is its meaning, or its density, that which grows out of it," thus reversing diametrically "the opinion of the empiricists that the meaning of an idea is that which it has grown from." In "An Empirical Survey of Empiricisms," John Dewey took special note of this

> phase of the philosophy of William James, namely, that validity is not a matter of origin nor to antecedents, but of consequents. This statement, associated with the philosophy of all pragmatism, is often treated as if it were directed merely against previous rationalisms. Its more direct objective of attack is previous empiricisms . . . the whole point of James's philosophy, which comes out better in some chapters of his *Psychology,* I think, especially in the last chapter of the second volume, than in his lectures on *Pragmatism,* is that the value of ideas is independent of their origin, that it is a matter of their outcome as they are used in directing new observation and new experience.

As James put it, most pungently of all, "by their fruits ye shall know them, not by their roots." James was a radical empiricist, yes; but even that philosophical commitment was meaningful essentially in its mediation of, and with, the human world.[49]

James's orientation to future results leads directly into his pluralism. In a sense, James's categorization of pluralism as tough-minded is an active loading of the dice in favor of the tough-minded. Pluralism would have seemed an ideal mediating characteristic. This tolerance, this willingness for a "strung-along" and not too "buttoned-down" situation seems perfectly situated (between starchy monism and something like relativism) to give every side its due, if no more. This arrangement would keep the symmetry

James has been establishing between, on the tender hand, one authoritative, certain meaning (a dogma, a religion, a reason for optimism, a set of ideals, an intellectual, rational system); and on the tough hand no meaning beyond the hard and potentially chaotic facts of sense data (scepticism, irreligiousness, pessimism, materialism, sensationalism, empiricism). Those facts could indeed be chaotic:

> Can we realize for an instant what a cross-section of all existence at a definite point of time would be? While I talk and the flies buzz, a seagull catches a fish at the mouth of the Amazon, a tree falls in the Adirondack wilderness, a man sneezes in Germany, a horse dies in Tartary, and twins are born in France. What does that mean? Does the contemporaneity of these events with each other and with a million more as disjointed as they form a rational bond between them, and unite them into anything that means for us a world? Yet just such a collateral contemporaneity, and nothing else, is the real order of the world. It is an order with which we have nothing to do but to get away from it as fast as possible. As I said, we break it: we break it into histories, and we break it into arts, and we break it into sciences; and then we begin to feel at home.[50]

Pluralism as a mediating characteristic would allow the tough diversity of meanings that is brought on by the diversity in human experience without utterly relativizing grounds for authority. Some kind of authority is, after all, an ambassador's best hope for a progressing discussion between sides, rather than continuous and unmoving declaration *at* each other. It is the only means to a mediated peace and cooperation.

James tries to balance — and he admits, precariously — tender, certain authority with the potentially chaotic diversity of tough sense experience in a mediate solution involving a diversity of authorities in between. But in locating pluralism in relativism's seemingly more appropriate place as tough-minded, he seems to put the emphasis of the "diplomatic" mission of pluralism there too — without any account of what one does with relativism, or why pluralism belongs there instead. In this abrupt and unargued siding with the tough-minded, it seems to me, James doomed his mission of mediation to at least partial failure — unnecessarily.

We have already met with most of the principles behind James's pluralism and behind the rhetoric that popularized it. Systems of knowledge are human constructs, devised to address particular needs, purposes, interests, and temperaments, which naturally threaten to conflict: "the greatest enemy of one of our truths may be the rest of our truths." His arguments against "imperialism" among systems were based firmly in this notion of the meaning of truth.

> Hands off — neither the whole of truth nor the whole of good is revealed to any single observer, although such observer gains a partial superiority of insight from the peculiar position in which he stands.

For the pluralistic James, preemptive monistic claims evidenced ignorance of what knowledge is—it was literally (in our terms, "ethically") unhealthy. "I am convinced that the desire to formulate truths is a virulent disease."[51] "He always left the impression that there was more," says Perry; "that he knew there was more; and that the more to come might, for all one knew, throw a very different light on the matters under discussion. He respected his universe too much to believe that he could carry it under his own hat." And James never tired of saying so. "There never can be a state of facts to which new meaning may not truthfully be added. . . . "[52]

James thought that pluralism's greatest attribute as a philosophic method was its wide-open strung-along compatibility with "the moral and dramatic expressiveness of life." "It seems wholly possible to argue," he said, "that life presents itself to us in terms which are not wholly comprehensible. Pluralism leaves us with mysteries on our hands, but it cannot well do otherwise."[53] Clearly pluralism had advantages as James's rhetorical method too; his open-hearted pluralism accounted for some of his character's appeal. But it was just this pluralism that exposed him to the fiercest criticism that his thought received and seems to reveal to us some limitations and vulnerabilities of his character. Yet, in the bargain, it revealed some virtues that his "tough-and-tender" lists never anticipated, virtues that perhaps constitute James's strongest argument for intellectual reconstitution—in several senses, an ethical argument.

Pragmatism came under an immediate hail of criticism by professional philosophers, including heavyweights like Bertrand Russell, G. E. Moore, and F. H. Bradley. The criticisms, on the whole, were distinguished by their tone of personal attack and their often startling misreading (and sometimes plain ignorance) of what James had in fact said. James responded to these criticisms both ably and amiably, eventually collecting his responses into the volume *The Meaning of Truth*. These first objections are of limited interest for our purposes, but let us at least examine the two predominant types.

The simpler criticism leveled at James was the charge of plain capriciousness, of utter relativism: that the stress on individual purposes, needs, interests, and temperaments would permit any belief or idea to be truth if it fulfilled those purposes and needs, satisfied those interests and temperaments. Thus, this argument runs, in James's system "truth" was predicated arbitrarily, without reference to any sharable, publicly validatable standard. But such criticism overlooked the difficulties in finding a belief or idea that would indeed "work" in James's sense—that would square with, would mediate between previous truths on the one hand and the particular new experience on the other, damaging previous truth and common sense as little as possible while leading to a sensible, verifiable terminus. "To affirm that values are relative to and dependent on our interests is not to say that they are dependent on our opinion about them"; while each interest "is subjective in the sense that an individual finds it emanating from himself, but objective in the sense that it is an empirical datum."[54]

A related line of criticism viewed James's pluralism as at best merely subjectivist, and at worst solipsistic. No "objective" reference to the external, shared world was possible if the knowledge each man has is merely an experienced relation within experience, if we each are sealed up within the subjective experiences that are made from our private and individual purposes, needs, interests, and temperaments. James isn't even *relativistic* toward the world, this argument claims; he can't relate with any confidence or authority to the world outside himself at all. In some respects, James does seem to suffer from this limitation, for example his resistance to the notion that there is an inherently public dimension to religion, a legitimate public interest in its discussion, and even an important potential for communal decisions in terms of it.

Yet this objection overlooks an essential — Patrick Dooley says the essential — insight of James's thought: the humanistic bent of his epistemology.[55] The human knower is not a disinterested spectator, but an actively involved selector; as early as the *Principles*, James was defining attention as an active process of selection. "As an 'interested selector,' man's knowledge is not a neutral apprehension of a static, finished reality, rather our ideas function as guides for interacting with reality." The knower is necessarily involved in the world, remaking it as it remakes him until they both successfully "work" together; and ultimately, James declares, "the existence of the object, whenever the idea asserts it 'truly,' is the only reason . . . why the idea does work successfully."[56]

But after *The Meaning of Truth* appeared and the first, seemingly impulsive criticisms had been answered, more thoughtful challenges emerged. James never managed to answer these more sophisticated objections as decisively as he had the earlier ones; in fact he confessed, gratefully, that they were objections well-taken, and he consciously tried to adapt.

In Patrick Dooley's words, "James has always been praised for insightfulness and cursed for his lack of continuity and consistency." Critics as sympathetic as the reverent Ralph Barton Perry and the enthusiastic Gordon Allport join with those as resolutely unsympathetic as A. O. Lovejoy to decry James's "looseness of argument," his "dearth of selectivity" — what James spoke of as his "lax popular rhetoric."[57]

Perhaps George Santayana phrased this criticism most articulately. While recognizing and honoring James's successes in popular education, he maintained that the source of his distinctive powers also accounted for certain distinctive shortcomings. Santayana suggested that a philosophy so essentially disorderly and unselective was inadequate precisely for those purposes and interests about which James cared most — for instance his explicit concern for "the moral and dramatic expressiveness of life."[58]

> James — and this is what gives such romantic warmth to these writings of his — disclaims all antecedent or superior knowledge, listens to the testimony of each witness in turn, and only by accident allows us to feel that he is swayed by the eloquence and vehemence of some of them rather than of others. This method is modest, generous, and impartial; but if James intended, as I think he did, to picture the *drama* of human belief, with its risks and triumphs, the method was inadequate. Dramatists never hesitate to assume, and to let the audience perceive, who is good and who is bad, who wise and who foolish, in their pieces; otherwise their work would be as impotent dramatically as scientifically. The tragedy and comedy of life lie precisely in the contrast between the illusions or passions of the characters and their true condition and fate, hidden from them at first, but evident to the author and the public. If in our diffidence and scrupulous fairness we refuse to take this judicial attitude, we shall be led to strange conclusions.[59]

Whether James's philosophy was able ultimately to account for life's drama as philosophy is somewhat beyond our study of his rhetoric; but we can readily discover how James's breezy, not overexact approach could invite trouble from his specialist colleagues while confusing his popular audiences.

Perhaps James's trouble with his colleagues can be illustrated best right where it began. When James was inundated by the tide of criticism of *The Will to Believe,* he admitted ruefully that he had started it all for himself by his terminology — started it in fact with the very name of the book: "a luckless title," he mourned, "which should have been the *Right* to Believe." Later, suffering the objections to *Pragmatism* that we have already discussed, James admitted "how unlucky a word pragmatism has been to attach to our theory of truth. It seems to most people to *exclude* intellectual relations and interests, but all it *means* is to say that these are subjective interests like all the others, and not the sole ones concerned in determining the beliefs that count as true."[60]

James did try to remedy the sloppiness which his critics pointed out; but privately, he was hurt by the constantly personal nature of their criticism. The nastiness with which James's colleagues consistently greeted him is worth a moment's notice. One index of the criticism's tone is the unusual degree of parody that this supposedly specialist analysis contained, parody of James's characteristic faults. *The Will to Believe* was discussed as *The Will to Deceive* and *The Will to Make-Believe; The Varieties of Religious Experience,* which appeared about the same time as did Ernest Thompson Seton's book of animal stories, was tabbed *Wild Religions I Have Known.* James's hurt here is understandable. For him, the philosopher was first and always a man; thought always represented character in an intimately, re-

vealingly personal way. Indeed, as we have seen, human feelings were ele-
mental to his philosophy. James liked to quote a colleague, Howison of
California: " 'what we philosophers really need is praise! Harris calls it
"recognition"—but what it is is really praise, just bald rank praise.' Dear
Howison! To tell the truth so simply!"[61] James the thinker always remained
James the man—indeed, this was a strength of his thought—and always felt
a little pained at personal assaults. Candidly, it is difficult to find a philosopher who, in supposedly professional criticism, was so often attacked in so
personal a way.

But not only did James's characteristic faults invite trouble from his
colleagues; they created a certain confusion in his democratic audiences. It
was a little like the vaguely edified confusion that Emerson induced; but
Emerson had by his character established a field of discourse in which that
could be meaningful. James, on the other hand, had spoken—sometimes at
least, and as we saw he learned more and more this way—as the exacting
empiricist. Once such a stance was established, it resisted and suspected—
and perhaps, as in Twain, tended to undermine—any such quick transition
back to the transcending sage. Audiences who were suddenly asked to cope
with oracular musings like "the art of being wise is the art of knowing what
to overlook" or "any author is easy if you catch the center of his vision"
tended to demand more information before being at all persuaded—precisely because they had been trained by James to discover what statements
mean exactly.[62]

Emerson and Twain had accustomed their audiences to certain kinds of
truths and screened out others by their characters. James's audiences had
been taught to ask some tough-minded questions, to use some methodical
ways of rooting out the truth. Now he seemed to be asking his audiences to
suspend all that, to unlearn those lessons for his special case. Democratic
audiences were resistant by their nature to such a special, unegalitarian,
unaccountedly aristocratic claim.

James was sensitive to these problems in his mediation. He attributed
them, interestingly, to his mode of composition.

By far the largest part of his writing (everything but *The Meaning of
Truth, Essays in Radical Empiricism,* and *Some Problems of Philosophy: A
Beginning of an Introduction to Philosophy*) began as lectures, and he felt
that this "free and easy and personal way of writing has made me an object
of loathing. . . . I am rather tired of awakening that feeling, which more
popular lecturing on my part will probably destine me to increase."[63] James
was recognizing in himself what we saw in Emerson and in Twain: his
rhetoric shaped his thought—not merely rhetoric in abstract theory, but in
its concrete practice on the circuit of public speech.

James declared a firm purpose of amendment—"I've had enough of
the squashy popular-lecture"—but promptly thereafter he agreed to take on

the Hibbert lectures at Manchester College. He collected these into another book, *A Pluralistic Universe,* which of course was decried for the familiar old flaws. So it went, characteristically, for James's philosophy.[64]

James never did persuade these critics; and without reflecting on the accuracy of their criticism, the sheer undeniable fact of it suggests that James did not entirely succeed in popularizing a mediation of thought. The ambassador had worked out some particular settlements, of course, but they did not add up to a comprehensive and continuing peace. Yet there was another sense, an important sense, in which James's characteristic style was effective for democratic education.

Just as James's tough-and-tender lists proved inadequate for complete philosophical mediation, they are inadequate for complete characterization too; what is appealing and effective in his democratic education involves not only "mediating" characteristics, but *reconciling* characteristics too. They can emerge most quickly and clearly if we look first at James's classroom rhetoric.

The Ambassador as Reconciler:
(A) Man Thinking Again

In a letter to a former student, James counseled, "let me advise you in your teaching to be as methodical as possible. Let them see the plan of the forest as well as the individual tree. I find my incurable disorderliness of method always stood in my way. Too incoherent and rambling." Yet his pupils saw actual advantages in James's characteristic style. As a student in James's 1881–1882 class on Mill's *Logic* recalled,

> The very fact that he had not well organized the course . . . gave him opportunity to show his own personal reactions. He was thinking his way clear in regard to the points discussed and took students with him in his thinking. He was refreshingly straightforward and frank, did not hesitate even to express a different view today from what he did yesterday, and to say, perhaps, that yesterday he was all wrong. . . .

This was certainly not the rigidly structured professional argumentation that James's critics demanded of him, and that he was frequently tempted to give them. Curiously, however, it was precisely the sort of "Teaching of Philosophy in Our Colleges" for which James had rather passionately argued in an article by that name. The article appeared in 1876 and was reworked and repeated thereafter on the circuit, just at the outset of his career as a teacher, a popular lecturer, and a publishing philosopher, at the point of his life when he had ceased wandering—when he had found himself.

> What doctrines students take from their teachers are of little conse-
> quence provided they catch from them the living, philosophic attitude
> of mind, the independent, personal look at all the data of life, and the
> eagerness to harmonize them.[65]

There is an echo of Emerson here, a resonance of the fundamental truths
accessible simply to a man thinking. As C. Hartley Grattan put it, James
"gave his thoughts, like Emerson, by a process of moral radiation rather
than by systematic exposition." The essential content of the rhetoric may
not always manage to be the systematic philosophy "pragmatism," exactly,
but that doesn't faze James. His deeper rhetorical concern has a different,
more ethical character. And even his distinctive flaws of disorderliness suggest that his thinking was most fundamentally of this character too.

> The philosophy of William James cannot be forced within the bounds
> of any orderly system. He had no interest in intellectual architecture: he
> was an explorer, and not a surveyor or map maker. Love of adventure,
> and insatiable curiosity were his profoundest traits. He was inventive
> and positive, quick to affirm the latest ideas that flashed upon him
> without asking the consent of the ideas which he had already af-
> firmed—more concerned with the new wine than the old bottles.

Santayana—student, then colleague of James at Harvard—drew this
dichotomy more sharply, insisting that the real content of James's intellectual activity was far less importantly a matter of what he knew than what
and who he was.

> What is a good life? Had William James, had the people about
> him . . . any notion of that? I cannot think so. They had much expe-
> rience of personal goodness, and love of it; they had standards of
> character and right conduct; but as to what might render human exist-
> ence good, excellent, beautiful, happy and worth having as a whole,
> their notions were utterly thin and barbarous.[66]

Whether or not one quite agrees with Santayana or finds any of the
other criticisms as devastating as they were so ferociously intended to be, it
is nonetheless the plain fact that James, as mediator of thought, had no
effective comprehensive plan for settlements. Pragmatism was not then,
nor is it now, universally accepted as a philosophic method. Pragmatism as
James practiced it even had failed to mediate more than half of those
conflicts it explicitly set out to mediate: while James was neither dogmatic
nor sceptical, neither religious nor irreligious, neither optimistic nor pessimistic, he did side with the tender-minded free-willists, and with the
tough-minded empiricists, sensationalists, materialists, and pluralists. So
while James's mediations were a productive start, they clearly fell short of
reconciling all the oppositions he detected and addressed.

Yet James had never felt it necessary to "settle the universe's hash"
definitively all by himself. It is unlikely he expected to resolve all conflicts,

and would probably have been the first to stir up trouble if someone else managed it. As Santayana put it,

> I think it would have depressed him if he had had to confess that any important question was finally settled. He would still have hoped that something might turn up on the other side, and that just as the . . . hangman was about to dispatch the poor convicted prisoner, an unexpected witness would ride up in hot haste, and prove him innocent.[67]

James merely tried, and manfully, to do what he could and to involve as many of his listeners in the process, acting as if a diversity of thoughts and characters were the greatest ally in the mediation and reconciliation of thought. His most compelling resource for this involvement — and for James, literally a source for his own involvement, his own philosophizing — was, in reconciliation as it was in mediation, still his character.[68] He used the appeals of his character to the process of philosophizing, to keeping the questions open and the discussion going. For James, again, the continued involvement of people — their purposes, needs, interests, and temperaments, in short their characters — was the best hope for the renewal, the reinvigoration of thought. Philosophy depended not on man thinking exclusively and independently, however transcendentally representative he might be. It depended instead on people thinking, in all their diversity, together.

To attract this diverse audience, James used a diversity of appeals besides his tough and tender and mediating characteristics. These included his resolute fairness; his ability to identify with all sorts of ideas and people; his warm sense of humor; and, ultimately, an almost inexhaustible versatility of further characteristics. This flexibility was enhanced — it "grew up" — in his efforts at mediation; a genuinely persuasive diversity, a pluralism of character was found in this function of reconciliation. Once again, in practicing the rhetoric of democratic education, a popularizer had found his voice.

James's uncanny ability to do justice — both philosophically and rhetorically — to other sides is precious rare in philosophers, in educators, in people generally. It was an innate, immediate empathy with whatever others needed to say (coupled with an affirmation of their right to say it) that seemed to issue from both his thought and his character.

> In his own person he was ready enough to face the mystery of things, and whatever the womb of time might bring forth; but until the curtain was rung down on the last act of the drama (and it might have no last act), he wished the intellectual cripples and the moral hunchbacks not to be jeered at; perhaps they might turn out to be the heroes of the play.[69]

The temptation here is, quite frankly, to release a flood of examples; for this is James's most frequent, as well as possibly his most winning characteristic. I forbear, mercifully, except to grant a taste.

James spent a week at Lake Chautauqua in the summer of 1896, and it seems the Chautauquans had made it seem like much longer—not because they were a resistant, bad audience, but because they were so solemnly, resolutely, unplayfully *good.*

> I've been meeting minds so earnest and helpless that it takes them half an hour to get from one idea to its immediately adjacent next neighbor, and that with infinite creaking and groaning. And when they've got to the next idea, they lie down on it with their whole weight and can get no farther, like a cow on a doormat, so that you can get neither in nor out with them.

For a week James wrote uncharacteristically complaining letters about the affectingly virtuous Chautauquans he'd met. If ever there was an audience to which he felt himself actually averse, this was surely, emphatically it. Nonetheless, he could not close without conceding: "Still, glibness is not all. Weight is something, even cow-weight." The extent of this capacity for empathy is reflected and mildly self-satirized in one of his favorite sayings: "if at the last day," he used to remark, "all creation was shouting hallelujah and there remained one cockroach with unrequited love, *that* could spoil the universal harmony." Perry summarized it this way: for James, "in metaphysics, as in human relations, the chief source of illumination is sympathy."[70]

I suspect that all this had roots in James's own powerful experience of melancholy, his "touching bottom" in the directionless years just after he received his M.D., just before he "found himself." But whatever the source, James—his consistently cheery vigor notwithstanding—never lost touch with this side of life.

> Unsuspectedly from the bottom of every fountain of pleasure, as the old poet said, something bitter rises up a touch of nausea . . . a whiff of melancholy, things that sound a knell, for fugitive as they may be, they . . . often have an appalling convincingness.

> In the deepest heart of all of us there is a corner in which the ultimate mystery of things works sadly.[71]

But the other side of this coin is shiny: James's sparkling, ever-present wit. It really was ever-present; no subject was too serious for some deflating. And it actually seems humor was one of those factors that could subvert the continuity and tone of his arguments. James, typically, told this anecdote on himself and one of his students.

> At a lecture one day, when I was in the full flood of my eloquence, his
> voice rose above mine, exclaiming: "but doctor, doctor! to be serious
> for a moment. . . . "[72]

Sometimes James's humor was as inadvertent as Emerson's; in James's
case, it was less a consequence of misjudging the audience than the distracting result of attempting too many things at once. "A friend has described a
scene at a little class that, in a still earlier year, met in James's own study. In
the efforts to illustrate he brought out a blackboard. He stood it on a chair
and in various other positions, but could not at once write upon it, hold it
steady, and keep it in the class's vision. Entirely bent on what he was doing,
his efforts resulted at last in his standing it on the floor while he lay down at
full length, holding it with one hand, drawing with the other and continuing the flow of his commentary."[73]

But humor was not always a distraction. James's keen sense of the
absurd and the amusing provided him the means to popularize difficult
ideas. For example, his class in the philosophy of nature was discussing
Spencer's law:

> Evolution is an integration of matter and concomitant dissipation of
> motion; during which the matter passes from an indefinite, incoherent
> homogeneity to a definite, coherent heterogeneity; and during which
> the retained motion undergoes a parallel transformation.

Not quite the stuff of parlor conversation — but under James's deft comic
touch, it came out rather more memorably.

> Evolution is a change from a no-howish untalkaboutable all-alikeness
> to a somehowish and in general talk-aboutable not-all-alikeness by con-
> tinuous stick-togetherations and somethingelseifications.

Surely this deft, gentle touch helped James to "get away with" more. Who
he was as a man enabled him to discuss things with an audience engagingly
that other speakers could not; who he was as a man enabled him to involve
his audiences in topics complicated enough to send their attention spans
scurrying for cover if it had come from someone else. Perry records one
student's reminiscence:

> I still remember vividly how James used to arrive . . . how handsome
> he looked on the edge of the platform and saying in a casual conversa-
> tional tone. "There is no primal reagibility in a protoplasm."[74]

What is striking about who James the reconciler seemed to be is how
much more there is to say, not only about the world, but about himself —
how many more persuasive characteristics he displayed. James as reconciler
was, for example, distinctively American; biographer Edward Moore's
premise was that

the intellectual biography of William James is almost an intellectual biography of America. To understand the problems which James coped with intellectually and to respond perceptively to the solutions which he arrived at is to understand the inner life of more individual Americans than would be the case if one studied any other representative thinker.

And James never was very reluctant to employ a specifically egalitarian appeal.

Why may not the world be a sort of republican banquet . . . where all the qualities of being respect one another's personal sacredness, yet sit at the common table of space and time?

In just this line of criticism, the somewhat unsympathetic Santayana even claimed that James was, at heart, neither a scholar nor a philosopher at all, but rather a closet anti-intellectual.[75]

All this was related to the vigorous part of James's personality, his sheer, vibrant physicality, how he struck his listeners as "alive to his fingertips," "an irresistible gust of life," with the vitality of a "nervous thoroughbred."[76] Surely his energy, his eagerness, his zestfulness were some of the most compelling aspects of his popularization. And in this he seemed very literally to characterize — to give a persuasive, authoritative human identity to — certain of his principles:

When a man's pursuit gradually makes his face shine and grow handsome, you may be sure it is a worthy one.

I have often thought the best way to define a man's character would be to seek out the particular mental or moral attitude in which, when it came upon him, he felt himself most deeply and intensely active and alive. At such moments there is a voice inside which speaks and says: "*This* is the real me!"[77]

The list of attributes goes on. But let us not commit James's sin here; let us not be so unselective that we fail to convey the real moral expressiveness of the man himself. The man himself must serve as summary; he is the only image rich enough. James, in his function as an ambassador of thought, was always man thinking. But immediately we must amend that: *a* man thinking. The difference between the way Emerson and James functioned in this regard is precisely that Emerson is Man in his most transcendent (and least individual) mode, and James is *a* man. This precious human individuality is, as we have seen, every bit as central to his enterprise as Emerson's transcendency was to the philosophy that he popularized. Of our three authors, James has shown the most flexible popularizing ethos. Precisely in the popularizing of his thought, he has shown us the most about himself. In this he seems not merely a man thinking, but a warm, empathetic, lively, curious, gentle, articulate, believable, thinking friend — who will stay a friend through the inevitable vagaries of thought.

This is not to say that we should forget his flaws. As students of rhetoric, and of James, we must in good faith note how his interests or his humor or his compassion or his melancholy or his curiosity or his doubt do occasionally tangle up with the tough continuity and consistency he elsewhere struggles to promote. This can be to his disadvantage as a mediator. But in a characteristically compelling way, it is to his advantage as a reconciler:

> the spirit would sometimes come upon him, and, leaning his head on his hand, he would let fall golden words, picturesque, fresh from the heart, full of the knowledge of good and evil. Incidentally there would crop up some humorous characterisation, some candid confession of doubt or of instinctive preference, some pungent scrap of learning; radicalisms plunging sometimes into the sub-soil of all human philosophers; and, on occasion, thoughts of simple wisdom and wistful piety, the most unfeigned and manly that anybody ever had.

Though his characteristics sometimes snarled his philosophy, William James has given us in his popularization a sense of how "a human life is greater than all its possible critics" and how that greatness can invigorate thinking.[78]

"Few teachers have been so loved and valued as a friend."[79] Few popularizers are respected so deeply or known so personally. Perhaps we can say that James, in his attempts at democratic education, fulfilled most fully the notion of character in its relation to thought that Emerson articulated, the notion behind this whole business of character in popularization: "But do your thing and I shall know you. Do your work and you shall reinforce yourself." For James's work as democratic educator ultimately did involve and identify his character.

> Let me repeat once more that a man's vision is the great fact about him. . . . a philosophy is the expression of a man's intimate character, and all definitions of the universe are but the deliberately adopted reactions of human characters upon it.[80]

James is a character we come to value most not in his particular functioning—his often (but not always) successful functioning—as mediator, but in his transcending identity as reconciling friend.

As a friend, he seeks to include us in his rhetoric, to keep our conversation going with matters of real substance at stake. In this, James's mediating, reconciling, meaningfully friendly rhetoric is particularly appropriate to a democratic audience; for democracy, as we have seen, characteristically depends for its survival and prosperity on its conversations continuing meaningfully and substantively—characteristically depends, that is, on the friendly rhetoric of men thinking together.[81]

Perhaps, then, it is the greatest compliment we can pay to James as a democratic educator, a man who "never took a day's journey in the realms of thought without *meeting* somebody," to say that when these meetings took place, James would make friends. James was often a successful mediator of past and present conflicts in thought; but his greatest rhetorical success lay in his reconciliation of men thinking, so that they might make their future — and themselves — together.[82] The thought which James characterizes, and with which his listeners identify, is, in the most rhetorically appealing and intellectually productive senses, ethical education.

> I merely point out to you that, as a matter of fact, certain persons do exist with an enormous capacity for friendship and for taking delight in other people's lives; and that such persons know more of truth than if their hearts were not so big.[83]

Education in Thought and Character:
The Rhetorical Reconstitution
of Democracy

> The problems that vex democracy seem unmanageable by demo-
> cratic methods.
>
> — Walter Lippman

> If there ever was a country where eloquence was a power, it is the
> United States. Is it not worth the ambition of every generous
> youth to train and arm his mind with all the resources of knowl-
> edge of method, of grace and of character, to serve such a constit-
> uency?
>
> — Ralph Waldo Emerson

> The rhetorical function is the function of adjusting ideas to people
> and of people to ideas.
>
> — Donald Bryant

IN democracy, the people rule — that is, they rule insofar as they make their own decisions. But those decisions grow more complex, more intellectually demanding every day. The average citizen — "Charley Six-Pack" as one politician described him — is called to deliberate on an increasingly formidable variety of issues, each demanding a different way of knowing. Decisions must be made on, among other things, problems of toxic waste disposal, the macroeconomics and ethics of the "supply side," the reliability of nuclear power plant construction and operation, the relative military and negotiating merits of the American cruise missile versus the Soviet backfire bomber, the proper limits and accountability of recombinant DNA research, the cost/benefit ratio of the space program, and whether exploration of the cosmos ought to be measured by some different standard — say, the program's capacity to rekindle our sense of wonder and shared adventure and national purpose. After settling these matters, he or she can go on to think about the optimum balance of economic, health, safety, and political considerations in the development of energy sources and conservation strategies; about how to improve the balance of payments; about the short- and long-term environmental tolerances of new pesticides; and about the selective stability of proposed weapons systems like the MX or the Midgetman, Stealth or the BlB, or the nuclear-pumped X-ray laser aboard a space platform. Exhausting as this very incomplete list of issues is, that's not the worst of it.

Each of these questions is so frightfully difficult that the "experts" are adamantly divided about how they should be answered, and even how they should be formulated. More exasperatingly, the questions are inextricably linked. More money for space leaves less in the public sector to distribute or less in the private sector to trickle down, and if that might decelerate inflation, it might also skyrocket interest rates and/or unemployment—but then again, maybe not. The use of farm exports as an instrument of foreign policy may or may not give us leverage over the Soviets, but how much leverage offsets the effects on the federal trade deficit and on the small farmer? Each issue seems to grow entangled in the next, and of each only one thing is sure: it is probably more complicated than we yet know and than politicians will be inclined to admit. Life in an increasingly technologized society imposes increasing intellectual demands on society's decision makers; public life is just as liable to future shock as private life, arguably more so and more quickly.[1] If in such an era democracy's decisions are to be made intelligently and effectively, the public must somehow be reconstituted intellectually.

But with the increased demands for an educated democratic audience, there has been an alarming growth in the media of public manipulation. Candidates can—and feel they must—arm themselves with TV image masters, pollsters, direct-mail money raisers, all calculating primarily how to manipulate, rather than inform, public opinion.[2] One need only scan the popular literature—Joe McGinniss's *The Selling of the President 1968,* say, or Jack Germond and Jules Witcover's *Blue Smoke and Mirrors*—to get a sense of the threat.[3] Perhaps that title is already the best description of our political discourse: our civic talk on urgent and complex issues, obscured by mirrors and blue smoke.

> Illusion. Mirrors and blue smoke, beautiful blue smoke rolling over the surface of highly polished mirrors, first a thin veil of blue smoke, then a thick cloud that suddenly dissolves into wisps of blue smoke, the mirrors catching it all, bouncing it back and forth. If somebody tells you how to look, there can be seen in the smoke great, magnificent shapes, castles and kingdoms, and maybe they can be yours. All this becomes particularly dynamic when the person telling you where to look knows how to adjust the mirrors, tilt one forward, walk to the

other side, and turn one on the base a few degrees to the right, suddenly causing the refractions to be different everywhere. And then going to the blue smoke lessening it, intensifying it, and all the time keeping those watching transfixed, hoping, believing himself. Believing perhaps more than anybody else in the room. And at the same time knowing that what he is believing in is mirrors and blue smoke.[4]

If in such an era the decisions people make are to be genuinely their own rather than the reflex of some electronically programmed response, people must be liberated personally, to think for, think *as* themselves.

Democracy is ever more pinched between these growing concerns: ever more complicated problems requiring ever more specialized and disciplined thinking, ever more skillful techniques of mass indulgence pandering ever more seductively to the inclinations they detect and the commonplaces they plant in the democratic audiences. Uniquely dismaying as they may seem, similar difficulties have confronted America before. One natural response has been to despair of democracy's future: as with Orestes Brownson in 1840, people are tempted to foreswear democratic ideals — along with the tedious and irksome public responsibilities implicit in those ideals — for some more elitist approach.[5] But if despair is no new reaction to the problem of the democratic audience, neither is its alternative. Whenever democracy has found itself in such a pinch, it has turned to popular education. Indeed, it is not too much to say that this inclination has become part of the American character; "one of the signal facts of our national experience," claimed historian Richard Hofstadter, is "our persistent, intense and sometimes touching faith in the efficacy of popular education."[6] If the tasks today seem unusually formidable, there may be both comfort and motivation in that. Prospects have seemed every bit as dismal before, and a measure of educational success was nonetheless clearly achieved. There may be something educational for us in turning back to the successes of the nineteenth century to find implications for the twenty-first.

On the lyceum and Chautauqua circuits, rhetoric was central to a publicly constitutive and personally liberating education of the democratic audience. It had to work within the peculiar limits and capacities of the democratic audience; the sorts of rhetoric that succeeded involved identification, a living connection of thought and character. But such rhetoric reconstituted more than the audience. To succeed, democratic education had to involve and fulfill its obligations to every element of the exchange — subject and speaker as well as audience — in adjusting ideas to people and people to ideas. Indeed, the most provocative implication of the circuit of public speech is a new concept of rhetorical success.

Recall that the nineteenth century's democratic audience was in need of education too. As an audience it was similarly exasperating but was similarly worthy of being addressed. Shifty of attention, shallow of commit-

ment, undifferentiatingly resistant to claims of special authority—almost
every attribute that could make education more difficult, this audience had
and prided itself upon. But with the vices came inextricable virtues: ambition, confidence, a certain independence of mind once that mind had been
engaged, an openness to new ideas, an eagerness to try them on and see
how they fit, see if the ideas became them.

Many new instruments of democratic education were invented in adaptation to these limits and capacities; nothing proved more distinctive of
American education in the nineteenth century than institutional innovation. Only the lecture circuit has been examined here. It is my suspicion,
however, that a great deal might be learned—by contemporary theorists of
education, by political thinkers intrigued by democracy, by students of the
American character—from further investigation of these institutions in all
their diversity and purposeful eccentricity and from reflection on the ideas
and aspirations they institutionalized.

But its singular success focused us on the circuit of public speech. To
examine its success is to see rhetoric from an unusual angle. It is a commonplace that rhetoric may be used for the indulgence of audiences, for playing
the pastry chef when the patient needs castor oil. One might even concede
that rhetoric might be used in mildly ambitious projects of vulgarization;
sometimes the body politic needs the nourishment of new ideas, and it is no
surprise that a resistant audience can be made to swallow them with a little
sugarcoating. Rhetoric thus can be tolerable, even in a sneaky way useful,
as long as the sugarcoating doesn't alter the chemistry of the exchange.

But to study the circuit is to find some successful popularizations. The
fact is unsettling and undeniable: some democratic educators used rhetoric
to articulate intellectual specialties and make them popular—make them
widely known and widely admired. But the success of their rhetoric challenges some of our own commonplaces. It reveals the inadequacy of our
very notions of success, and it implies that rhetoric may have something of
a proper role to play in democratic society, may have a distinct office to
fulfill. This book itself may serve as a popularization insofar as it prods us
to criticize and reconstitute, rather than indulge, our commonplaces about
what rhetoric is and what it can do among us.

What rhetoric did was provide some solution to the problem of the
democratic audience. The audience's shiftiness could be conscripted in the
cause of new ideas; its resistance to claims of superior authority could be
circumvented, even reshaped into an educable independence of mind. The
audience's rhetorical problem could be handled when its democratic character was recognized, in a sense embraced in strategies of identification.

The solution was ingenious. Education needed firm authority in order
to question the mass habits of thought and replace them with the liberating,
individuating assumptions and premises from which a new discipline, a new

way of thinking could be built. Democratic audiences resisted claims of personal superiority, admiring instead more direct representation. Rhetorics of identification, paradoxically, allowed claims of extraordinary authority on just this basis. Americans identified with, granted authority to those like them; in the full capabilities and virtues his discipline gave him, an Emerson or Twain or James could be representative of them—like them, only more so. The audience, by being drawn to his character, was drawn to the thought that clearly helped make him. The reconstitutive power of this rhetoric lay in the identification of thought and character.

In this identification is a glimpse of the light rhetorical studies can shed on the American condition, the democratic condition, and perhaps—if the contemporary rhetorical theorists are right—on the human condition. For rhetorical studies can describe the variety of identifications that were successful and can explore the nature of that success. The range of these identifications and of their successes delineate the range of identities that were meaningful and valuable and powerful in the American community at that time. The decisions the community would then make, the alternatives it would understand and consider were charged with these meanings and values and powers. It is, from the perspective of rhetorical practice, an incomplete description of democracy to regard it not as a distinctive culture, but simply as a procedural mode of organizing administrative relationships.[7] To understand how it worked at a given time is to understand how it was a distinctive culture of character, made of and moved by who its citizens were and who they wanted to be. Those identifications are nowhere more clearly and accessibly represented than in the practice of rhetoricians who successfully identified themselves as like their audiences, only somehow more so.

But the public reconstitutions of audiences also had to be, for democratic purposes, personally liberating. In a way of life that otherwise lent itself to a tyranny of the majority, it was crucial that rhetoric not homogenize listeners into simply another mass with slightly shuffled commonplaces. Rhetorics of identification proved marvelously flexible in this way. They could involve disciplines as different as Transcendentalism and Pragmatism, characteristics as different as Twain's subversive wit and Emerson's affirming solemnity, purposes as different as James's persistent reconciling and Twain's restless rebellion. Indeed, success in democratic education seems to have depended on our authoritative, liberatingly personal connection of thought and character. The diversity of such connections suggests just how much personal liberation could be found in rhetorics of identification.

Emerson was persuasively "tender-minded," Twain persuasively "tough-minded," James persuasively flexible. Emerson had troubles with transition, as befits one who sees the truth of the universe as one and transcending; if there is but one Point to make, what is the need for transition? Twain had trouble with endings, as befits one who proceeds empirically, seeing each successive object of contemplation with his own innocent eye; it is difficult to come to a conclusion when there is no end to empirical data. And notwithstanding his attempts to satisfy such opposite demands with a reconciling rhetoric, James was perhaps closer to Twain than to Emerson; his essential commitment was to "radical empiricism." But in sharing characteristics with both Emerson and Twain, James sometimes found himself suffering both kinds of structural problems.

All three popularizers could in a sense be said to have seen through "innocent eyes." Twain rebelled furiously against the dominant culture, but the mild Emerson himself willingly endured and even courted controversy to "say what he saw." He did, after all, deliver the "American Scholar" speech, a plea for an overthrow of foreign cultures and traditions in favor simply of Man Thinking at the 1837 Phi Beta Kappa convocation, before professional scholars of those cultures and traditions. And a year later, he did deliver his most self-consciously unorthodox religious meditation before the Harvard Divinity School itself. James, for his part, continually exasperated professional philosophers with his loose yet muscular, "strenuous" way of thinking, so foreign to their conventions.

The differences here lay in the way the popularizers responded to their visions: Emerson simply affirmed, without explicit reference to or argument against any other side. Twain mostly subverted, referring—usually implicitly, but sometimes directly—to another side, that of the dominant culture. James was aware of a multiplicity of sides, each in their way worthwhile. Although he both subverted and affirmed, James perhaps resembles Emerson more closely in his inclusion of every point of view, his suggestion that the only accurate perspective on any subject is that which most appreciatively affirms its virtues.

James's mediate position, his flawed yet still potent attempt at flexible thought, may explain the distinctive reaction that his character evoked from the democratic audience. Emerson was deeply respected by his audiences, but there is no evidence that he was liked in any warm, personal way (this might be confirmed in part by our own reaction to him). Of course a personal relation would get in the way of his prophecy, his being a credible vehicle of higher truth. Twain on the other hand was genuinely liked; even in our own reading, it is easier to establish a personal relation with him, even if it is a relation that sometimes gets wildly out of hand. But Twain was never too solemnly respected—a rebel couldn't be. Nothing could be viewed with too much solemnity if a little honest subversion was to take place.

James's role can be seen as the most inclusive in that he was both properly respected and personally liked. He saw and said more kinds of things, gave his audiences more kinds of characteristics with which to identify, represented more alternatives of identity for men thinking. At last, I have argued, he didn't use or say his message perfectly well; Emerson and Twain each articulated their own particular sort of truths more clearly and efficiently. But James was able to make different sorts of appeals, to include in his audiences listeners who responded to different sorts of characteristics. Thus the heights of success James reached may not have been as high, but his valleys were never quite as low. James left no audience so nonplussed as Emerson left the town that was expecting a comedian and in fact thought that they had heard one, however unfunny; James left no audience so unpersuaded as Twain left his listeners at the Whittier dinner. Ultimately, James may not himself have been the most successful in terms of greatness or popularity. But he did demonstate the potentials of pluralistic rhetoric for inclusiveness, for reconciliation, for keeping the conversation going.

This is an obligation to democracy, the fulfillment of which is an aspect of rhetorical success. If the persuasion is to stay meaningful, democracy must survive; and democracy depends on — and in a sense exists in, and through — rhetoric. Democracy depends on the course of its civic conversation, imperfect but ongoing, to communicate and even constitute its res publica, its common thing. Bernard Crick gets at the same point another way: "the moral consensus of a free state is not something mysteriously prior to or above politics. It is the activity, the civilizing activity, of politics itself."[8] Thus a rhetoric is successful insofar as it reconstitutes and frees audiences to participate in the constitutive conversation for themselves — participate *as* themselves, as women and men thinking, or rebels or reconcilers or whatever new character with which (no, with *whom*) the listener may identify.

We have seen so far how rhetoric can be central to a publicly constitutive, personally liberating education for the audience. But in the adjustment of ideas to people and people to ideas, audiences are only one aspect of successful reconstitutions and liberations.

Rhetoric as we have also seen functions to reshape the subjects of discourse. Emerson, Twain, and James repeatedly tried out their material on the circuit before putting it into print. This did not have to mean dummying down the message, but could mean instead fitting the message into the community and the patterns of living in which it is to be meaningful. As in the cases of our three popularizers, the subject can be invigorated by a whole new vocabulary in which to be articulated, new examples to speak to, new topics to consider, and new concerns to feel and think about. Sometimes on the circuit, disciplines of thought undeniably were vulgarized or worse. But some identifications were strong enough to pull in the opposite direction, not to degrade disciplines into venal chitchat, but to elevate and incorporate the common sense.

I've claimed that this sort of democratic education is an obligation to democracy; it also is an obligation to the discipline itself, the fulfillment of which is another aspect of rhetorical success. This is true in an imminently practical sense. If the public is allowed to misapprehend the nature and effects of, say, genetic engineering (or if the course of that engineering were not accountable to the interest of the public), support – access to the public facilities for research, release time – and money for such research might disappear. If the public is not instructed in the role of distributive justice in thinking about the allocation of medical resources, graver injustices might become irresistible. But the obligation applies in a more intrinsic sense, in the sense Tocqueville worried about "the lights that guide us" going out, our losing touch in the same way the Chinese did with the basic principles that animate our constitutive intellectual disciplines.[9] Disciplines must for their own survival attract and engage the best minds possible that they may in their turn probe and push their frontiers. A rhetoric of democratic education is successful insofar as it reconstitutes ways of thought so as to get people to think them. It is successful insofar as it frees the discipline to be all it can be – to be satisfying, as James would say – for the human beings who animate and practice and extend it.

So far, we have formulated rhetorical success in terms of publicly constitutive, personally liberating rhetorical functions for audiences and subject matters. In the adjustment of ideas to people and people to ideas there remains only the function most directly concerned with identification: the constitution and liberation of speakers themselves.

A rhetoric of identification is "ethical" rhetoric in two senses. Clearly it establishes and argues from the authority of the speaker's ethos. But rhetoric is also ethical insofar as it reconstitutes and liberates the speaker's ethos, insofar as it quite literally identifies him and his way of discourse: the most important reality made in any rhetorical interaction is people, including the speaker himself. Emerson, Twain, and James all found their voices on the circuit – found what it was that made them persuasive and powerful, even what it was that made them purposeful in their public careers and personal lives. In the popularization of their ways of thinking, they truly became themselves, only more so in the identifications they effected, in their distinctive connection of thought and character.

This may be the most productive aspect of the shift of focus in contemporary rhetorical theory from *persuasion,* a leveraging of people "out there" by a removed and uninvolved creator of rhetoric, to *identification,* an enrichment of the field of selves in which the speaker, a creator and creature of rhetoric, finds himself. Each of us is a creature "who can find his 'self' only through his communal building of selves, who can find his life, in fact, only by losing himself back into the society of selves that made him."[10] This is the ultimate lesson for democratic education of Emerson's, Twain's, and James's success: rhetoric is successful insofar as its public reconstitutions are personally liberating. To see and practice rhetoric this way is, in the American expression, "self-interest rightly understood."

These obligations to audience, subject, and self, these functions of adjusting ideas to people and people to ideas define a role, a distinctive office for rhetoric in democracy: rhetoric as central to a publicly constitutive, personally liberating education, an ever fuller identification of thought and character.

NOTES

CHAPTER 1

1. In *The Orator,* Cicero complained of an education that separated training in how to think about public issues from training in how to use language; he envisioned as a solution a public education constituted around rhetoric, and a rhetoric designed to be a liberating, constitutive center of public concern and action. In *The Institutes of Oratory,* Quintillian articulated a practical system of education based on this premise. After the rediscovery of the complete texts (in 1414 and 1419), such a scheme of education was reinstated. Today, in the midst of widespread dissatisfaction with public education, there is an extensive push "back to basics" without comparably extensive reflection on what those basics are, and are to do. In response, several scholars in a variety of fields have called for an education that would link training in the effective uses of language more closely with training in thought about practical public issues. See, for example, the excellent anthology *The Rhetorical Tradition and Modern Writing,* ed. James J. Murphy (New York: Modern Language Assocation of America, 1982).

2. Senator Claiborne Pell (D-RI), quoted in CBS Radio "News Update," 16 January 1984.

3. In 1978 Boys' Town administrators were found to have misled the public concerning the way money had been and was to be spent. *New York Times,* 24 November 1978, 15.

4. An early attack on the split was Wolfgang Köhler, *The Place of Value in a World of Facts* (New York: Liveright, 1938). More recent works especially worth noting along this line are Michael Polanyi, *Personal Knowledge* (Chicago: Univ. of Chicago Press, 1958) and Stephen Toulmin, *Human Understanding* (Princeton, N.J.: Princeton Univ. Press, 1972).

5. This argument is made extensively in an analysis of the fact/value distinction and its rhetorical effects: Wayne C. Booth, *Modern Dogma and The Rhetoric of Assent* (Chicago: Univ. of Chicago Press, 1974). The range of the argument makes the book itself an artful work of popular education. At first blush it may seem doubtful that a confessed and unregenerate rhetorician like Booth will have something of worth to say about so profound a philosophical question. But such a doubt already assumes a firm distinction between a pristine philosophical reality and the, well, sometimes sleazy world of rhetoric. It is the point of Booth's book, insofar as it succeeds, that such an assumption itself is questionable philosophically. One of the points of this book, insofar as it may succeed, is that such an assumption is questionable historically, indeed that it breaks down in the American experience, and that the study of rhetoric has something to say about what we are, who we can and ought to become in our intellectual and moral constitution.

6. Alexis de Tocqueville, *Democracy in America,* trans. George Lawrence, ed. J. P. Mayer (Garden City, N.Y.: Doubleday, Anchor Books, 1969), 12.

7. Quoted in Raymer McQuiston, *The Relation of Ralph Waldo Emerson to Public Affairs* (Lawrence, Kans.: published by the university in *Bulletin of the University of Kansas Humanistic Studies* 3 no. 1,1923):15.

8. One point of this study gets an etymological push: "education" is related to the Latin *educere,* to lead forth: *Oxford English Dictionary,* compact ed., s.v. "education." This study examines rhetoric that attempted to lead individuals out of their mass habits of thought, to reconstitute individuals intellectually.

9. See Charles Dickens's satire of the circuit's dilettantes, *Martin Chuzzlewit.*

10. Tocqueville, *Democracy in America,* 430.

11. Ibid., 434, 435, 430.

12. Plato, *Gorgias,* 503a, 464d.

13. Ibid., 474a.

14. Plato, *Phaedrus,* 265a, trans. J. Harward, *Great Books of the Western World* (Chicago: Univ. of Chicago Press, 1952). For Plato, true philosophy absolutely required this sort of engagement. About the teaching and learning of his own philosophy, he wrote:

> This much, at least, I can say about all writers, past or future, who say they know the things to which I devote myself, whether by hearing the teaching of me or of others, or by their own discoveries—that according to my view it is not possible for them to have any real skill in the matter. There neither is nor ever will be a treatise of mine on the subject. For it does not admit of exposition like other branches of knowledge; but after much converse about the matter itself and a life lived together, suddenly a light, as it were, is kindled in one soul by a flame that leaps to it from another, and thereafter sustains itself.

Plato, *The Seventh Letter,* 341 b, c, and d, trans. J. Harward, *Great Books of the Western World.*

15. Kenneth Burke, *A Rhetoric of Motives* (Berkeley: Univ. of California Press, 1950), 19, his italics.

16. Booth, *Modern Dogma and the Rhetoric of Assent,* xvi.

17. Wayne C. Booth, "Mere Rhetoric, Rhetoric and Reality," 11 April 1978, lecture at Woodward Court, University of Chicago.

CHAPTER 2

1. Arthur M. Schlesinger, Jr., *The Age of Jackson* (Boston: Little, Brown, 1953), 401.

2. See Chap. 3, 27-29.

3. Orestes Brownson, "Democracy and Liberty," reprinted in *The Brownson Reader,* ed. Alvan S. Ryan (New York: P. J. Kenedy 1955), 59.

4. Glyndon G. Van Deusen, *The Jacksonian Era: 1828–1848* (New York: Harper & Row, 1959), 16.

5. The ramifications of Jackson's "Bank War" are examined specifically in Chap. 3, 41–43.

6. Schlesinger, *The Age of Jackson,* 334–35.

7. Robert V. Remini, *The Revolutionary Age of Andrew Jackson* (New York: Harper & Row, 1976), 6.

8. Van Deusen, *Jacksonian Era,* 116–17.

9. Ibid., 146.

10. Richard Hofstadter, *Anti-Intellectualism in American Life* (New York: Alfred A. Knopf, 1966), 156.

11. Edward Pessen, *Jacksonian America: Society, Personality, and Politics* (Homewood, Ill.: Dorsey Press, 1969), 156, 177.

12. Nicholas Biddle to Herman Cope, 11 August 1835, quoted in Robert Gray Gunderson, *The Log-Cabin Campaign* (1957; reprint, Westport, Conn.: Greenwood Press, 1977), 73.

13. Gunderson, *The Log-Cabin Campaign,* 65; Schlesinger, *The Age of Jackson,* 292.

14. Van Deusen, *Jacksonian Era,* 147; Pessen, *Jacksonian America,* 177, 58.

15. Ibid., 177.

16. Most of these new coinages passed out of currency, which suggests something about how useful people found them in their normal employment of language. Two have, however, become very familiar parts of the language. Arthur Schlesinger, Jr., makes the assertion, hotly contested, that "Okay" was introduced by the slogans of Martin Van Buren, who hailed from Old Kinderhook, New York: Martin Van Buren. O.K., another four years." *(The Age of Jackson,* 298). Manifestly, the Democrats' sloganeers were the less adroit, but in any case the Whigs had still another ally, one that may have proven, at least in this election, more influential. Glyndon Van Deusen records that "booze" as a word denoting alcoholic beverages entered the American vocabulary when the Harrison campaign served the hard cider of the E. C. Booz Company *(Jacksonian Era,* 147–48).

17. James Fenimore Cooper, *The American Democrat* (New York: Penguin Books, 1967), 13.

18. Ibid. Such groggeries may not even have been the most persuasive gimmick of the campaign: Robert Gunderson reports that "Whig maidens refused to consort with Loco-Foco swains. Tennessee belles wore sashes proclaiming their intentions: 'Whig husbands or none.' " *The Log-Cabin Campaign,* 139.

19. Gunderson, The *Log-Cabin Campaign,* 1.

20. Columbus *Ohio State Journal,* 18 November 1840.

21. Brownson, "Democracy and Liberty," 32: Schlesinger, *The Age of Jackson,* 401; Brownson, "Democracy and Liberty," 59–60.

22. Schlesinger, *The Age of Jackson,* 401; Brownson, "Democracy and Liberty," 61.

23. Schlesinger, *The Age of Jackson,* 385, 509.

24. Russell Blaine Nye, *Society and Culture in America: 1830–1860* (New York: Harper & Row, 1974), 17–18.

CHAPTER 3

1. James Bugg, Jr., *Jacksonian Democracy: Myth or Reality?* (New York: Holt, Rinehart & Winston, 1962), 4; Robert V. Remini, *The Revolutionary Age of Andrew Jackson* (New York: Harper & Row, 1976), 18.

2. A most helpful and comprehensive attempt at a history of that heritage is A. J. Beitzinger's *A History of American Political Thought* (New York: Dodd, Mead, 1972); Alexis de Tocqueville, *Democracy in America,* trans. George Lawrence, ed. J. P. Mayer (Garden City, N. Y.: Doubleday, Anchor Books, 1969), 22–30.

3. Frederick Jackson Turner, "The Significance of the Frontier in American History," in *The Annual Report of the American Historical Association for the Year 1893* (Washington, D.C.: U.S. Government Printing Office, 1894), 200, 201.

4. What is more, Turner is only concerned with opportunities for white males. It comes as something of a shock to find a historian of the late nineteenth century still contending that "when American history comes to be rightly viewed, it will be seen that the slavery question is an incident" (ibid., 217).

5. Malcolm Knowles, *The Adult Education Movement in the United States* (New York: Holt, Rinehart & Winston, 1962), 22; Glyndon Van Deusen, *The Jacksonian Era: 1828–1848* (New York: Harper & Row, 1959), 1; Tocqueville, *Democracy in America,* 455.

6. John William Ward, *Andrew Jackson: Symbol for an Age* (New York: Oxford Univ. Press, 1953), 176.

7. Charles A. and Mary R. Beard, *A Basic History of the United States* (New York: Doubleday, 1944), 79; Tocqueville, *Democracy in America,* 222n.

8. Richard Hofstadter, *The American Political Tradition and the Men Who Made It* (New York: Vintage Books, 1974), 62–63.

9. Edward Pessen, *Jacksonian America: Society, Personality, and Politics* (Homewood, Ill.: Dorsey Press, 1969), 161.

10. Ibid., 162.

11. Ibid., 40.

12. Harold Syrett, *Andrew Jackson: His Contribution to the American Tradition* (New York: Bobbs-Merrill, 1953), 43.

13. Washington McCartney, "Eulogy [on the Death of Andrew Jackson]," in Ward, *Andrew Jackson: Symbol for an Age,* 1.

14. Remini, *The Revolutionary Age of Andrew Jackson,* i.

15. Ibid., 4.

16. *Salem Gazette,* 23 September 1814; *Boston Daily Advertiser,* 3 February 1815; *National Intelligencer,* 4 October 1814; *Boston Patriot,* 28 January 1815; *New-York Evening Post,* 25 January 1815; *Washington Republican,* 3 February 1815.

17. *Cincinnati Spirit of the West,* 5 February 1814; *National Intelligencer,* extra, 4 February 1815; *Boston Patriot,* 11 February 1815.

18. Ward, *Andrew Jackson: Symbol for an Age,* 5–6; *Enquirer,* 18 February 1815; *New Hampshire Patriot,* 21 February 1814.

19. Robert Remini, *Andrew Jackson,* Rulers and Statesmen of the World Series, ed. Hans Trefousse (New York: Twayne, 1966), 64, 66.

20. Ibid., 72.

21. Richard Hofstadter, *Anti-Intellectualism in American Life* (New York: Alfred A. Knopf, 1966) 34; Van Deusen, *Jacksonian Era,* 1.

22. Hofstadter, *The American Political Tradition,* 74.

23. Syrett, *Andrew Jackson: His Contribution to the American Tradition,* 25.

24. James Fenimore Cooper, *The American Democrat,* (New York: Penguin Books, 1967), 20.

25. Pessen, *Jacksonian America,* 173; Schlesinger, *The Age of Jackson,* 206; Hofstadter, *The American Political Tradition,* 69.

26. U. S., *Constitution,* Amend. XII, sec. 2.

27. Pessen, *Jacksonian America,* 155; cited in Van Deusen, *Jacksonian Era,* 148.

28. Schlesinger, *The Age of Jackson,* 19; Van Deusen, *Jacksonian Era,* 27.

29. Ibid., 20.

30. Hofstadter, *Anti-Intellectualism in American Life,* 23, 57, 157.

31. Van Deusen, *Jacksonian Era,* 27; Remini, *The Revolutionary Age of Andrew Jackson,* 52.

32. Schlesinger, *The Age of Jackson,* 6; Van Deusen, *Jacksonian Era,* 31; Tocqueville, *Democracy in America,* 200–201.

33. Cooper, *The American Democrat,* 31.

34. Remini, *The Revolutionary Age of Andrew Jackson,* 34.

35. Senate, *Message,* 21st Cong., 1st sess., 8 December 1829, 1:8.

36. Pessen, *Jacksonian America,* 337; Remini, *The Revolutionary Age of Andrew Jackson,* 78. The "spoils" malady has continued to afflict American public life continuously, down to recent days when a Republican U.S. attorney following up charges of corruption against a Democratic congressman can be replaced in the middle of the investigation by a Democratic president — on the advice of the congressman under investigation. President Carter was exonerated from any wrongdoing (to everyone's relief, but hardly anyone's surprise) by his Department of Justice. Yet it is significant that even this chief executive — elected as the morally upright outsider, owing no debts and making no deals — could blandly defend the removal as a political matter of course. "To the victors," as William Marcy was only the first to put it, "belong the spoils of the enemy."

37. Robert Gray Gunderson, *The Log-Cabin Campaign* (1957; reprint, Westport, Conn.: Greenwood Press, 1977), 88.

38. Pessen, *Jacksonian America,* 337.

39. Remini, *The Revolutionary Age of Andrew Jackson,* 14–15.

40. *Senate Journal,* 22d Cong., 1st sess., 1831–1832, 446.

41. Hofstadter, *The American Political Tradition,* 77.

42. *Congressional Debates,* 23d Cong., 1st sess., 1833–1834, 10:1334.

43. Van Deusen, *Jacksonian Era,* 98–99.

44. Syrett, *Andrew Jackson: His Contribution to the American Tradition,* 34.

45. Alexander Hamilton, John Jay, and James Madison, *The Federalist Papers,* with an introduction by Edward Mead Earle (New York: Modern Library, 1937), nos. 68, 39.

46. Quoted in Hannah Fenichel Pitkin, *The Concept of Representation* (Berkeley: Univ. of California Press, 1967), 169.

47. Joseph Tussman, quoted in Pitkin, *The Concept of Representation,* 43.

48. John Adams, "Letter to John Penn" and "Defense of the Constitution of Government of the United States of America," quoted in Pitkin, *The Concept of Representation,* 60, 61.

49. Pitkin, *The Concept of Representation,* 61.

50. This notion of representation seemed to reach — and perhaps to exceed — its limits in American democratic society during the hearings that considered the nomination of G. Harrold Carswell to the Supreme Court. The proceedings, as even his staunch supporters were forced to admit, had revealed Carswell to be at best a very ordinary candidate, and at worst obviously unqualified. But Senator Roman Hruska (R-Neb.) persevered undaunted in his support of Carswell's candidacy on the grounds that mediocre and even ignorant people deserved "representation" too. It is interesting that, far from winning his confirmation as it was presumably intended to do, the comment actually made Carswell a laughing-stock and insured his resounding defeat. But then, Carswell was later arrested on morals charges, raising the possibility that he would have misrepresented even the peculiar constituency imputed to him.

This line of argument should not, however, be considered peculiarly American in nature; no less a figure than Lord Booth himself explained his position on the proper representative makeup of British Parliament this way:

> Ideally, the House of Commons should be a social microcosm of the nation. The nation includes a great many people who are rather stupid, and so should the House.

Quoted in Anthony H. Birch, *Representative and Responsible Government* (Toronto: Univ. of Toronto Press, 1964), 232.

51. All quotations from Remini, *The Revolutionary Age of Andrew Jackson,* 177.

52. Syrett, *Andrew Jackson: His Contribution to the American Tradition,* 215; Tocqueville, *Democracy in America,* 394; Van Deusen, *Jacksonian America,* viii.

53. Remini, *The Revolutionary Age of Andrew Jackson,* 39.

54. Ward, *Andrew Jackson: Symbol for an Age,* 55.

55. Hofstadter, *The American Political Tradition,* 56.

56. Syrett, *Andrew Jackson: His Contribution to the American Tradition,* 22.

57. Pessen, *Jacksonian America,* 57.

58. Hofstadter, *The American Political Tradition,* 80; Van Deusen, *Jacksonian Era,* 63.

59. Remini, *The Revolutionary Age of Andrew Jackson,* 79; Pessen, *Jacksonian America,* 3.

60. Tocqueville, *Democracy in America,* 436.

61. Ibid., 440–41, 461.

62. Ibid., 461, 464–65.

63. Ibid., 430; Hofstadter, *Anti-Intellectualism in American Life,* p. 157. Also see Chap. 2, 39.

64. Tocqueville, *Democracy in America,* 430, 434, 435.

65. Walt Whitman, *Leaves of Grass,* ed. Emory Holloway (Garden City, N. J.: Doubleday, 1926), "One's-Self I Sing," 11.1–2, 8.

66. Ibid., 323–24, "I Was Looking a Long While," 11.1, 2, 6, 7.

67. Ibid., 25–77, "Song of Myself," I,11.1–3; LII,1.27; XXXVII,11.2,3; XL,11.1,2,4,5; XXXIII,11.70–71; XV,1.66.

68. Cooper, *The American Democrat,* 121; Tocqueville, *Democracy in America,* 197.

69. Cooper, *The American Democrat,* 129.

70. Ibid., 70, 142, 143, 197; Tocqueville, *Democracy in America,* 250, 259.

71. Cooper, *The American Democrat,* 197. Tocqueville, *Democracy in America,* 436.

72. Cooper, *The American Democrat,* 131; Tocqueville, *Democrary in America,* 197.

CHAPTER 4

1. James Bryce, *The American Commonwealth,* 2d ed. rev., (New York: Macmillan, 1891) 2:276.

2. Glyndon Van Deusen, *The Jacksonian Era: 1828–1848* (New York: Harper & Row, 1959) 14.

3. Alexis de Tocqueville, *Democracy in America,* trans. George Lawrence, ed. J. P. Mayer (Garden City, N. Y.: Doubleday, Anchor Books, 1969), 292.

4. Malcolm Knowles, *The Adult Education Movement in the United States,* (New York: Holt, Rinehart & Winston, 1962), 13.

5. Donald M. Scott "The Popular Lecture and the Creation of a Public in Mid-Nineteenth Century America," *Journal of American History* 66 (1980):791.

6. Even though it was always a sort of minority voice, there was a tradition of persistent American affection for books and learning that is rarely recognized or fully appreciated. Its roots reach back to the first settlement of the country. When the original colonizers were packing for the hazardous journey to America, they must have felt that their choices about what to bring along and what to leave behind were matters of life and death. Space was at a premium on the tiny ships, and every bit of clothing and ammunition that could be packed would be needed in establishing a new life in the wilderness. Nonetheless, many of the settlers allocated some of their precious cargo space for books. And even when they reached their destination and were beset by problems of basic survival, the new Americans maintained their old respect for learning; "one of the first concerns of the colonists after they established themselves in the wilderness was the provision of some kind of education." Ibid., v.

The same impulse is visible in our own day, for example, in Lyndon Johnson's expenditures on education as a keystone in the construction of the Great Society. No small part of that society's subsequent malaise stemmed from the apparent failings of education to solve social problems or even maintain its own quality.

7. Another instructive comparison is with the regimented methods of technical education occuring in Tocqueville's native France. See Frederick B. Artz, *The Development of Technical Education in France 1500–1850* (Cambridge, Mass.: Society for the History of Technology and M.I.T. Press, 1966), especially 109–11.

8. Ibid., Lyman Bryson, *Adult Education* (New York: American Book, 1936), 13–14.

9. Joseph E. Gould, *The Chautauqua Movement: An Episode in Continuing American Revolution* (New York: State Univ. of New York Press, 1961), vii.

10. Carl Bode, *The American Lyceum: Town Meeting of the Mind* (New York: Oxford Univ. Press, 1956), 37, italics his; Rebecca Richmond, *Chautauqua: An American Place* (New York: Duell, Sloan & Pearce, 1943), 117; Marian Scott, *Chautauqua Caravan* (New York: Appleton-Century, 1937), 246.

11. Tocqueville, *Democrary in America,* 95, 96.

12. Ibid., 95.

13. Ibid., 188, 189–90, 191.

14. Ibid., 526.

15. Ibid., 526, 527.

16. Bode, *The American Lyceum,* 7; Bode points out an intriguing similarity: the leadership in each of these movements of popular education did not comprise many people; rather, in each country where it appeared, the movement was led only by one or two men. Ibid., 8.

17. *Who's Who in the Lyceum,* ed. A. Augustus Wright (Philadelphia: Pearson, 1906), 19.

18. Josiah Holbrook, "The Constitution for the American Lyceum of Science and the Arts," reprinted in *The Massachusetts Lyceum During the American Renaissance; Materials for the Study of Oral Tradition in American Letters,* ed. Kenneth Walter Cameron (Hartford, Conn.: Transcendental Books, 1969), 46.

19. Bode, *The American Lyceum,* 12; Paul Stoddard put it delicately: "Holbrook's passion for education was just a little colored by the desire for profit." Paul Wakelee Stoddard, "The American Lyceum" (Ph.D. diss. Yale Univ., 1947), 61.

20. Ibid., 186–87; Richard L. Weaver II, "Josiah Holbrook: Feeding the Passion for Self Help," *Communication Quarterly* 24, no. 4 (1976):14.

21. Bode, *The American Lyceum,* 186.

22. *American Journal of Education* 14 (Sept. 1864) 541.

23. Bode, *The American Lyceum,* 157.

24. Scott "The Popular Lecture," 791.

25. Bode, *The American Lyceum,* 250. For example, the Salem, Massachusetts, lyceum between 1831 and 1838 drew about 75 percent of its lectures from Salem and rarely went beyond Boston for a lecture. By 1845 only one in ten lectures was delivered by Salem residents and almost half the lectures came from outside the state. Scott, "The Popular Lecture," 797.

26. Wright, *Who's Who in the Lyceum,* 25.

27. Adapted from Bode, *The American Lyceum,* 48.

28. Charles F. Horner, *Strike the Tents: The Story of Chautauqua* (Philadeliphia: Dorrance, 1954), 33; Bode, *The American Lyceum,* 206, 190.

29. Ibid., 190.

30. Ibid., 188, 214.

31. Knowles, *The Adult Education Movement in the United States,* 13.

32. John Dewey, *Democracy and Education* (New York: Macmillan, 1916), 101, 5.

33. Ibid., 375, 5.

34. Scott, "The Popular Lecture," 808-89.

35. Dewey, *Democracy and Education,* 101.

36. Ibid.

37. Tocqueville, *Democracy in America,* 488, 435, 640.

38. Ibid., 255.

39. Edward C. Lindemann, *The Meaning of Adult Education* (New York: New Republic, 1926), 126–27.

40. Scott, "The Popular Lecture," 802–3.

41. Lindemann, *The Meaning of Adult Education,* 135; Dewey, *Democracy and Education,* 225; Lindemann, *The Meaning of Adult Education,* 49.

42. David Mead, *Yankee Eloquence in the Middle West, 1850–1870* (East Lansing, Mich.: Michigan State College Press, 1951), 179.

43. Quoted in Bode, *The American Lyceum,* 201.

44. Ibid., 217; quoted ibid., 235.

45. Ibid., 30; David Mead, *Yankee Eloquence in the Middle West,* 36–37.

46. Bode, *The American Lyceum,* 49, 15; Mead, *Yankee Eloquence in the Middle West,* 98.

47. Ibid., 188.

48. Bode, *The American Lyceum,* 124–25.

49. Ibid., 217.

50. Mead, *Yankee Eloquence in the Middle West,* 152.

51. Quoted in Bode, *The American Lyceum,* 147; Mead, *Yankee Eloquence in the Middle West,* 152; Bode, *The American Lyceum,* 231.

52. As cited ibid., 251.

53. Theodore Morrison, *Chautauqua* (Chicago: Univ. of Chicago Press, 1974), 177. Morrison's book is by far the most comprehensive and incisive book I have seen on the topic.

54. Irene Biggs and Raymond F. Da Boll, *Recollections of the Lyceum and Chautauqua Circuits* (Freeport, Me.: Bond Wheelright, 1969), 66; as quoted in *The World Almanac and Book of Facts for 1924,* 375.

55. Morrison, *Chautauqua,* 31; J. L. Hurlbut, *The Story of Chautauqua* (New York: G. P. Putnam, 1921), 23; Morrison, *Chautauqua,* 33.

56. Ibid., 178.

57. Adapted from Morrison, *Chautauqua,* 149–9.

58. This is not to say that even such eminent figures always achieved complete rhetorical success: "One Redpath superintendent, when asked what 'Fighting Bob' La Follette talked about, said 'About four hours. The first two hours, the farmers wanted to rush to Washington and shoot Speaker Joe Cannon. After that, they were for Cannon and wanted to shoot La Follette.' " Ibid., 120.

59. Ibid., 95, 96.

60. Gould, *The Chautauqua Movement,* ix, 11.

61. Horner, *Strike the Tents,* 77, 173, 198.

62. Gould, *The Chautauqua Movement,* 82, 75, 82.

63. Richmond, *Chautauqua: An American Place,* 12, 14, 144.

64. Gould, *The Chautauqua Movement,* 98.

65. Harry P. and Karl Detzer, *Culture Under Canvas: The Story of Tent Chautauqua* (New York: Hastings House, 1958), xvii.

66. But this observation needs its pessimism qualified. It is interesting—and in a way, heartening—to note that as soon as each circuit decisively committed itself for commercial reasons to indulgence and was popularly recognized to have done so, Americans abandoned it. Something of the same character may be visible today in the change of public attitudes toward the news media.

67. Gould, *The Chautauqua Movement,* subtitled *An Episode in Continuing American Revolution.*

CHAPTER 5

1. While such an approach is not rhetorically ambitious enough for our purposes, it should not be dismissed before noting the degree of art in this approach. To flatter an audience believably is obviously more difficult for some objects of indulgence than for others, and the audience that most hungrily demanded such indulgence was invariably the most difficult in which to find anything to flatter.

2. Carl Bode, *The American Lyceum: Town Meeting of the Mind* (New York: Oxford Univ. Press, 1956), 126.

3. Ibid., 221.

4. Cited in James Eliot Cabot, *A Memoir of Ralph Waldo Emerson* (Boston: Houghton Mifflin, 1893) 1: 321; Vivian C. Hopkins, *Spires of Forms* (Cambridge: Harvard Univ. Press, 1951), 159.

5. Quoted in Bode, *The American Lyceum,* 224.

6. Cited in Raymer McQuiston, *The Relation of Ralph Waldo Emerson to Public Affairs* (Lawrence: Univ. of Kansas, 1923), 15.

7. Ralph Waldo Emerson, "The American Scholar," *The Complete Essays and Other Writings of Ralph Waldo Emerson,* ed. Brooks Wilkinson (New York: Modern Library, 1950), 49; *The Heart of Emerson's Journals,* ed. Bliss Perry (Boston: Houghton Mifflin, 1937), 217.

8. Alexis de Tocqueville, *Democracy in America,* trans. George Lawrence, ed. J. P. Mayer (Garden City, N. Y.: Doubleday, Anchor Books, 1969), 430.

9. Carl Bode, "Enough of His Life to Suggest His Character," reprinted in *Ralph Waldo Emerson: A Profile,* ed. Carl Bode, American Profiles Series, (New York: Hill & Wang, 1968), xii; Carl Bode, *The American Lyceum,* 235.

10. Ralph Waldo Emerson, in "Self-Reliance," *Essays, First and Second Series* (New York: E. P. Dutton, 1909), 42, 44, 37.

11. Places like these still remain touchstones of American popular culture. H. R. Haldeman expressed this when he gauged the success of the various versions of the Nixon Watergate explanations with the question "Will it play in Peoria?" As long as it did, Richard Nixon remained president despite what people in New York and Boston and the capital itself were thinking; only when it no longer played in Peoria and Madison and Independence and Davenport did the administration fall.

12. Bode, *The American Lyceum,* 176. Even the calm Emerson must have blanched somewhat upon hearing himself introduced as "Walph Raldo Emerson"; Mead, *Yankee Eloquence in the Middle West 1850–1870* (East Lansing: Michigan State College Press, 1951), 53.

13: Phillips Russell, *The Wisest American* (New York: Brentano's, 1929), 241.

14. Edward Wagenknecht, *Ralph Waldo Emerson: Portrait of a Balanced Soul* (New York: Oxford Univ. Press, 1974), 124.

15. Emerson, *Essays, First and Second Series,* "Compensation," 66.

16. Quoted in J. Arthur Hill, *Emerson and His Philosophy* (London: William Rider, 1919), 58.

17. Reprinted in Regis Michaud, *Emerson, the Enraptured Yankee,* trans. George Boas (New York: Harper, 1930), 219. Characteristically, Emerson also used the stuff of this private letter for publication as "Friendship" in *Essays, First Series.*

18. Quoted in Hill, *Emerson and His Philosophy,* 61.

19. Ralph L. Rusk, "Emerson in Love," reprinted in *Emerson: A Profile,* 39.

20. Bode, "Enough of His Life to Suggest His Character," reprinted ibid., vii.

21. The major reforms of this democratization are discussed in Chap. 3, 26–29.

22. Tocqueville, *Democracy in America,* 434; Cabot, *A Memoir of Ralph Waldo Emerson,* 1: v; Aristotle, *On Sophistical Refutations,* Chap. 2, 165b, trans. W. A. Pickard, Cambridge, Great Books of the Western World (Chicago: Univ. of Chicago Press, 1952); Chaim Perelman and L. Olbrechts-Tyteca, *The New Rhetoric* (Notre Dame, Ind.: Univ. of Notre Dame Press, 1971) 53.

23. Tocqueville, *Democracy in America,* 435.

24. Quoted in McQuiston, *The Relation of Emerson to Public Affairs,* 16.

25. Ralph Waldo Emerson, "The Uses of Great Men," reprinted in *Representative Men: Seven Lectures* (Boston: Houghton Mifflin, 1892), 28–29.

26. Hopkins, *Spires of Form,* 159; Cooper, *The American Democrat,* 131.

27. The other most eminent American figure in this formal rhetorical tradition was of course Daniel Webster.

28. Michaud, *Enraptured Yankee,* 21, 32. Michaud's reliability as a source must always be tempered by a perception of his own Emersonian disregard for factual exactitude. His often shaky hold on biographical detail and his sometimes breathtaking use of poetic license suggest that Michaud was possessed of no small rapture himself.

29. Hopkins, *Spires of Form,* 159.

30. Henry K. Oliver, "Address," reprinted in *The Massachusetts Lyceum During the American Resaissance: Materials for the Study of the Oral Tradition in American Letters,* ed. Kenneth Walter Cameron (Hartford, Conn.: Transcendental Books, 1969), 11.

31. See Chap. 3, 45–46.

32. Quoted in Russell, *The Wisest American,* 252.

33. Quoted in McQuisten, *The Relation of Emerson to Public Affairs,* 52.

34. The ultimate rhetorical poverty of this approach may come home more emphatically in an example from our own day: the way we talked—and made our decisions—about the war in Vietnam. Our fundamental communal assumptions were never effectively made the object of the public debate about the war. Rather, we deliberated about it using our everyday, commonplace terms of cost accounting. Even when the consensus turned for withdrawal and against our presence there, it was not understood as a contradiction or an embarrassment that one of the many costs accounted was the "body count." We lacked the very language to understand the war in deeper terms—say as an authentic national tragedy; what drove us from South Vietnam was a complicated and in its own way grisly calculation of inefficiency, not a national sense of shame, or failure, or even the finitude of commitment. Even now, years after the end of the war, confusion persists about what its enduring lessons, foreign and domestic, really were. For a fuller discussion see E. A. Goerner, "Privacy, Libertarian Dreams and Politics," in Robert Meagher, *Toothing Stones* (Chicago: Swallow Press, 1972), 99–115.

35. Perelman and Olbrechts-Tyteca, *The New Rhetoric*, 53.

36. Emerson, *Representative Men*, 17.

37. Ralph Waldo Emerson, "Master Minds," reprinted in *The Complete Writings of Ralph Waldo Emerson* (New York: William H. Wise, 1929) 2:v.

38. Emerson, " Literature" in *The Early Lectures of Ralph Waldo Emerson*, ed. Stephen E. Whicher and Robert E. Spiller (Cambridge: Belknap Press of Harvard Univ., 1966) 11:57.

39. Emerson, "The Christian Minister: Part 1," in *Young Emerson Speaks, Unpublished Discourses on Many Subjects* by Ralph Waldo Emerson, ed. Arthur Cushman McGiffert Jr. (Boston: Houghton Mifflin, 1938), 26.

40. Bode, *The American Lyceum*, 226; Edwin Percy Whipple, "Some Recollections of Ralph Waldo Emerson," reprinted in *Emerson: A Profile*, 13.

41. It appears to be a precept of the modern rhetoricians who work as network television programmers that appealing characters can be churned out formulaically, by a sort of ethical recipe. The repetition has been endless: "An Attractive Woman" should be blonde, ample-bosomed, funny gently and only inadvertently, perhaps wily in her way but vulnerable, needful, and sufficiently witless not to threaten even the shakiest male ego. "Old People" must be cuddly: if they are occasionally feisty, it ought not be in any serious way; deep inside they must always be sweet enough to break down and smile—or wink, or hug, or perform whatever other form of friendly motor activity they can manage. It helps if they are secretly hip, or at least potentially hip, or hep, or whatever the word is this week: closet Jagger freaks populating Florida and Arizona as far as the eye can see. Above all an old person must never, under any circumstances, be detectably and discomfitingly sick, disabled, or in any way inconsolably embittered about life. "A Black Youth" is almost necessarily portrayed—and it is a sadness to see continued willingness to make this portrayal—as loudmouthed, jive talking, perhaps protuberant eyed but always ready with a carnivorously wide smile, and if possible possessed of some other equally endearing physical deformity, appalling obesity being the favorite.

What is interesting about the appeal of these characters is that they cannot—programming policies to the contrary—be multiplied indefinitely. "Charlie's Angels" soared for years, new cherubs notwithstanding, but "Flying High" was promptly grounded and forgotten. "Love Boat" cruises on, for the most part serenely, but "Supertrain," was quickly and unceremoniously derailed. Even so, if a "Simon and Simon" succeeds, can a "Riptide" be far behind? Let "Knight Rider" gain the slightest detectable momentum, and "Automan" will appear automatically.

This all ignores the fact — and one imagines that this would strike the most devoted worshippers of the great gods Nielsen and Arbitron first of all — that the characters who sustain interest and grow in appeal are often those who break the stereotypes: Mary Tyler Moore as Mary Richards; John Amos, playing black men whose dignity consists of something clearly more than swagger; the unsmiling, unwinking, terminally unhip John Houseman; and the articulately, buoyantly stable Sergeant Phillip Freemason Esterhaus, projected by the late Michael Conrad on "Hill Street Blues."

42. Frederic Ives Carpenter, *Emerson Handbook* (New York: Henricks House, 1953), 16.

43. Samuel McChord Crothers, *Ralph Waldo Emerson: How to Know Him* (Indianapolis: Bobbs-Merrill, 1921), vii; Emerson, *Essays, First Series,* "Self-Reliance," 35.

44. Ibid., 31, 40, 48.

45. Cabot, *A Memoir of Ralph Waldo Emerson* 1:53.

46. Emerson, *Essays, First Series,* "Self-Reliance," 30.

47. Quoted in Cabot, *A Memoir of Ralph Waldo Emerson,* 320; Ralph Waldo Emerson, "The Times," in *Nature,* reprinted in *The Complete Writings* 1:81.

48. Jay B. Hubbell, "Emerson and the South," reprinted in *Emerson: A Profile,* 147–48.

49. Ralph Waldo Emerson, "Success," in *Society and Solitude,* reprinted in *The Complete Writings* 1:709.

50. Irving Rein, "The New England Transcendentalists: Philosophy and Rhetoric," *Philosophy and Rhetoric* 1(1969):115. Three other assessments of Emerson by traditional standards of rhetoric are Otis Aggertt, "The Public Speaking of Ralph Waldo Emerson," M.A. thesis, Univ. of Illinois, 1947; John Lawton, "A Rhetorical Analysis of Representative Ceremonial Addresses of Ralph Waldo Emerson," Ph.D. diss., State Univ. of Iowa, 1957; Ralph Pomeroy, "Ralph Waldo Emerson as a Public Speaker," Ph.D. diss., Stanford Univ., 1960.

51. To see Emerson's rhetoric in untraditional terms is hardly an unprecedented idea. An interesting study of the relation between Emerson's philosophy and his doctrine of audience adaptation is John H. Sloan, " 'The Miraculous Uplifting': Emerson's Relationship with His Audience," *Quarterly Journal of Speech* 52(1966):10–15. An excellent study of the relation between Emerson's rhetoric and his epistemology is Roberta K. Ray, "The Role of the Orator in the Philosophy of Ralph Waldo Emerson," *Speech Monographs* 41(Aug. 1947):215–25.

52. Newton Dillaway, *Prophet of America* (Boston: Little, Brown, 1936), 118; Michaud, *Enraptured Yankee,* 267; Rebecca Richmond, *Chautauqua: An American Place* (New York: Duell, Sloan & Pearce, 1943), 24.

53. Jeffrey L. Duncan, *The Power and Form of Emerson's Thought* (Charlottesville: Univ. Press of Virginia, 1973), 43.

54. Ralph L. Rusk, *The Life of Ralph Waldo Emerson* (New York: Charles Scribner 1949), 259; Wagenknecht, *Portrait of a Balanced Soul,* 108.

55. Whipple, "Some Recollections of Ralph Waldo Emerson," 3; Hill, *Emerson and His Philosophy,* 59–60.

56. Ralph Waldo Emerson, "Fate," in *The Conduct of Life,* reprinted in *The Complete Writings* 1:522.

57. Wagenknecht, *Portrait of a Balanced Soul,* 216; Dillaway, *Prophet of America,* 22. Here we have an excellent example of ethical argument gone awry in the disconnection of thought from character.

58. Quoted in Dillaway, *Prophet of America,* 299; Hill, *Emerson and His*

Philosophy, 92. Emerson occasionally shared his gentle humor with his friends. In trying to convince Thoreau he spent too much time in the woods, Emerson argued that if God had intended Thoreau to live in a swamp, he would have made him a frog. Throeau's reply, perhaps mercifully, is not recorded. Quoted in Wagenknecht, *Portrait of a Balanced Soul,* 108.

59. Quoted in Charles Eliot Norton, "Emerson—The Brahmin View," reprinted in *Emerson: A Profile,* 143; Quoted in Michaud, *Enraptured Yankee,* 111.

60. Quoted in Michaud, *Enraptured Yankee,* 111.

61. Emerson, "Fate" 1:522.

62. Phillips Russell argues that " 'Self-Reliance' was an elixir to a famished Young America," *The Wisest American,* 77; Stephen E. Whicher, *Freedom and Fate: An Inner Life of Ralph Waldo Emerson* (Philadelphia: Univ. Pennsylvania Press, 1953), 173.

63. Dillaway, *Prophet of America,* 111. Leonard Nick Neufeldt, "Editor's Preface," in *Ralph Waldo Emerson, New Appraisals: A Symposium,* ed. Leonard Nick Neufeldt (Hartford: Transcendental Books, 1973), 5; Quoted in Dillaway, *Prophet in America,* 55; Wagenknecht, *Portrait of a Balanced Soul,* 230.

64. Samuel McChord Crothers, *Emerson,* 8; Dillaway, *Prophet of America,* 113; John Dewey, "Ralph Waldo Emerson," reprinted in *Emerson: A Collection of Critical Essays,* ed. Milton A. Konvitz and Stephen E. Whicher (Englewood Cliffs, N.J.: Prentice-Hall, 1962), 29.

65. Many of the ideas in this section were refined in a very helpful discussion with Professor William J. Brandt of the University of California at Berkeley.

66. Quoted in Dillaway, *Prophet of America,* 116.

67. See Russell, *The Wisest American,* 54; Quoted in Wagenknecht, *Portrait of a Balanced Soul,* 190, 181.

68. Moncure Daniel Conway, *Emerson at Home and Abroad* (New York: Hasdell House, 1968), 242; Quoted in Rusk, *The Life,* 435; George Santayana, "Emerson," in *Emerson: A Collection of Critical Essays,* 37; Rusk, *The Life,* 293.

69. Emerson, "The Progress of Culture," in *Social Aims,* reprinted in *The Complete Writings* 1:81.

70. Emerson, "The Times," ibid.; Emerson, "The Transcendentalist," ibid. 1:101.

71. Emerson, *Essays, First and Second Series,* "Self-Reliance," 31, 35, 36.

72. Quoted in Rusk, *The Life,* 248. To Lowell, "Emerson seemed to merit Ben Jonson's praise of Bacon as the one noble speaker of his time, full of gravity and nobly censorious in his language and so pithy in his thought that his hearers could not cough or look aside from him without loss." Ibid., 439.

73. Whipple, "Some Recollections of Ralph Waldo Emerson," 10.

74. Emerson, *First and Second Series,* "Self-Reliance," 37, 38, 39, 34, 43, 41. Although there is no hard statistical evidence, my sense is that only the King James Bible and Shakespeare produced as many of our language's familiar expressions as Emerson. Two more examples: "Strike, says the smith, the iron is white"; ("Prudence," *Essays, First Series,* in *The Complete Writings* 1:193); "if a man has good corn, or wood, or board, or pigs, to sell, or can make better chairs or knives, crucibles or church organs, than anybody else, you will find a broad, hard-beaten road to his house, though it be in the woods" (quoted in Russell, *The Wisest American,* 254. Over the years, this has been misquoted as "build a better mousetrap and the world will beat a path to your door").

75. Hill, *Emerson and His Philosophy,* 76.

76. *Ohio Register,* 21 March 1867.

77. Morse Peckham, "Emerson's Prose," in *Emerson: New Appraisals,* 66; Hill, *Emerson and His Philosophy,* 69; Quoted in Hubbell, "Emerson and the South," 156–57. There are critics (Hopkins, Buell) who have found Emerson not altogether so bereft of transition and order. I find these analyses largely unpersuasive, but I do find myself very much in sympathy with the effort. There seem to me to be at least two sorts of reasons to suspect that Emerson's scrambled topics occur in accordance to some subtle sort of pattern: first, our convictions about the quality of Emerson's mind; and second, our convictions about what will hold a audience. By this I mean my suspicion, which I expect you somehow to share, that genuine transitionless chaos would eventually have driven his listeners from the lecture hall.

78. Reprinted in Mead, *Yankee Eloquence in the Middle West,* 40–41.

79. *Rusk, A Life,* 411; Wagenknecht, *Portrait of a Balanced Soul,* 100.

80. Russell, *The Wisest American,* 303; Rusk, *A Life,* 287.

81. Emerson, "Behavior," in *The Conduct of Life,* reprinted in *The Complete Writings* 1:579; Maurice Gonnaud, "Human Seer: Humor and Its Avators in Emerson," reprinted in *Emerson: New Appraisals,* 79; Stephen Whicher, "Emerson's Tragic Sense," reprinted in *Emerson: A Collection of Critical Essays,* 39; Leonard N. Neufeldt, "The Law of Permutation—Emerson's Mode," reprinted in *Emerson: New Appraisals,* 20.

82. Ralph Barton Perry, *The Thought and Character of William James* (Boston: Little, Brown, 1935) 1:41; Henry James, Sr., as quoted in ibid, 43.

83. Whipple, "Some Recollections of Ralph Waldo Emerson," 2, 3, 2.

84. Quoted in Conway, *Emerson at Home and Abroad,* 139; David Macrae, quoted in Wagenknecht, *Portrait of a Balanced Soul,* 123.

85. Hill, *Emerson and His Philosophy,* 40.

86. Ralph Waldo Emerson, "Experience," in *Essays, Second Series,* reprinted in *The Complete Writings* 1:261.

87. Quoted in Hill, *Emerson and His Philosophy,* 58; Hopkins, *Spires of Form,* 19.

88. Lawrence Buell, *Literary Transcendentalism* (Ithaca, N.Y.: Cornell Univ. Press, 1973), 310; Hill, *Emerson and His Philosophy,* 59.

89. Emerson's letter to Margaret Fuller, reprinted in Michaud, *Enraptured Yankee,* 219; Hill, *Emerson and His Philosophy,* 59.

90. Ray, "The Role of the Orator," 221; Emerson, "The Christian Minister: Part 1," 26.

91. Duncan, *The Power and Form of Emerson's Thought,* 42; Whicher, "Emerson's Tragic Sense," 40; Peckham, "Emerson's Prose." 73.

92. See Whicher and Spiller, "Introduction," *The Early Lectures* 1, 13.

93. Emerson, *Essays, First and Second Series,* "Compensation," 59; 67; 57–58.

94. Ibid., 59, 60, 75, 66, 62, 71, 76.

95. Michaud, *Enraptured Yankee,* 277.

96. Emerson, *Essays, First and Second Series,* "Compensation," 73.

97. Ibid., 70.

98. Quoted in Crothers, *Emerson: How to Know Him,* 20.

99. Emerson, *Essays, First and Second Series,* "Compensation," 76.

100. Wagenknecht, *Portrait of a Balanced Soul,* 30.

101. Bode, "Enough of His Life to Suggest His Character," xi.

102. Still, since rhetoric helps make the man, it is difficult wholly to disengage judgments of the rehetoric from judgments of the man and of mankind.

103. Emerson, *Essays, First and Second Series,* "Compensation," 63.

104. Evelyn Barish Greenberger, "The Phoenix on the Wall: Consciousness in Emerson's Early and Late Journals," in *Emerson: New Appraisals,* 54. Emerson's reaction to Waldo's death has been given much critical notice. The example Greenberger quotes is typical: "I am not friendly to myself. I bite and tear myself . . . when will the day of peace and reconcilement come when, self-united and friendly, I shall display heart and energy to the World?"

105. Bode, "Enough of His Life to Suggest His Character," vii.

106. Emerson, "Experience" 1:253.

107. Emerson, "Experience" 1:263; Emerson, "Eloquence," in *Society and Solitude,* reprinted in *The Collected Writings* 1:763, 766.

108. Bode, *The American Lyceum,* 226; Emerson, "Art and Criticism," in *The Natural History of Intellect,* reprinted in *The Complete Writings* 2:1335.

109. Rusk, *The Life,* 281.

110. *Cincinnati Times,* 28 January 1857, quoted in Mead, *Yankee Eloquence in the Middle West,* 223.

111. Henry Nash Smith, "Emerson's Problem of Vocation," in *Emerson: A Collection of Essays,* 61: Quoted in Russell, *The Wisest American,* 162; Whicher, *Freedom and Fate,* 173.

CHAPTER 6

1. Samuel Clemens, *Mark Twain's Autobiography,* ed. Charles Neider (New York: Harper, 1917), 165.

2. Samuel Clemens, *Complete Essays of Mark Twain,* ed. Charles Neider (Garden City, N.Y.: Doubleday, 1963), xviii.

3. Paul Fatout, *Mark Twain on the Lecture Circuit* (Bloomington, Ind.: Indiana Univ. Press, 1960), 98–99, 16.

4. Fatout, *Twain on the Lecture Circuit,* 134–35; Samuel Clemens, "Salutatory," reprinted in *Essays,* 1.

5. Hamlin Hill, *Mark Twain: God's Fool* (New York: Harper & Row, 1973), xxiii; Fatout, *Twain on the Lecture Circuit,* 165, 135; cited in Robert Regan, *Unpromising Heroes: Mark Twain and His Characters* (Berkeley: Univ. of California Press, 1966), 27.

6. *Chicago Daily Tribune,* 8 January 1869; the dating of Twain's three stages is intended to be approximate and flexible. He did some rhetorically serious work both in his beginning phase and in his decline, and by no means was his middle period innocent of rhetorical indulgence of both his audience and himself, as for example his frank request for applause interrupting his delivery of "Woman: An Opinion"; reprinted in Clemens, *Mark Twain's Speeches* (New York: Harper, 1923), 31–33.

7. Fatout, *Twain on the Lecture Circuit,* 68, 123; Justin Kaplan, *Mr. Clemens and Mark Twain* (New York: Simon & Schuster, 1966), 29.

8. Fatout, *Twain on the Lecture Circuit,* 46; Kaplan, *Clemens/Twain,* 29.

9. Ibid.

10. Gladys Carmen Bellamy, *Mark Twain as a Literary Artist* (Norman: Univ. of Oklahoma Press, 1950), 115. In a more direct statement of this sort, a reply to Rebecca Richmond's interview question about Twain's favorite tree, Twain said "any

that bears forbidden fruit." Richmond's papers were recently discovered in the archives of the Grand Rapids Public Library, as reported in the *Grand Rapids Press,* 12 October 1978.

11. Fatout, *Twain on the Lecture Circuit,* 46.

12. Hill, *God's fool,* 177; Kaplan, *Clemens/Twain,* 366.

13. Fatout, *Twain on the Lecture Circuit,* 273.

14. This was probably behind his later claim to the title "Professor of Moral Culture and the Dogmatic Humanities," Bellamy, *Twain as Literary Artist,* 112, 114.

15. "R. C. B.," in the *Critic,* 25 April 1896, quoted in Twain, *Essays,* xiii; Phillip Foner, *Mark Twain as Social Critic* (New York: International, 1958), 237, 309.

16. Quoted in Hill, *God's Fool,* 9; Maxwell Geismar, *Mark Twain: An American Prophet* (Boston: Houghton Mifflin, 1970), 205.

17. Clemens, *Essays,* 682.

18. Geismar, *An American Prophet,* 112; Regan, *Unpromising Heroes,* 62; Bellamy, *Twain as Literary Artist,* 192, 218.

19. Bellamy, *Twain as Literary Artist,* 139, 110, 323, 265.

20. Foner, *Twain as Social Critic,* 309.

21. Clemens, *Essays,* xvi.

22. Reprinted in *Mark Twain's Speeches* (New York: Harper, 1923), 104–8.

23. Henry Nash Smith, *Mark Twain, The Development of a Writer* (Cambridge, Mass.: Belknap Press of Harvard Univ. Press, 1962), vii.

24. The word selection here ("bag") illustrates Paul Fatout's very emphatic contention that Twain laid "considerable stress on what he called 'that elusive and shifty grain of gold, the right word.' He once remarked 'that the difference between the almost right word and the right word is the difference between the lightning bug and the lightning.' " *Twain on the Lecture Circuit,* 250.

25. One should perhaps temper the reading of this particular passage by recalling Twain's definition of a classic as "a book which people praise and don't read." "Pudd'nhead Wilson's New Calendar," reprinted in Clemens, *The Art, Humor and Humanity of Mark Twain,* ed. M. M. Brasher and R. M. Rodney, with an introduction by Edward Wagenknecht (Norman: Univ. of Oklahoma Press, 1959), 399.

26. Perhaps the most impressive aspect of this familiarity is that we readers, at a century's remove, can share so fully in it. The language in which Twain communicates his commonsense values "dates" better than the language of perhaps any other nineteenth-century American orator.

27. Smith, *Twain, Development of a Writer,* viii; Allison Ensor, *Mark Twain and the Bible* (Lexington: Univ. of Kentucky Press, 1969), 27.

28. Ibid., 75–96.

29. Geismar, *Mark Twain: An American Prophet,* 58.

30. Albert E. Stone Jr., *The Innocent Eye* (New Haven: Yale Univ. Press, 1961).

31. Walter Blair, *Horse Sense in American Humor* (New York: Russell & Russell, 1942), v.

32. Hill, *God's Fool,* 272; 77; Regan, *Unpromising Heroes,* ix.

33. *London Spectator,* 18 October 1873.

34. William Dean Howells, "Mark Twain: An Inquiry," *North American Review* 222 (Feb. 1901), 306–21. Reprinted in *Mark Twain: Selected Criticism,* ed. and introduction by Arthur L. Scott (Dallas: Southern Methodist Univ. Press, 1967), 82; Geismar, *Mark Twain: An American Prophet,* 6.

35. Clemens, "The American Vandal," reprinted in *Mark Twain's Speeches,* 22.

36. Clemens, "The Sandwich Islands," reprinted ibid., 14–15.

37. Clemens, "The Weather," reprinted ibid., 56–57.

38. Clemens, "Plymouth Rock and the Pilgrims," reprinted ibid., 86–87, 88–89.

39. Clemens, "Theoretical and Practical Morals," reprinted ibid., 191–92.

40. Clemens, "Literature," reprinted ibid., 207–8.

41. Fatout, *Twain on the Lecture Circuit,* 134.

42. Quoted in Smith, *Twain, Development of a Writer,* 98.

43. Samuel Clemens, *Mark Twain's Letters,* arranged and with comment by Albert Bigelow Paine (New York: Harper, 1917) 1:316; Kaplan, *Clemens/Twain,* 210; Smith, *Twain, Development of a Writer,* 99, 98.

44. Kaplan, *Clemens/Twain,* 225.

45. Clemens, "The Babies," reprinted in *Mark Twain's Speeches,* 58, 59, 60.

46. Ibid., 61–62.

47. Smith, *Twain, Development of a Writer,* 97.

48. Clemens, "Turncoats," reprinted in *Mark Twain's Speeches,* 114.

49. Clemens, "Consistency," 121.

50. Clemens, *Essays,* xxiv; Regan, *Unpromising Heroes,* vii.

51. Bellamy, *Twain as Literary Artist,* 105; Clemens, *Mark Twain's Letters* 2:527; Blair, *Horse Sense in American Humor,* v; Bellamy, *Twain as Literary Artist,* 56.

52. Wayne C. Booth, *A Rhetoric of Irony* (Chicago: Univ. of Chicago Press, 1974), 13.

53. Bellamy, *Twain as Literary Artist,* 115.

54. Fatout, *Twain on the Lecture Circuit,* 123, 124; Clemens, *Mark Twain's Letters* 2:527.

55. Bellamy, *Twain as Literary Artist,* 115n.; Kaplan, *Clemens/Twain,* 146.

56. *Boston Daily Advertiser,* 11 November 1869.

57. Samuel Clemens, *Mark Twain Speaks for Himself,* ed. Paul Fatout (West Lafayette, Ind.: Purdue Univ. Press, 1978), 195–97.

58. Kaplan, *Clemens/Twain,* 283n.

59. In his *Autobiography,* Twain called it a *responsibility* for the speaker who wished both to entertain and to instruct to memorize his speech in order to get it properly "limbered up, broken up, colloquialized." When he learned to memorize his prepared materials, "they transformed themselves...with all their obstructing preciseness and formalities gone out of them for good." Clemens, *The Autobiography,* 176.

60. Clemens, "The Galveston Orphan Bazaar," reprinted in *Mark Twain's Speeches,* 204–6.

61. Kaplan, *Clemens/Twain,* 361.

62. Ibid., 24, 14–15.

63. Regan, *Unpromising Heroes,* 36.

64. Ibid., 13–14.

65. Hill, *God's Fool,* 176.

66. Clemens, *Mark Twain's Letters* 2:640.

67. Reprinted in Hill, *God's Fool,* 176–77.

68. Ibid., 177.

69. Cited, ibid.

70. Clemens, *Essays,* xxiv.

71. Clemens, "Seventieth Birthday," reprinted in *Mark Twain's Speeches,* 254–62. This passage is helpful in illustrating to some extent Twain's gift for timing; for

example, that fine progression in which one can almost hear Twain: "then the worm turned (pause). I was the worm (pause); it was my turn to turn (long pause) and I turned." But such gifts of delivery are part of Twain's art that are peculiarly difficult for us to appreciate at first hand since they were impossible to record. But the people who heard him almost unanimously marveled at Twain's timing, and Twain himself revealed that he had reflected extensively on this matter of "the pause—that impressive silence, that eloquent silence, that geometrically progressive silence" (*The Autobiography,* 181).

72. Clemens, *Essays,* xxiv.

CHAPTER 7

1. See Charles Wegener, *Liberal Education and the Modern University* (Chicago: Univ. of Chicago Press, 1978).

2. George Santayana, *Character and Opinion in the United States* (New York: Charles Scribner, 1920), 64; Ralph Barton Perry, *The Thought and Character of William James* (Boston: Little, Brown, 1935) 1:129.

3. Ibid. 1:383.

4. Gay Wilson Allen, *William James* (New York: Viking Press, 1967), x.

5. Ibid., 41.

6. Perry, *Thought and Character* 2:125; H. S. Thayer, foreword to William James, *Pragmatism* (Cambridge: Harvard Univ. Press, 1975), xxxi.

7. William James, "The Present Dilemma in Philosophy"; reprinted in *Pragmatism: A New Name for Some Old Ways of Thinking* (New York: Longmans, Green, 1907).

8. Ibid., 15.

9. Ibid., 6, 12.

10. Ibid., 6, 13, 37.

11. Quoted in Perry, *Thought and Character* 2:457.

12. Ralph Waldo Emerson, in "Self-Reliance," *Essays, First and Second Series* (New York: E. P. Dutton, 1909), 29–55.

13. Samuel Clemens, *Life on the Mississippi* (New York: Signet Books, 1961), 67–68.

14. William James, *A Pluralistic Universe,* introduction by Richard Bernstein (Cambridge: Harvard Univ. Press, 1977), originally delivered as the Hibbert Lectures at Manchester College, 4–28 May 1908.

15. James, "The Present Dilemma of Philosophy," 40.

16. Ibid., 5. See also note 69.

17. See above, 165–66.

18. *The Letters of William James,* ed. and introduction by his son Henry James (Boston: Atlantic Monthly, 1920) 2:11.

19. William James, *The Varieties of Religious Experience* (New York: Longmans, Green, 1902), 337.

20. Eusapia Paladino, the European medium, is perhaps the most famous of this sort; see James "President's Address before the Society for Psychical Research," reworded as "What Psychical Research Has Accomplished," in *The Will to Believe and Other Essays in Popular Philosophy* (New York: Longmans, Green, 1905), 299–327.

21. Ibid., 299–300.

22. James, *Pragmatism,* 7.

23. James, *Letters* 2:3; William James, *Principles of Psychology* (New York: Henry Holt, 1927) 2:299; William James, "The Sentiment of Rationality" reprinted in *The Will to Believe,* 63–110, 63.

24. William James, *Talks to Teachers on Psychology: And to Students on Some of Life's Ideals* (New York: Henry Holt, 1912), 266.

25. James, *Principles* 2:675n.; Perry, *Thought and Character* 1:734.

26. William James, *Collected Essays and Reviews* (New York: Longmans, Green, 1920), 427–28; James, *Varieties,* 31.

27. James, *Letters* 1:131; Ibid. 2:127.

28. Ibid. 2:76.

29. Santayana, *Character and Opinion,* 76-77.

30. James, *Pragmatism,* 109, 142–43; Patrick Kiernan Dooley, *Pragmatism as Humanism: The Philosophy of William James,* Professional/Technical Series (Chicago: Nelson-Hall, 1974), 107; James, *Varieties,* 489.

31. James, *Pragmatism,* 201; James, *Will to Believe,* 61; Perry, *Thought and Character* 1:737.

32. See, for example, *Varieties,* 522, *Pragmatism,* 229, *A Pluralistic University,* 141; James, *Will to Believe,* 61; James, "Is Life Worth Living" in *Will to Believe,* 32–62, 61.

33. James, *Letters* 2:39; ibid. 1:58; James, *Varieties,* 88.

34. James, *Pragmatism,* 257.

35. Ibid., 290–91.

36. C. Hartley Grattan, *The Three Jameses: A Family of Minds* (New York: Longmans, Green, 1932), 132.

37. Cited in Perry, *Thought and Character* 1:322.

38. Ibid. 1:654; James, *Letters* 1:147.

39. Perry, *Thought and Character* 1:655.

40. James, *Letters* 1:247; William James, *Essays in Radical Empiricism* (New York: Longmans, Green, 1919), 41; Quoted in Allen, *William James,* 324.

41. James, "What Pragmatism Means," reprinted in *Pragmatism,* 67; James, "Some Metaphysical Problems Pragmatically Considered," reprinted ibid., 95; James, "The One and the Many," reprinted ibid., 132; James, "The Notion of Truth," reprinted ibid., 236; James, "Pragmatism and Humanism," reprinted ibid., 257; James, *Letters* 2:187, 203.

42. George Santayana, *Character and Opinion in the United States* (New York: Charles Scribner, 1920), 71; Perry, *Thought and Character* 2:682.

43. Quoted in James, *Letters* 2:174–75, 1:135.

44. Quoted in Perry, *Thought and Character* 1:348–49, 327.

45. James, *Letters* 2:147, 102.

46. James, *Varieties,* 456–57.

47. James, *Essays in Radical Empiricism,* iv–v.

48. William James, *Memories and Studies* (New York: Longmans, Green, 1911), 14–15.

49. Julius Seelye Bixler, *Religion in the Philosophy of William James* (Boston: Marshall Jones, 1926), 40; Edward C. Moore, *William James* Great American Thinkers Series (New York: Washington Square Press, 1966), 79; John Dewey, "An Empirical Survey of Empiricisms," in *Studies in the History of Ideas* (New York: Columbia Univ. Press, 1935) 3:20–21; James, *Varieties,* 20.

50. James, *Principles,* 20.

51. James, *Pragmatism,* 78; James, *Talks to Teachers,* 264; James, *Letters* 2:199.

52. Perry, *Thought and Character* 2:704; James, *Varieties,* 429.

53. Quoted in Bixler, *Religion in the Philosophy of William James,* 60, 64.

54. Ibid., 105, 106.

55. Dooley, *Pragmatism as Humanism,* xi. Dooley's very comprehensive summary of the criticisms, 127–43 is most helpful, and its influence is evident here.

56. Ibid., 143; quoted ibid.

57. Ibid., xii; Perry, *Thought and Character* 2:515; Gordon Allport, "The Productive Paradoxes of William James," *Psychological Review* 50(1943):96; A. O. Lovejoy, *The Thirteen Pragmatisms and Other Essays* (Baltimore: Johns Hopkins Univ. Press, 1963).

58. See ibid., 239n.5.

59. Santayana, *Character and Opinion,* 77–78.

60. Both quoted in Perry, *Thought and Character* 2:475, 488.

61. `Both cited in Bixler, *Religion in the Philosophy of William James,* 1, 173.

62. James, *Principles* 2:369; James, *A Pluralistic Universe,* 44.

63. James, *Letters* 2:300–301.

64. Quoted in Perry, *Thought and Character* 2:338. James never did get to finish the book of systematic philosophy that he wanted to write. The closest James came to a sustained effort of this nature was the fragmentary *Some Problems in Philosophy: A Beginning of an Introduction to Philosophy,* published—in fact, discovered—posthumously.

65. Quoted in Perry, *Thought and Character* 2:443, 444; William James, "The Teaching of Philosophy in Our Colleges," *Nation* 23 (1876):178.

66. Grattan, *Three Jameses,* 156; Perry, *Thought and Character* 2:449; Santayana, *Character and Opinion,* 85.

67. George Santayana, quoted in Allen, *William James,* 437; Santayana, *Character and Opinion,* 82.

68. To push the "ambassador" metaphor a bit further, James's use of his character as a resource for this diplomacy has historical precedents: a Metternich, a Castlereagh, or in our time a Kissinger. I find this part of the analogy somewhat misleading, however, somewhat unflattering to James.

69. Santayana, *Character and Opinion,* 304–5. With his line about intellectual cripples and moral hunchbacks, Santayana might have been discribing the brilliant but arrogant, cranky, and eventually almost anti-social Charles Sanders Peirce. For almost a quarter century James scrounged appointments for Peirce, all of which were squandered bullheadedly. Finally, James set up a trust fund for Peirce, noting in exasperation (*Letters* 2:177): "There's no excuse for him, I admit. But God made him; and after kicking and cuffing and prodding him for twenty years, I have now come to believe that he ought to be treated in charity pure and simple (even though that be a vice)."

70. James, *Letters* 2:120; quoted in Bixler, *Religion in the Philosphy of William James,* 59; Perry, *Thought and Character* 2:704.

71. Quoted in Bixler, *Religion in the Philosophy of William James,* 18; James, *Will to Believe,* 32.

72. James, *Memories and Studies,* 349.

73. Allen, *William James,* 300.

74. Perry, *Thought and Character* 1:428; Ibid. 2:695.

75. Moore, *William James,* 1; James, *Will to Believe,* 270; Santayana, *Character and Opinion* 2:9, 92.

76. Allen, *William James,* 277, 287.

77. James, *Memories and Studies,* 195; James, *Letters* 1:199.

78. Santayana, *Character and Opinion,* 96; James, *Memories and Studies,* 142.

79. Allen, *William James,* vii.

80. Allen, *A Pluralistic Universe,* 14.

81. See Chap. 4, 467–70.

82. Perry, *Thought and Character* 1:541.

83. James, *Talks to Teachers,* 267.

CHAPTER 8

1. The most celebrated study of this problem is Alvin Toffler, *Future Shock* (New York: Bantam Books, 1971). A particularly grim analysis of technological society's demands and public communication's capacity to respond is advanced by Jacques Ellul, *The Technological Society,* trans. John Wilkerson (New York: Vintage Books, 1967).

2. For an interesting study of the various forms of political consultants infecting the present political culture, see Larry J. Sabato, *The Rise of Political Consultants* (New York: Basic Books, 1981). Two other useful books are Dan Nimmo, *The Political Persuaders of Modern Election Campaigns* (Englewood Cliffs, N.J.: Prentice-Hall, 1970) and Stanley Kelley, Jr., *Professional Public Relations and Political Power* (Baltimore: Johns Hopkins Univ. Press, 1956). An account of political consulting by a thoughtful practitioner is Joseph Napolitan, *The Election Game and How to Win It* (New York: Doubleday, 1972).

3. Joe McGinniss, *The Selling of the President 1968* (New York: Trident Press, 1969); Jack W. Germond and Jules Witcover, *Blue Smoke and Mirrors: How Reagan Won and Why Carter Lost the Election of 1980* (New York: Viking Press, 1981).

4. Jimmy Breslin, *How the Good Guys Finally Won* (New York: Ballantine Books, 1975), 31–32.

5. The nineteenth century was of course not alone in perceiving the democratic condition with astounded and somewhat stricken despair. An important argument for the institutionalization of an especially authoritative role for experts in the democratic process is Walter Lippmann, *Public Opinion* (New York, Macmillan 1922). In this, Lippman may be seen as this century's Orestes Brownson.

6. Richard Hofstadter, *Anti-Intellectualism in American Life* (New York: Alfred A. Knopf, 1963), 299.

7. Some of the ideas implicit in this section arose from conversations with Professor Dante Germino about democracy as the "open society."

8. Bernard Crick, *In Defense of Politics* (Chicago: Univ. of Chicago Press, 1962), 2 4. This intriguing book is finally a disappointment in its failure, indeed its refusal to discriminate good politics from bad politics, good rhetoric from bad rhetoric. It seems that for Crick, any accommodation that is "politically" achieved is a tolerable one, any rhetoric is successful as long as it is thoroughly popular. In his concern for toleration, Crick sees no qualitative difference among rhetorics, and specifies no need for moral stature or intellectual content to guide the public discussion. But even the doctrinaire democrats felt the need for some discipline of thought and character to guide the public discussion. Even Jefferson, the first and most articulate "popular" president, conceded that "though the will of the majority is in all cases to prevail, that will to be rightful must be reasonable"; Thomas Jefferson,

"First Inaugural," in *Inaugural Addresses of the Presidents of the United States* (Washington, D.C.: U.S. Government Printing Office, 1961), 14. In the chapters on Emerson, Twain, and James, I hope I have shown ways in which a qualitative rhetorical difference—true popularization, not mere indulgence or even vulgarization—makes a difference worth recognizing and responding to.

9. See Chap. 3.

10. Booth, *Modern Dogma and the Rhetoric of Assent* (Chicago: Univ. of Chicago Press, 1974), 196.

SELECTED BIBLIOGRAPHY

SOURCES ON RHETORIC

Aristotle. *On Sophistical Refutations.* Trans. W. A. Pickard. Great Books of the Western World. Chicago: Univ. of Chicago Press, 1952.

_____. *Rhetoric.* Trans. W. Rhys Roberts. Great Books of the Western World. Chicago: Univ. of Chicago Press, 1952.

Booth, Wayne C. *Modern Dogma and the Rhetoric of Assent.* Chicago: Univ. of Chicago Press, 1974.

_____. *A Rhetoric of Irony.* Chicago: Univ. of Chicago Press, 1974.

_____. "Mere Rhetoric, Rhetoric, and Reality." A Lecture at Woodward Court, University of Chicago, 11 April 1978.

Burke, Kenneth. *Language as Symbolic Action: Essays on Life, Literature and Method.* Berkeley: Univ. of California Press, 1968.

_____. *A Rhetoric of Motives.* Berkeley: Univ. of California Press, 1950.

Crick, Bernard. *In Defence of Politics.* Chicago: Univ. of Chicago Press, 1962.

Perelman, Chaim, and Olbrechts-Tyteca, L. *The New Rhetoric.* Notre Dame, Ind.: Univ. of Notre Dame Press, 1971.

Plato. *Gorgias.* Trans. Benjamin Jowett. Great Books of the Western World. Chicago: Univ. of Chicago Press, 1952.

_____. *Phaedrus.* Trans. Benjamin Jowett. Great Books of the Western World. Chicago: Univ. of Chicago Press, 1952.

_____. *The Seventh Letter.* Trans. J. Harward. Great Books of the Western World. Chicago: Univ. of Chicago Press, 1952.

BOOKS ON AMERICA AND
AMERICAN POPULAR CULTURE

Beard, Charles A. and Mary R. *A Basic History of the United States.* New York: Doubleday, 1944.

Beitzinger, A. J. *A History of American Political Thought.* New York: Dodd, Mead, 1972.

Bode, Carl. *The Anatomy of American Popular Culture, 1840–1861.* Berkeley: Univ. of California Press, 1959.

Brownson, Orestes. *The Brownson Reader.* Ed. Alvan S. Ryan. New York: P. J. Kenedy, 1955.

Bryce, James. *The American Commonwealth.* 2d ed., rev. New York: Macmillan, 1891.

Cooper, James Fenimore. *The American Democrat.* New York: Penguin Books, 1967.

de Tocqueville, Alexis. *Democracy in America*. Trans. George Lawrence, ed. J. P. Mayer. Garden City, N.Y.: Doubleday, Anchor Books. 1969.

Gunderson, Robert Gray. *The Log-Cabin Campaign*. Lexington, Ky.: Univ. of Kentucky Press, 1957. Reprint. Westport, Conn.: Greenwood Press, 1977.

Hamilton, Alexander; Jay, John; and Madison, James. The *Federalist Papers*. Introduction by Edward Mead Earle. New York: Modern Library, 1937.

Hofstadter, Richard. *The American Political Tradition and the Men Who Made It*. New York: Vintage Books, 1974.

_____. *Anti-Intellectualism in American Life*. New York: Alfred A. Knopf, 1966.

Knowles, Malcolm. *The Adult Education Movement in the United States*. New York: Holt, Rinehart & Winston, 1962.

Nye, Russell Blaine. *Society and Culture in America; 1830–1860*. New York: Harper & Row, 1974.

Santayana, George. *Character and Opinion in the United States*. New York: Charles Scribner, 1920.

OTHER SOURCES ON AMERICA

Goerner, E. A. "Privacy, Libertarian Dreams, and Politics." In *Toothing Stones,* ed. Robert Meagher. Chicago: Swallow Press, 1972.

Jefferson, Thomas. "First Inaugural Address." In *Inaugural Addresses of the Presidents*. Washington, D.C.: U.S. Government Printing Office, 1961.

Turner, Frederick Jackson. "The Significance of the Frontier in American History." In *The Annual Report of the American Historical Association for the Year 1893*. Washington, D.C.: U.S. Government Printing Office, 1894.

Whitman, Walt. *Leaves of Grass*. Ed. Emory Holloway. Garden City, N.J.: Doubleday, 1926.

BOOKS ON JACKSON AND JACKSONIAN AMERICA

Bugg, James, Jr. *Jacksonian Democracy: Myth or Reality?* New York: Holt, Rinehart & Winston, 1962.

Pessen, Edward. *Jacksonian America: Society, Personality, and Politics*. Homewood, Ill.: Dorsey Press, 1969.

Remini, Robert. *Andrew Jackson*. Rulers and Statesmen of the World Series, ed. Hans Trefousse. New York: Twayne, 1966.

_____. *The Revolutionary Age of Andrew Jackson*. New York: Harper & Row, 1976.

Schlesinger, Arthur M., Jr. *The Age of Jackson*. Boston: Little, Brown, 1953.

Syrett, Harold. *Andrew Jackson: His Contribution to the American Tradition*. New York: Bobbs-Merrill, 1953.

Van Deusen, Glyndon. *The Jacksonian Era: 1828–1848*. New York: Harper & Row, 1959.

Ward, John William. *Andrew Jackson: Symbol for an Age*. New York: Oxford Univ. Press, 1953.

OTHER SOURCES ON JACKSON AND JACKSONIAN AMERICA

Boston Daily Advertiser, 3 February 1815.
Boston Patriot, 28 January 1815, 11 February 1815.
Cincinnati Spirit of the West, 5 February 1815.
Columbus Ohio State Journal, 18 November 1840.
Enquirer, 18 February 1815.
National Intelligencer, 4 October 1814, Extra, 4 February 1815.
New Hampshire Patriot, 21 February 1814.
New York Evening Post, 25 January 1815.
Salem Gazette, 23 September 1814.
U.S. Congress. Senate. *Message,* 8 December 1829. 21st Cong. 1st sess. 1829–1830. Vol. 1.
_____. *Journal.* 22d Cong. 1st sess. 1831–1832.
_____. *Register of Debates in Congress.* 23d Cong. 1st sess. 1833–1834. Vol. 10.
Washington Republican, 3 February 1815.

SOURCES ON THE CIRCUIT OF PUBLIC SPEECH

American Journal of Education. 14 September 1864.
Bode, Carl. *The American Lyceum: Town Meeting of the Mind.* New York: Oxford Univ. Press, 1956.
Briggs, Irene, and Da Boll, Raymond. *Recollections of the Lyceum and Chautauqua Circuits.* Freeport, Me.: Bond Wheelright, 1969.
Gould, Joseph E. *The Chautauqua Movement: An Episode in Continuing American Revolution.* New York: State Univ. of New York Press, 1961.
Harrison, Harry P., and Detzer, Karl. *Culture Under Canvas: The Story of Tent Chautauqua.* New York: Hastings House, 1958.
Holbrook, Josiah. "The Constitution for the American Lyceum of Science and the Arts." Quoted in *The Massachusetts Lyceum During the American Renaissance; Materials for the Study of Oral Tradition in American Letters,* ed. Kenneth Walter Cameron. Hartford, Conn.: Transcendental Books, 1969.
Horner, Charles P. *Strike the Tents: The Story of Chautauqua.* Philadelphia: Dorrance 1954.
Hurlbut, J. L. *The Story of Chautauqua.* New York: G. P. Putnam, 1921.
Mead, David. *Yankee Eloquence in the Middle West, 1850–1870.* East Lansing, Mich.: Michigan State College Press, 1951.
Morrison, Theodore. *Chautauqua.* Chicago: Univ. of Chicago Press, 1974.
Richmond, Rebecca. *Chautauqua: An American Place.* New York: Duell, Sloan & Pearce, 1943.
Scott, Donald M. "The Popular Lecture and the Creation of a Public in Mid-Nineteenth Century America." *Journal of American History* 66 (1980):791 809.
Scott, Marian. *Chautauqua Caravan.* New York: Appleton-Century, 1937.
Stoddard, Paul Wakelee. "The American Lyceum." Ph.D. diss., Yale Univ., 1947.
Weaver, Richard L. II. "Josiah Holbrook: Feeding the Passion for Self-Help." *Communication Quarterly* 24(1976):10–15.
Wright, A. Augustus, ed. *Who's Who in the Lyceum.* Philadelphia: Pearson, 1906.

QUOTED SOURCES BY EMERSON

Emerson, Ralph Waldo. *The American Scholar.* In *The Complete Writings of Ralph Waldo Emerson.* New York: William H. Wise, 1929.
_____. "The Christian Minister: Part 1." In *Young Emerson Speaks, Unpublished Discourses on Many Subjects by Ralph Waldo Emerson,* ed. Arthur Cushman McGibbert, Jr. Boston: Houghton Mifflin, 1938.
_____. *The Conduct of Life.* In *The Complete Writings of Ralph Waldo Emerson.* New York: William H. Wise, 1929.
_____. *Essays, First and Second Series.* New York: E. P. Dutton, 1909.
_____. "Literature." In *The Early Lectures of Ralph Waldo Emerson,* ed. Stephen E. Whicher and Robert E. Spiller. Cambridge: Belknap Press of Harvard Univ. Press, 1966.
_____. "Master Minds." In *The Complete Writings of Ralph Waldo Emerson.* New York: William H. Wise, 1929.
_____. *Nature.* In *The Complete Writings of Ralph Waldo Emerson.* New York: William H. Wise, 1929.
_____. *Representative Men: Seven Lectures.* Boston: Houghton Mifflin, 1892.
_____. *Social Aims.* In *The Complete Writings of Ralph Waldo Emerson.* New York: William H. Wise, 1929.
_____. *Society and Solitude.* In *The Complete Writings of Ralph Waldo Emerson.* New York: William H. Wise, 1929.

BOOKS ON EMERSON

Buell, Lawrence. *Literary Transcendentalism.* Ithaca, N.Y.: Cornell Univ. Press, 1973.
Cabot, James Eliot. *A Memoir of Ralph Waldo Emerson.* Boston: Houghton Mifflin, 1893.
Carpenter, Frederic Ives. *Emerson Handbook.* New York: Henricks House, 1953.
Conway, Moncure Daniel. *Emerson at Home and Abroad.* New York: Haskell House, 1968.
Crothers, Samuel McChord. *Ralph Waldo Emerson: How to Know Him.* Indianapolis: Bobbs-Merrill, 1921.
Dillaway, Newton. *Prophet of America.* Boston: Little, Brown, 1936.
Duncan, Jeffrey L. *The Power and Form of Emerson's Thought.* Charlottesville: Univ. Press of Virginia, 1973.
Hill, J. Arthur. *Emerson and His Philosophy.* London: William Rider, 1919.
Hopkins, Vivian C. *Spires of Form.* Cambridge: Harvard Univ. Press, 1951.
McQuiston, Raymer. *The Relation of Ralph Waldo Emerson to Public Affairs.* Lawrence: Univ. of Kansas, 1923.
Michaud, Regis. *Emerson: The Enraptured Yankee.* Trans. George Boas. New York: Harper, 1930.
Rusk, Ralph L. *The Life of Ralph Waldo Emerson.* New York: Charles Scribner, 1949.
Russell, Phillips. *The Wisest American.* New York: Brentano's, 1929.
Wagenknecht, Edward. *Ralph Waldo Emerson: Portrait of a Balanced Soul.* New York: Oxford Univ. Press, 1974.
Whicher, Stephen E. *Freedom and Fate: An Inner Life of Ralph Waldo Emerson.* Philadelphia: Univ. of Pennsylvania Press, 1953.

OTHER SOURCES ON EMERSON

Aggertt, Otis. "The Public Speaking of Ralph Waldo Emerson." M. A. thesis, Univ. of Illinois, 1947.

Bode, Carl, ed. *Ralph Waldo Emerson: A Profile*. American Profile Series. New York: Hill & Wang, 1968.

Cincinnati Times, 28 January 1857.

Konvitz, Milton R., and Whicher, Stephen E., eds. *Emerson: A Collection of Critical Essays*. Englewood Cliffs, N.J.: Prentice-Hall, 1962.

Lawton, John. "A Rhetorical Analysis of Representative Ceremonial Addresses of Ralph Waldo Emerson." Ph.D. diss., State Univ. of Iowa, 1957.

Neufeldt, Leonard Nick, ed. *Ralph Waldo Emerson, New Appraisals: A Symposium*. Hartford: Transcendental Books, 1973.

Ohio Register, 21 March 1867.

Pomeroy, Ralph. "Ralph Waldo Emerson as a Public Speaker." Ph.D. diss., Stanford Univ., 1960.

Ray, Roberta K. "The Role of the Orator in the Philosophy of Ralph Waldo Emerson." *Speech Monographs* 41(Aug. 1974).

Rein, Irving. "The New England Transcendentalists: Philosophy and Rhetoric." *Philosophy and Rhetoric* 1 (1969).

Sloan, John H. " 'The Miraculous Uplifting': Emerson's Relationship with his Audience." *Quarterly Journal of Speech* 52(1966).

QUOTED SOURCES BY SAMUEL CLEMENS

Clemens, Samuel. *Complete Essays of Mark Twain*. Ed. Charles Neider. Garden City, N.Y.: Doubleday, 1963.

———. *Life on the Mississippi*. New York: Signet Books, 1961.

———. *Mark Twain's Autobiography*. Ed. Charles Neider. New York: Harper, 1917.

———. *Mark Twain's Letters*. Arranged and comment by Albert Bigelow Paine. New York: Harper, 1917.

———. *Mark Twain Speaks for Himself*. Ed. Paul Fatout. West Lafayette, Ind.: Purdue Univ. Press, 1978.

———. *Mark Twain's Speeches*. New York: Harper, 1923.

BOOKS ON MARK TWAIN

Bellamy, Gladys Carmen. *Mark Twain as Literary Artist*. Norman: Univ. of Oklahoma Press, 1950.

Blair, Walter. *Horse Sense in American Humor*. New York: Russell & Russell, 1942.

Ensor, Allison. *Mark Twain and the Bible*. Lexington: Univ. of Kentucky Press, 1969.

Fatout, Paul. *Mark Twain on the Lecture Circuit*. Bloomington, Ind.: Indiana Univ. Press, 1960.

Foner, Phillip. *Mark Twain as Social Critic*. New York: International Publishers, 1958.

Geismar, Maxwell. *Mark Twain: An American Prophet.* Boston: Houghton Mifflin, 1970.
Hill, Hamlin. *Mark Twain: God's Fool.* New York: Harper & Row, 1973.
Kaplan, Justin. *Mr. Clemens and Mark Twain.* New York: Simon & Schuster, 1966.
Regan, Robert. *Unpromising Heroes: Mark Twain and his Characters.* Berkeley: Univ. of California Press, 1966.
Smith, Henry Nash. *Mark Twain: The Development of a Writer.* Cambridge, Mass.: Belknap Press of Harvard Univ. Press, 1962.
Stone, Albert E., Jr. *The Innocent Eye.* New Haven: Yale Univ. Press, 1961.

OTHER SOURCES ON TWAIN

Boston Daily Advertiser, 11 November 1869.
Brashear, M. M., and Rodney, R. M. *The Art, Humor, and Humanity of Mark Twain.* Intro. Edward Wagenknecht. Norman: Univ. of Oklahoma Press, 1959.
Chicago Daily Tribune, 8 January 1869.
Critic, 25 April 1896.
Grand Rapids Press, 12 October 1978.
Howells, William Dean. "Mark Twain: An Inquiry." In *Mark Twain: Selected Criticism.* Ed. Arthur L. Scott. Dallas: Southern Methodist Univ. Press, 1967.
London Spectator, 18 October 1873.

QUOTED BOOKS BY WILLIAM JAMES

James, William. *Collected Essays and Reviews.* New York: Longmans, Green, 1920.
_____. *Essays in Radical Empiricism.* New York: Longmans, Green, 1912.
_____. *The Letters of William James.* Ed. Henry James. Boston: Atlantic Monthly, 1920.
_____. *A Pluralistic Universe.* Introduction by Richard Bernstein. Cambridge: Harvard Univ. Press, 1977.
_____. *Pragmatism.* New York: Longmans, Green, 1907.
_____. *Principles on Psychology.* New York: Henry Holt, 1927.
_____. *Talks to Teachers on Psychology: And to Students on Some of Life's Ideals.* New York: Henry Holt, 1912.
_____. *The Varieties of Religious Experience.* New York: Longmans, Green, 1902.
_____. *The Will to Believe and Other Essays in Popular Philosophy.* New York: Longmans, Green, 1905.

SOURCES ON WILLIAM JAMES

Allen, Gay Wilson. *William James.* New York: Viking Press, 1967.
Allport, Gordon. "The Productive Paradoxes of William James," *Psychological Review* 50:(1943).
Bixler, Julius Seelye. *Religion in the Philosophy of William James.* Boston: Marshall Jones, 1926.

Dewey, John, ed. "An Empirical Study of Empiricisms." In *Studies in the History of Ideas*. New York: Columbia Univ. Press, 1935.

Dooley, Patrick Kiernan. *Pragmatism as Humanism: The Philosophy of William James*. Professional/Technical Series. Chicago: Nelson-Hall, 1974.

Grattan, C. Hartley. *The Three Jameses: A Family of Minds*. New York: Longmans, Green, 1932.

Lovejoy, A. O. *The Thirteen Pragmatisms and Other Essays*. Baltimore: The Johns Hopkins Univ. Press, 1963.

Moore, Edward C. *William James*. Great American Thinkers Series. New York: Washington Square Press, 1966.

Perry, Ralph Barton. *The Thought and Character of William James*. Boston: Little, Brown, 1935.

Thayer, H. S. Foreword to *Pragmatism*. Cambridge: Harvard Univ. Press, 1975.

OTHER SOURCES

Artz, Frederick. *The Development of Technical Education in France 1500–1850*. Cambridge, Mass.: Society for the History of Technology and M.I.T. Press, 1966.

Birch, Anthony H. *Representative and Responsible Government*. Toronto: Univ. of Toronto Press, 1964.

Bryson, Lyman. *Adult Education*. New York: American Book, 1936.

Dewey, John. *Democracy and Education*. New York: Macmillan, 1916.

Lindemann, Edward C. *The Meaning of Adult Education*. New York: New Republic, 1926.

Ortega y Gasset, Jose. *The Revolt of the Masses*. London: George Allen & Unwin, 1932.

Pitkin, Hannah Fenichel. *The Concept of Representation*. Berkeley: Univ. of California Press, 1967.

Wegener, Charles. *Liberal Education and the Modern University*. Chicago: Univ. of Chicago Press, 1978.

The World Almanac and Book of Facts for 1924.

INDEX